S0-AAZ-980

# I Have Tasted the Sweet Mangoes of Cebu

# I Have Tasted the Sweet Mangoes of Cebu

*George Estrada*

iUniverse, Inc.
New York  Lincoln  Shanghai

# I Have Tasted the Sweet Mangoes of Cebu

All Rights Reserved © 2003 by George Estrada

No part of this book may be reproduced or transmitted in any form or by any means, graphic, electronic, or mechanical, including photocopying, recording, taping, or by any information storage retrieval system, without the written permission of the publisher.

iUniverse, Inc.

For information address:
iUniverse, Inc.
2021 Pine Lake Road, Suite 100
Lincoln, NE 68512
www.iuniverse.com

ISBN: 0-595-27955-4

Printed in the United States of America

# ACKNOWLEDGEMENTS

I want to thank my lovely wife and handsome son for all their love & patience & strength. This book is about them as much as it is about me. I wish my late mother and father could've seen them, as well as this book. They would've been proud. I miss mom and dad more than words can express. Many thanks, as well, to all my cousins, aunts and uncles in San Francisco, Sacramento, Cincinnati, Toronto and the Philippines. *Hoy!*

I also want to recognize the journalism faculties of the University of Texas at Austin and Humboldt State University for all their support. I'm told I should also thank the copyright holders of *And I Love Her* (Northern Songs) and *Can We Still Be Friends* (Earmark Music Inc.) for using some of their lyrics in my story.

Lastly, I want to thank the people of the Philippines for being so courageous and true. You give me strength! *Gitagaan ko ninyo'g kusog. Binigyan ninyo ako ng lakas.*

# 1

## *Mangoes Here, Man Goes Here*

This place was making me stupid. This place was making me happy. This place was making me so stupid-happy that I couldn't wipe the big, ridiculous mango grin off my face.

Why was I in such a state of delirium? What was it about Cebu?

Was it the deep history and the dark Christian mysticism of the place that so grabbed me? Was it the brave, suffering Cebuano people, so elegant in their simplicity, so stunning in their complexity? Was it the language, the food, the culture, the maddening heat, the cheesy music everywhere, the sputtering jeepneys, the welcoming smiles, the attainability of everything?

Was it all of this that was making me so spellbound, so out of my mind?

Or was it the girl?

Her name was Liza, and she worked in a department store in Cebu. Her skin was the color of an exotic desert. Her eyes were those of a surprised, laughing child. Her smile was pure, utter acceptance, with a radiance that shot out beams of eternity. Her long hair was black silk falling like rain over the terrain of her frail body.

I fell in love with Liza the very first moment I laid eyes on her.

Now I was here in Cebu, pledging all of my love to her again. Telling her tales of our future together, again. Promising everything and anything American to her, again and again and again.

Liza was all I needed now. I have everything else, and now I needed her. This I tell her again and again. And each time I do, she would squeeze my hand gently, close her eyes and dream of things she never could dream of before.

She was a young woman of the Philippines, land of magic, myth, crushing poverty and mangoes. I was an American, bringing promises of baseball, suburban lawns, 401Ks and pumpkin pies.

1

Displaced and loving it, I was a stupid-happy American manchild in this land of strange fruit, and I was about to taste the sweet mangoes of Cebu, REALLY taste them, for the very first time.

Her name is Liza, the lady of light, and I have come for her.

As the tropical heat shrouded me in its sweet madness, and as the taxi took me through the hysterical streets of Cebu to Liza's side, my thoughts drifted off to other times in my life, and how far away they seemed now. I thought of my four-year struggle to get my Ph.D. at the University of Texas, I thought of my nine years as a newspaper reporter in Oakland, I thought of my undergraduate days at Berkeley, my childhood years in Oakland. I thought of my mother. I thought of mangoes.

My mother had a masterful way with mangoes. She would slice them into thirds. The middle portions she'd set aside because they had large, oblong seeds that were in the way of the sensuous treat to come. The first and third portions would be saved for their yellow-orange treasure, dripping with sensuality, promising eternity.

She would take the knife and carve little tic-tac-toe grids into this quivering flesh. Then she would push the rind side up through the squares and push the little mounds of tasty flesh up and out. And there they'd stand, proud, erect, offering their succulence to any hungry lips passing in the night.

I tasted the sweet mangoes of the tropics while growing up in America. Even then, with an unrefined palate, with taste buds that were becoming dulled and standardized and homogenized, I could tell that these complex fruits my mother brought home from Oakland Chinatown were unlike any others here in the new land. Something about their texture, milky and meaty, that bathed my mouth with a tropical lushness. Something about their taste, an explosion of peach and melon and cream with a sassy backbite, spoke to me. It said that this was the harvest of the homeland, lad, all sensuous and warm and lush. These fruits come from the land of your birth, the Philippines.

Remember this, and never forget.

But I did forget. And I didn't remember for a long, long time. I didn't remember because my new land, America, had new demands on my attention: school, sports, money, careers, rock and roll, money, cars, money, bigger cars, money, money, more money. No time to be Filipino in the midst of all that America. No time, amidst all that, to stop and savor the mango moment.

Then, all of a sudden, Liza came into my life and everything changed. She brought light where there was darkness, and I found myself chasing that light halfway around the world, back to the land of my birth. It was here that the madness came, followed by a great revelation:—

I am Filipino and I am American. I am both and I am neither.

I am a Filipino-American. I am part East and part West, part savage and part intellectual, part Catholic and part pagan, part fish-head and part cheeseburger. I am part Spanish, part Malay, part Chinese, all American, and—like many of my fellow Fil-Ams—totally confused about who and what I am.

Maybe, in the end, this is why Cebu stuck to my soul like manga paste: the schizophrenia of the place resonated to the split in my own personality.

Maybe this is why Liza was such a riddle to me, and I to her. Maybe, in the end, this is why the beam of eternity in her eyes flickered on and off, off and on, and on and off again, leaving the dream in delirium's wake.

My name is George. I am both Filipino and American—and I am neither. This is my story.

# 2

## *The Lady of Light*

Her name was Liza. I accidentally met her one day on a computer.

I was in a University of Texas computer lab surfing the Internet, looking for faculty jobs, and for the moment I fancied the idea of teaching at a university in the Philippines for a year or two. Why not? I'm a Filipino-American, and it surely would be an interesting experience to live and work in the country of my birth. So I typed the word "Philippines" into the search engine and I was presented with a menu of many different topics. What grabbed my attention first, though, was the listing of a Web site offering Philippine women "penpals."

Right!

I'd heard of these things before, and I never paid them much mind before. They were for losers and desperate loners, I reckoned, not for me. But I had a few minutes to kill before starting my job search in earnest, so I went ahead and clicked on the *Filipina Dream Girls* page—just for fun.

A few clicks later, I was looking face to face at my future. I was looking in the eyes of the most magnificent woman I had ever seen.

She was extremely beautiful, and she was gorgeous in a delicate, natural way, not a posed, salacious, heavily made-up way. She was slim, almost too slim, about 5 feet 2, with straight, long, black hair, and a sweet, vulnerable smile that said, "I am a warm, caring, unassuming, shy but happy person who is looking for a better life and a loyal husband, and if you're good enough to win my heart, I will love you forever."

She had soft, moist, sympathetic eyes that whispered to me, "I see you with all your faults. I can feel your pain and I know all of your sins, but I will accept you as you are. I will love you as you are."

I had seen that face before, and I had seen those eyes before. I had seen them in my dreams. I had seen them in my imaginings, and I had heard those words in my fantasies, lying awake in the morning alone. And at this point in my strange and twisted life—freshly broken up from a long relationship that had turned very sour in the end, and working like a dog, under crushing pressure to finish my doctoral dissertation at the University of Texas—I was especially open to someone who emitted that kind of gentle, loving, welcoming vibe.

Oh, the irony of it! Liza Trujillo, the girl of my longlost dreams, was on a Web site featuring young Filipino women looking for "pen pals," preferably American ones. She was a "mail-order bride," the derisive term coined by non-thinking Americans who view these women as somehow debased, somehow less than human, commodities that can be purchased through the mails.

Perhaps I once thought in this cruel way too, being an American who has bought into a whole set of simplistic American ideas. But this day was different. This girl was different. And my soul was in turmoil.

I stared at this picture of Liza Trujillo, 22 years old, dubbed by this Web site as Cebu Sweetheart #C032.

I wanted to meet this woman. She was the one who had been lurking in the back of my mind my whole life, the one who had frolicked along the island paradises of my soul. I see her now, finally, in front of me, not in the flesh, but in the cold, Pentium luminescence of my computer screen. I had to make her mine. A voice inside was speaking to me: "Liza. Liza. LEASE-ahhh…Go to her."

I shook my head from side to side, to drive the voice away. I needed to think clearly about this. I looked intently at the photo and the accompanying text. I wanted to find out all I could about this woman.

She's a "Cebu Sweetheart," eh? Cebu? What is that? Oh, it's a big city in the Philippines, I see. I'm a Filipino-American, and I didn't even know about Cebu City. The truth is I don't know much about the Philippines at all. I'm a cultural disgrace, what some Filipino-Americans call a "flip flop." After a lifetime of whitewashing my island roots, and trying to become an accomplished American, I'm now a flop at being a Filipino. I don't speak any of the Philippine languages; I only speak English. I don't normally eat Philippine foods, except during holiday parties at the homes of relatives.

Liza Trujillo had a smile that made me forget every American thing I'd ever done and every American woman I'd ever known. Race didn't matter here, nothing mattered because of that smile, because it all came down to that smile, that loving, caring, luminescent, moist smile with a brilliance that shot beams of eternity at me all the way from Cebu City, Philippines, to this computer lab in Austin, Texas.

And I couldn't stop looking at that face. The inviting eyes, the smile, the love that must be waiting there. Oh, how I ached for her! How I wanted her! She's not like all the other girls on this Web site, I was convinced. She's not a hustler. She's different. She's gentle, she's kind, she's beautiful, she's sincere and dewy and moist and dripping with love. She's smiling for me and me alone. She's been waiting for me my entire life, but I was too blind to see.

Was I going mad? Perhaps I was. Was my brain unraveling because of all the pressure to finish my dissertation and get my Ph.D.? Perhaps it was. Perhaps I had begun the descent into madness long ago, the day my mother and I first set foot in America and tore my soul in half.

I am a Filipino-American. I am Filipino and I am American. I am both and I am neither. I am fully accepted by neither world.

The Philippines, the homeland of mad heat and dirty tropical passion, had been washed out of my brain by the need to become sanitized and American. Throughout my life, I did everything I could to get this brown off my skin. Recently, though, I'd felt something gnawing at my gut. I felt something missing from my body and my soul. I didn't know what it was until it faced me on this computer screen on this day. I see the light now, and Liza Trujillo, Cebu Sweetheart #032, was the bringer of this divinity.

*You must meet her and bathe in her warmth*, the voice was guiding me now. *Let her heal you, let her give you redemption.*

I sat in front of my screen for many long moments that day in November 1996, when I first stumbled on Liza's picture on the Internet. I looked at her mysterious smile, a "Mona Liza" smile, mysterious and knowing. I looked at her slim legs, her delicately arching calves, and I imagined the sleek, elegant lines hidden behind her black skirt and white smock. I noticed how her arms wound around her torso, like an affectionate cat caressing its master's leg with its tail, and I noticed how her hand protectively clutched her black bag. What was in that bag that was so precious that she would clutch it so eagerly? What pleasures waited for me there? Was my heart in her bag too, waiting for the caress of those delicate arms?

The room she was standing in appeared to be two degrees above shanty-town squalor. The back wall looked like a slab of green sheetrock, and it was partially covered with a shiny material that looked like a discarded shower curtain. On it hung one of those K-Mart-style battery operated clocks with tacky red trim that said it was 11:42 when this picture was taken. The floor was uneven, covered with cheap linoleum remnants. In a corner was a cluttered, plastic bookshelf, on which rested assorted magazines, a clothes iron and an oversized fan.

The photo told me a lot.

The fan meant there was no air-conditioning in this boarding house. The clothes iron said that this woman is impeccable about her appearance, even in the face of poverty. The assorted notebooks, magazines and stray items on this shelving unit told me that these shelves were meant to hold things, not display things. No cute little knick-knacks, no picture frames, no tacky little displays that bragged about vacations and disposable income. No, these shelves said, "I am in use; I hold the basic things you need to get you through your day."

I could make her life so much better, I thought to myself. I could give her so much.

Yes, a part of me told me I must meet this Liza Trujillo and make her fall in love with me. She is a Filipino and so am I, so I have the perfect right to do so. This is my birthright!

The other part of me, the American part, said, "Shame on you. Shame!" Yes, I had shared the dominant idea, and I thought that these young penpal girls from the Philippines were also somehow low. I, like most "decent" Americans, thought they were desperate and poor, and that the men who wrote to them were losers who couldn't get a "real" woman, an American woman.

But on this day, as I stared into this computer screen, I heard something calling to me, something telling me to reclaim what is mine, something telling me to come back home. *Resist the dominant idea and reclaim your right to happiness!*

I summoned my colleague, Chris Williams, a fellow graduate student at the University of Texas, over to the screen and pointed to Liza's face.

"See that girl?"

"Cute. Yeah, so what?"

"I'm going to marry her, Chris."

My friend tried not to show surprise, perhaps out of professional courtesy, perhaps because he was thinking that I might be violently disturbed. He rubbed his chin stoically, looked sideways at me, then turned and pondered the image of Liza.

"Well, George, she's gorgeous, all right. But I'm afraid she's a little too gorgeous for you. You know what I mean?"

"What? What do you mean?"

"Girls that beautiful are usually bad news. You know that. C'mon, you're smart. You just came off a bad relationship. You don't need any more bad news in your life."

"But…"

"And she's on a mail-order bride Web site, for God's sake. George—HELLO!—Get real!"

Silence. The young doctor-to-be had made his point. But this young doctor-to-be was about to make his. I stared him down for a moment. Another moment.

"I don't care if this is one of THOSE Web sites, or whatever it may be. You find gold where you can find it, right? And, she's too beautiful, you say? Well, my friend, you don't know the Philippines. You're too stuck in your American way of thinking. It's different in the Philippines. You can trust women there, beautiful or not. Women there are loyal. Women there are sincere. Listen, I'm a Filipino-American. I know about these things."

He shrugged. "Yeah right, so how come you never married one?"

Pause. Shoulder shrug. "Well, I'm real picky."

"Yeah, you're so picky that you always seemed to run with white women."

Ouch. That one hurt. It was true, it was brutal and it hurt.

"Chris, I've never found a Filipino girl here who was exactly what I was looking for. And come on, think about it. Real Filipino girls are impossible to find here. They change after they come here. They start acting American. They date white American men. Chris, I've just seen something different. I've seen perfection, and she's here on the Internet and she's waiting for me in the Philippines. Look at what she wrote here on her fact sheet."

On this Web site, Liza stated in her own handwriting that she was looking for someone "understanding, thoughtful, loving responsible"; that her hobbies are "cooking, watching movies, gardening, reading, writing to penpals"; that her ideal man is "educated, well dress, very formal."

Another graduate student, Dustin Harp, had joined the scene and she started an informal checklist: "Well, educated, yes, that's you. But the well-dressed and very formal, uh, well." Dustin looked me up and down and lingered on my black sweatpants and unwashed "Hook 'Em Horns" T-shirt.

"Uh…"

"Hey," I always had a comeback. "Don't sweat the small stuff. I can always put on better clothes and act like a refined person. That's nothing. Listen, this is the one, my friends. I've wanted to find one like her my whole life. And here she is, right here! I'm gonna write to her. I'm gonna tell her I love her. I'm gonna marry her!"

My friends scoffed and muttered something under their breath about how I'd finally snapped. They walked away and went back to their research with haughty steps that told me I really should do the same. After all, time was a-wasting, and there were more books to read, more footnotes to add, a dissertation to write, a doctorate to earn. Maybe Chris was right, maybe I had lost my mind. Maybe I should get back to my dissertation. Maybe I should put aside romance, put aside love, put aside fantasy—just as I'd done for the past four years—and get back to work.

Work, work, work, always work first. That's how one gets a Ph.D. in America. And that's how one becomes a professor. Yes, it was important for me to get my degree and become a professor. I'd been working hard for these goals. Maybe too hard. Maybe that's why my prior relationship of many years—yes, with a white woman—went bad. Because I'd become a workaholic and a cold, analytical person. Maybe that's why I was feeling desperately attracted to this warm, glowing, dewy, moist, dripping-with-love image named Liza Trujillo, Cebu Sweetheart #C032, that I had found on the Internet.

Maybe so. Maybe a lot of things. My friend Chris clearly didn't understand, though. How could he?

The next day was like all the others in Austin, Texas. I left my small loft apartment on West 25th St., near fraternity row, and walked four blocks through the sweltering Texas day. The sun was relentless like a good Texas sun always is, the dampness was pervasive, and sweat had already begun to seep through my T-shirt by the time I reached the College of Communication building on Guadalupe. (Pronounced GWAD-a-loop in Texan.) This was the same School of Journalism built by Jesse Jones, the founder of the *Houston Chronicle*. The same College of Communication that was host to the weekly stagings of *Austin City Limits*. The same College of Communication, rumor has it, that wouldn't hire Walter Cronkite on the faculty because Cronkite doesn't have a Ph.D.

The Ph.D. is everything in the world that I wanted to live in, the world of the big American university. The Ph.D. is the key to the kingdom. To not have it is to be denied a position on a respectable faculty. To not have it makes you a nonperson. The Ph.D. is the union card. It is what separates mere mortals from the gods. It is what transforms you from servant to master. It was what I wanted. It is what drove me every day. It is what I left my California home and moved to Austin, Texas, for. To get a Ph.D. To become a professor. To become something my immigrant parents could never have imagined. To become something bigger than what I was.

I took the elevator up to the journalism department office on the sixth floor, like I always did. Checked my mail, like I always did. Said hello to Maggi Fitch, the department secretary, like I almost always did. And then I walked to my closet-sized office to prepare for Journalism 312, the introductory reporting class I taught. The bigger offices, the ones with the picture-window views of the Austin skyline, went to the big-name professors, the kings. We graduate students had to share these cramped broom closets. It was their way of telling us we hadn't arrived yet, that we were nothing, that we were less than nothing, and that we lived in a ghetto, that the shining mansions on the hill awaited us if we could research brilliantly, footnote properly and publish like demons.

Seemed simple enough. And so it was, day after day after sweltering day. There was the research, there was the teaching, there was the grading of undergraduate papers, there was the preparing of lectures for the next day. Our work at school finished, we would go home and read, read, read, hoping to find nuggets of enlightenment somewhere/somehow in some dusky tome to help us on our long journey to the dissertation.

It was drudgery. Pure and simple. It was a marathon. It was an exercise in endurance, in pain, in tolerance. It was a test of gratification delay, a trial of self-denial. Read, read, read and read more. Then write, then footnote, then write, then footnote, then write, then revise, then write, then revise, then write and revise and write and revise some more until your fingers bleed and your vision grows dim and your mind goes blank and your senses are dulled and you can't stay awake one more minute.

God, I hated this! But I wanted that damned Ph.D.

I deplored this hazing. Who invented this Ph.D. thing, anyway? I later found out it was the Germans—who else could come up with such torture?—back in the early 1800s. A German scholar by the name of Johann Fichte, the first dean of philosophy at the University of Berlin, pioneered the first Doctor of Philosophy degree and conceived of the dissertation as the rite of passage. The first Ph.D. in America was awarded by Yale University in 1861. The Ph.D. became the coin of the realm in American universities, and so if you wanted to become a high priest of the Anglo-Saxon intellectual world, you had to prove your worth by earning a doctor of philosophy degree.

I was a dissertation away from my goal. I was about to become an Anglo-Saxon king. I was about to reach a point as far removed as possible from my backward, tropical island roots. Yes, the keys to this New World kingdom were in my reach, and I could see that proverbial light at the end of the tunnel.

The light.

Liza.

The light.

Liza, the lady of light. Her light somehow calmed me down, made me lose my fierce intensity for the moment. Her light, her soft glowing light, threw its goodness over my battered soul. God help me, I can't get her out of my mind. She was making me lose my focus, and that would surely lead to failure in my quest for the kingdom. I had to do something and do it now.

Here's an idea: Let's write Liza a letter today. Let's make this the start of something new. Let's bring the light back into this life. This was going to be a day like none of the others, after all.

I put away my research material, and fired up my Macintosh laptop. The computer was ready for my words, the blank screen was my canvas, the keyboard was my palette. I had to create a masterpiece, I had to paint beautiful pictures with words. But what would I write?

"Hello, my name is George and I noticed your picture on the *Filipina Dream Girls* Web site…" Naw, too basic and unimaginative.

"Hello, I normally don't do this kind of thing, but I saw your picture on the Internet and…" Naw, too defensive, too condescending.

"Hey, babe, what's up? I saw what ya got and it's looking good, see what I'm saying, and so I thought I'd write." Naw, too pimpy.

After several pathetic attempts, I finally came up with this:

---

*Dear Liza,*

*I saw your picture in the Filipina Dream Girls pages, and I was inspired to write to you. You are so very, very beautiful! What a gorgeous smile you have! I have often thought about what my dream girl would look like, and you look very much like the girl I've always imagined! Of all the girls in the Filipina Dream Girls pages, you are the one I want to meet. I can't tell you how much I am overwhelmed by your beauty! I hope that you are also a nice girl, and I hope that you will write to me.*

*My name is George Estrada, I am a Filipino-American, and I am studying at the University of Texas. I hope to get my Ph.D. degree in May. Then I will be a professor and a Doctor of Journalism. I am currently looking for a teaching job at a good university.*

*You seem like a very nice girl. I would like very much to meet you someday. Are you planning to visit America soon? Do you currently have a boyfriend? I had an American girlfriend here in Texas, but we recently broke up. I'm looking for a new girlfriend, but I'm not in a rush. I want to be careful. I want to find someone who is nice, loving, caring, kind, and willing to commit to a long relationship. Also, I want someone who likes music, movies, books, and who can understand that I am a very busy man. I am very dedicated to my work, and my girlfriend has to understand this and must be very dedicated to me. In return, I can give that girl all my love and a secure future. I know that one day I will find that one special girl…*

*Please write to me soon, Liza. You are very attractive, and from what you wrote in your description of yourself, you seem to be a very nice girl. Tell me about your dreams, your hopes, your family life..."*

Yes, tell me everything about yourself, Liza. Are you a nice girl or do you have a wild streak like many Filipino girls do? Will you be loyal to me? Will you stay with me through thick and thin, through sickness and in health? Would you still love me if I was poor? Do you like rock music or jazz? Do you like baseball? Will you go to Oakland A's games with me? How about football? Have you ever heard of the Oakland Raiders? How many children would you like to have?

Just your basic questions. They form my own axis of deep culture. But I had to stop myself from asking the more forward questions—about sex and love, mostly—because they might put her off. This is a simple girl, a delicate flower, a woman from a different time and place. She must not see the crude, full-bodied American that I really am—at least not for now.

First, I have to get her used to the idea of meeting someone new, someone from a different world, someone of her race but not of her culture. Then I have to get her to fall in love with me over the great distance that separates us. This is my goal, and it's a worthy one.

The rest of the letter spoke of how I used to be a reporter for a newspaper in Oakland, California, and how I'd interviewed a lot of famous people in my life and how, despite being a rather accomplished and well-connected person, I am earthy and real enough to fall in love with a girl like her.

Of course, this was all a pipe dream. Maybe Chris was right. Maybe this Web site was a scam. Maybe this Liza was a piece of fiction. After all, any lonely soul who wanted her mailing address would only have to fork over $2 to the proprietors of the *Filipina Dream Girls* Web site.

But what have I got to lose? Two dollars? Go for it! I wrote a check and dropped it in the mail to some address in Washington state. About 10 days later, I got my answer: Liza Trujillo, c/o Shoe Mart Dept. Store, North Reclamation Area, Cebu City 6000, Philippines.

What? She receives her mail at a department store? What is this Shoe Mart, anyway? Is that owned by Imelda Marcos or something? Is that where Imelda got her 2,000 pairs of shoes? All manner of stupid questions went through my head. Now was the moment of decision. Should I send her this letter or not? I'd written it about two weeks ago, but now I have this girl's address, and it looks like it could be the real thing. Are we serious about this, or what? Is this a game or is this the real thing? Do I have a chance with this girl or am I setting myself up for a big fall? How many letters has she gotten already? How many lonely hearts have already been broken? Just exactly who is this helpless, frail, young girl who has captivated my heart?

And what if she responds, what if we have a romance, what if we end up getting married? What would my friends and colleagues say when they found out that we met through the Internet? Would I be humiliated? Would we be laughed at and whispered about in the community? What would people say? Would people mark her as one of those "mail-order brides from the Philippines"? Would people think of us as desperate losers?

After thinking it through, I decided that none of this mattered. I'd probably be happy spending the rest of my life next to that girl, close to that smile.

I bought a 60-cent international airmail stamp, dropped the letter in the mailbox and hoped for the best.

# 3

# *Whispers From Afar*

Thanksgiving break was to be a do-or-die time for me and my dissertation. If I was going to finish it by summer—and start a new teaching job by fall—I needed to make some serious progress on this thing. I didn't want to become one of those students who takes five years or more to finish a doctoral program. I wanted to do it in four, thus I'd have to complete my dissertation in one. This was possible, I figured, because my training as a print journalist on a daily paper enabled me to crank out lots of copy real fast. It may not end up being a perfectly elegant piece of research, but by God, it'd be done. As one recently graduated doctor of philosophy told me: "Don't worry about getting it right. Just write it!"

Words to live by.

This pocket of free time was particularly important because when school is in session there is little time for marathon research-and-writing sessions. And as everyone who'd done it will tell you, writing a dissertation involves at least two dozen of these marathon sessions. Not to mention the time you need to spend psyching yourself into it.

My fall semester workload was particularly heavy: I was taking an advanced, graduate-level Spanish class (a language requirement for the journalism Ph.D. at Texas); I was teaching a beginning reporting class; and I had mounted a national job search for a permanent, full-time, tenure-track faculty position. This search consisted of scanning the *Chronicle of Higher Education's* job listings, sending out resumes and query letters, and begging professors for recommendation letters. All of that left not much time to do anything else. I'd also acquired a taste for playing pinball at the UT student union (a psyching-up activity for the marathon writing sessions), and listening to John Coltrane CDs for relaxation.

It's amazing what one can do when properly psyched-up. And I was definitely motivated. It's also amazing what one can do when focused. And I was definitely developing a hard case of tunnel vision. It's amazing what one can do when the smell of money is in the air. And all I could smell was more money going down a rathole if I had to stay in graduate school another year. I was already in hawk $30,000 in school loans. The dissertation had to get done, and it had to be finished by summer.

So during this Thanksgiving break, while everyone in Texas was eating turkey, watching the Dallas Cowboys on TV, drinking beer, laughing, joking, living their American lives of too much food, too much privilege, too much leisure, I was sitting in my West Campus apartment hacking away at my little Mac laptop.

It rained most of the first evening, and the ceiling sprang a leak, just to the left of where I sat working at my desk. I put a bucket under the drip, and decided not to call maintenance. That would've been too much of a distraction. Instead, I let the drip, drip, drip serve as a steady percussion to the symphony I was composing. And soon that steady drip, drip, drip began to hypnotize me, began to elevate me to another state. I was becoming obsessed, mad with desire, immaculate in my insanity. I was creating a symphony and Mother Nature herself was providing the rhythm section.

*Yes, a symphony. I was Beethoven. I was Mozart. And I'm making beautiful, delirious music for emperors and kings. And now I'm a postmodern madman, and I'm a battered genius and I'd rather die than give up control. I'm creating intellectual anarchy to free the masses. And now I am Foucault, and I am Baudrillard and I am Habermas and I am writing things that only the true visionaries can understand; and I am working myself into a lather, and I am screaming inside, and I am pounding, I am hacking, I am riffing, I am screaming, and my riffs and screams are from hell, and I am wrenching demons from the dark pits of my psyche; and I am torturing myself, and I am killing myself, and God, God, please help me through this ordeal.*

*Give me strength, give me words, fill the pages with meaning, crush these coals into diamonds, transform this lead into gold, help me make something out of nothing. God, give me the strength. Give me the will!*

Over the four-day break, I wrote 75 pages.

They weren't 75 great pages, but they were 75 pages. And I had written a big chunk of my dissertation. Maybe another 150 or 170 more pages to go? Goodness, I might be a third done! Could it be? Am I one-third done with this thing? Good God in heaven, I surprise myself sometimes.

When my "break" was done, I slept for the better part of three days, and I sleepwalked through classes. I had descended into madness during my writing marathon and my soul was a wreck, so I needed this time to heal a bit. A relatively quiet week passed, as I waited to hear my dissertation adviser's assessment of the chapters I'd just produced.

It was a day like any other in Austin, Texas, when a letter with strange stamps and a foreign postmark arrived. When I saw who it was from—Liza Trujillo, Cebu, Philippines—my heart leapt. When I read the letter, I knew that everything was about to change.

---

*Nov. 25, 1996*
*Dear George,*

*May God shower her Blessings to you and to your daily task. And also to your work. And I hope that everything is fine upon accepting this letter of mine.*

*By the way, I received your letter last Nov. 21, 1996 and I'm very surprised when I received your unexpected letter.*

*Well—asking me here, I'm still fine through the help of our Almighty God. And I'm living here, in Cebu City in one boarding house together with my sister and my cousin, and I'm working in Shoe Mart Department Store as a sales clerk.*

*Before, George, I'm studying in Manila. I'm taken the course of computer secretarial but due to poverty had not finished yet due to financial problem because my father was died already. As of now I'm working at the Dept. Store to support my brother and sister.*

*George, you ask so many questions here your letter. So, I will answered your questions with clear and honest answer.*

*First, about my dreams. My dreams is to finish studying so that we can find a good job, and good future someday.*

*Second, my hopes in my family life. I hope we can find a good lifetime partner someday and who is understanding, caring and kind. This about my town here in province of Cebu, its so nice. A lot is here, we can smell a fresh air. You are asking me also the American movies. Sometimes I will watching movies but I don't have a favorite actor. About music, I'm always also listening music.*

*And you are asking for how close to Cebu to Manila. It is easy to travel to Cebu from Manila.*

*That's enough until here my letter. Regards to you, your relatives, your friends. Take care always.*

*Your friend,*

*Liza Trujillo*

Yes, it was from her, my Liza, the shining gem in my computer screen. It was her, the one with the laughing face, the dewy eyes, the kind smile. She of the caressing arms, the fine bones, the silken black hair. She who lives with such beauty, she who walks in such poverty. It is her, the most distant woman in the world, the most perfect woman in the world, whose eyes shot beams of eternity through the ether, beams of heavenly light that had pierced the darkness of my life.

"She's too beautiful for you," my friend had told me in the computer lab those many weeks ago, but here she is now, in my life, in my living room, in the paper in my hands. It is her.

Her English seems a little rough, but I guess I should've expected that. She doesn't seem to know the basic rules of grammar, but so what? I understand perfectly what she's trying to say. She is telling me that she's intrigued. My letter had stirred up some curiosity in her. She wants to know more.

And she seems humble. She is poor, she is working hard and barely making it. People depended on her and her meager sales-clerk salary just to get by.

She is religious: "May God shower Her blessings to you…" Hah! If I didn't know better, I'd think she was a feminist, calling God a "her." But I know this isn't the case here. It is just a mistake in pronoun use—common among Filipinos who haven't mastered English. I appreciated the sentiment, and I welcomed the blessing.

I hurriedly plugged in my laptop and knocked out another letter.

---

*Dec. 5, 1996*
*Dear Liza:*

*Thank you so very much for your letter. It was so good of you to reply so quickly. It made me feel like I somehow touched your soul. That was my goal. I hope now that we can be good friends and regular penpals. Maybe more…*

*Reading your letter I was happy to find that your English is good! Unfortunately, I do not speak Tagalog. I can understand a little bit when I am with my relatives and they are speaking Tagalog, but my comprehension of it is very limited. You see, when I was growing up in California my parents only spoke English at home. And that is why I only speak English now. They wanted me to learn the language of America, and not get confused with the Tagalog, Visayan and Ilocano languages they also knew. They would speak the native languages with others, but not with me. This has its good points and its bad points. The good thing is that now, because of my parents, I am extremely proficient with English—I have to be in order to function as a university professor. But I feel that something deep inside is missing because I cannot speak the language of the Philippines. Oh well…maybe someday I will learn. (Will you help me? I hope so.)*

*Right now, I am forced to study Spanish because of my degree requirements. I'd rather learn Tagalog, but they do not offer Tagalog classes in Texas. I guess it's because there are not too many Filipinos here. In California, there are lots of Filipinos. I think you'd love San Francisco because there are lots of Pinoys and Pinays there. My favorite cousins, Joyce and Rickey, live there. Most likely I'll be moving back to San Francisco after I finish in Texas, to start working as a professor at San Francisco State University. There are other colleges interested in my services, so I'm not 100 percent sure about San Francisco as my final destination. but right now it seems the most probable. I have taught there before, and they told me that I could probably get a permanent faculty position there after I got my Ph.D. Nothing is certain, though. We'll just have to see what develops, right?*

*There is one thing I know for sure: I would like to find a nice Filipino girl who is unspoiled by all the corrupting influences of America. If I could find that girl, I would like to bring her to America to be with me. You see, I think girls who grew up in America are too conceited, too flirtatious, too disloyal. I want someone who is pure of heart, someone who is adventurous and spirited but who will be true to me, someone who will love me for what I am, someone who is ready to commit a lifetime to me. I don't know if it's right for me to be saying these things to you, Liza, since we just started exchanging letters and since we really don't know each other yet. But I want to be honest, and I want you to know exactly what it is I'm looking for in a woman. And let me tell you right now: when I saw your picture, and when I saw that beautiful smile of yours, I was immediately moved to write to you. I said to myself: "If you can find a girl who is that beautiful, that intelligent, and that nice, you would be the luckiest man in the world." I believe that with all my heart.*

*And so that is why I wrote to you—to find out more about you. To find out about the girl behind the gorgeous smile. I'm hoping that we can be friends, but I'm praying that maybe there can be more than just friendship. Please don't think I'm being too forward, or too arrogant, or too conceited. I'm just being honest. I think you are incredibly beautiful. I would love to have a girl as magnificent as you. Is this possible? I don't know. We live a vast distance apart. And it would be hard for us to meet. I have the money to visit, but I don't know when I can find the time. Do you have the time or the desire to visit America? If so, then the money for your fare possibly can be arranged. But, again, I'm going too fast here. For now, let's continue writing letters to one another and see what happens, OK?*

*I have an idea : Do you have a cassette tape recorder? If so, I could send you a tape-recorded message and you can hear my voice. Also, you could send me a voice message in return. Finally, if you want to call me, you can call collect. This means that I will pay for the call. All you have to do is tell the operator that you want to make a collect phone call to America. My phone number is 512-555-0599. Try it! The best time to call is during the weekend, Saturday or Sunday. Remember, there is a big time difference between here and the Philippines. When it's midnight there, it's 10 in the morning here. When it's 10 in the morning there, it's 8 at night here. Maybe you can call then. That would be fun! It would be exciting to talk with you. And you wouldn't have to pay for the call because I will be the one paying for it. I hope you can call me. That would be very exciting.*

*Well, that's it for now. I think I said a lot. I hope it was not too much. I'm sorry if I seemed too aggressive about expressing my feelings. But, when I see a woman as beautiful and rare as you, I am moved to do and say surprising things. I even surprise myself with the things I am saying in this letter!! When you write again, please send a picture, if you have one. The only picture I have of you is the one I saw on the Internet page. I'd love to have another one. As I promised, I'm sending you some money to help you pay for your postage. I know it's expensive to send a letter overseas, so maybe this will help you. Maybe in the next letter you send you can also send me a picture of you and your relatives. That would be so nice!*

*Until we communicate again, please take care. You are a rare and wonderful person. I want more than anything to know you better. Please write again soon. I will be waiting for your letter.*

*Warm regards from your admirer in Texas,*

*George Estrada*

I went to the post office and bought another 60-cent international airmail stamp. Then I took two one-dollar bills from my wallet and inserted them inside my folded letter. This money was to help her pay for postage for a return letter. The fact that she might also like the scent of American greenbacks was not lost on me. I dropped the letter in the mail.

Christmas break was more of the same. Writing, researching, reading, more writing, more researching, more reading. The chapters I'd written during Thanksgiving break got a lukewarm reception from my adviser, Prof. Chuck Whitney.

"Not great, but serviceable," he said. "It works, though."

He gave me a list of things I could do to improve things. For a week or two after, I did nothing with it. I was tired of looking at these pages, and I didn't relish the thought of re-visiting and re-writing old material. On top of that, it felt like a move backward. I thought I was a third done, but it turns out I was only half-baked. And even though Dr. Whitney was civil enough in his critique, I could read between the lines.

I imagined what he really was saying: "Look, George, this is not great, so don't go mistaking it for being a groundbreaking piece of research. Get used to that right now. But I understand your situation. You're an older guy, you've been out there in the world, you came back to school to get a Ph.D., you want to be a professor, you've got some good job possibilities out there and you want to finish this by summer, right? You don't want to be a career graduate student. You want to rejoin the middle class. I'm fine with that. So just keep working your butt off, keep on producing serviceable chapters, don't write anything stupid, and just do what I say and don't ask so many silly questions. Let me take care of things and it'll get done."

I was fine with this arrangement too. I certainly didn't want to make life more difficult for him, since he was the chairman of the Graduate Studies Committee and seemed to be involved in several big-time research projects at once. I just wanted to write the damned thing and move on. There was no room in my life for perfection in research, for I had found perfection in love. I had fallen for a gleaming, perfect image with a smile to melt your heart. I had fallen for a slip of a girl from my home country who wrote in a pigeon English that was so inept, so incompetent, so incorrect, so sweet, so genuine, so endearing, so charming and so unlike the high-flown scholarly English that was routinely bandied about in these halls of enlightenment.

Liza Trujillo was exactly the opposite of everyone around me. Maybe that's why I was so infatuated with her.

I couldn't bring myself to tell my intellectual mentor about my love for Liza because he would've asked where and when I met her, and I would've had to tell him that I'd never actually met her in the flesh and then I'd have to tell him about the *Filipina Dream Girls* pages and he would've started wondering about my mental stability. So I didn't go there. I simply nodded, took his list of things to do, and promised to return shortly with the revisions.

That was about a week and a half ago. In the meantime, Liza's second letter had arrived.

*Jan. 06, 1997*
*Dear George*

*Hi…Hello George. Here I am with another letter to you. I hope everything is okay with you and your family upon receiving this letter of me.*

*Thanks for your response. I get your letter last Jan. 02, 1997. I didn't expect your response my letter. I know you are busy regarding your job there. Well, George, sorry for my handwritten and also my English. I might think this is wrong grammar but I need your correction, please. And this is the one thing to write a penfriend in other country coz I want to developed my English and I want some friends in other places. You write also here your letter you want to learn how to speak in Tagalog, Visayan and Ilocano. The Tagalog and Visayan it is easy to learn that language. But Ilocano I don't know how to speak that.*

*Well, I have a question to you. Are you Catholic? And do you celebrate a Christmas season there because here in the Phil. most people are so busy last Dec. to celebrate Christmas. And this about you, did you celebrate also? Please tell me about the happenings of Christmas there. Well, George, never mind to send me a money for a postal. The only thing I want to have is your response when the time you receive my letter, to share a good idea that we have done. And I want to have our communication to be last long.*

*Well, inside me I might think that we are not compatible to each other because you are belong to a higher rank. Until here my letter see you next letter.*

*I do hope you write me back. Please take care yourself. Kindly regards to all your friends and all your relatives there and the most to you, my friend.*

*Your friend,*

*Liza Trujillo*

I was floored. I read the letter over and over again. Was this actually going to happen? Was I actually making contact with the girl of my dreams? Again, that atrocious English. But who cares? Let's look at some of these things she said.

First, she said she didn't expect that I'd send a second letter. How very modest and unassuming. I love that. What else…she wants a penpal who will correct her English. Well, that's what I do for a living, and I certainly can help you if you insist, but I'm not looking for a student, I'm looking for a love! Of course, if you want me to learn Tagalog or Visayan or Cebuano or whatever dialect it is you speak, I'd be happy to.

Yes, I am Catholic, but I don't go to church much anymore. Only during special events with my family. Of course, I can start going every Sunday if you were with me here. I'd have to do a monster confession, though, because I've got about 30 years of sinning I need to tell the priest about. Christmas? Let's see, what do we do for Christmas here? I usually try and visit my family in San Francisco and Daly City, and we eat a lot of Philippine food and we all watch the kids open their presents. It's all about kids, isn't it? I'd love to have children with you, Liza. They'd be smart because I am smart, and they'd be beautiful because of you. What lucky children! Let's start making them!

And what is this about us not being compatible? Opposites attract, ying goes good with yang. Haven't you ever read about Cinderella? I love storybook endings. How about you?

I hacked out another letter, this time more passionate and more direct. I want to find a nice Filipina girl to marry. She must be beautiful, thoughtful and honest. You are beautiful, you seem to be very considerate of other people and you seem to be very honest. So let's keep on writing and see what's what. If you are the one, I am ready to go all the way with this. What do you think about that? Is it you? Are you my dream girl forever? Are you my future wife?

I enclosed two more dollars and also included a picture of me that was taken a few years back, when I was living in California. I am wearing bicycle shorts and a red jacket, and I am standing atop a cliff overlooking the Pacific Ocean. As I recall, this picture was taken somewhere along Highway 1 on the way to Santa Cruz.

It was a carefree time. It was a sunny day, a gentle sea breeze was tossing my hair, and I was smiling lovingly at the camera. I was also trim and buff from regular workouts at the gym. I remembered that the picture was taken by my then-girlfriend, Lauralee.

Lauralee and I had a stormy on-and-off relationship that started in 1978. She was 5-foot-9—a classic tall Texas blonde—and built like a model. She was a sexual dynamo. She was also from a very conservative Houston family. I had no business being with a girl like this, and her family didn't exactly approve of us. But Lauralee was one of those free spirits who came of age in the late 1960s and early 1970s, and she did pretty much what she wanted to do.

We first discovered each other during a group camping trip to Yosemite National Park. She was a carefree college girl on summer vacation who was into new age spiritualism and back rubs and I was a smart-ass Filipino-American kid from Oakland who was into Hunter Thompson and Led Zeppelin and we were totally wrong for each other and, of course, that is why we fell into each other's arms down by the river one night and fell in lust and fell in love and launched a wild, stormy 20-year affair.

It was to become the most passionate, absorbing, life-changing love affair of my life. Lauralee was the owner of my heart and the focus of my desire for the better part of two decades.

After a few years apart in the late 1980s, we got back together in 1991 and it seemed like a dream come true. You know, boy finds love of his life, boy loses love of his life, boy wins back love of his life. It was a good story, and there was supposed to be a happily-ever-after ending, with she and I having a wonderful family and growing old together.

But that's not how it turned out. After a period of long-distance romancing with Lauralee, I sold my house in Oakland and moved into her South Austin home in 1994. It was perfect! I'd live with the lady of my life and start attending the University of Texas to earn a Ph.D. What a perfect fit! But this dream scenario turned into a nightmare. She kicked me out after only two years.

Why? Well, to put it simply, she didn't want me in her house anymore because I'd become such an asshole. She didn't put it in those terms exactly, but that's the gist of what she said—and she was right! Grad school will do that to you. I didn't predict, couldn't predict, that the pressure of graduate school would turn me into a different person, an argumentative, analytical, workaholic person that a gentle soul like Lauralee couldn't bear to have in her home.

And so, last summer, the summer before my critical dissertation year was to begin, Lauralee told me she couldn't take it any more. The truth is that she was becoming a bit intolerant too because of pressures at work, so we were both to blame, really. Maybe the simple fact is that our love ran out of gas and neither of us wanted to get out and push the car up the hill anymore.

It was my fault that this epic love affair would end in such an unseemly way. Hell, I wouldn't want me living in my house either, at that point.

And so it was that I came to be living in a small, leaky loft apartment on fraternity row just three blocks west of the University of Texas campus, spending all of my waking hours polishing my resume, networking for a faculty job, coordinating my travel itinerary, studying Spanish, grading undergraduate papers, and pounding away hour after hour, footnote after freaking footnote, on this damned dissertation.

It was a good life.

It was no life at all.

And it drained every ounce of life from my body.

Even after I moved out, Lauralee and I remained friends. And every now and then we'd go out for a movie or a meal and we'd sit and chat about the good times. As I looked at that picture of me taken a few years ago—a picture I'd be sending to Liza—I thought of Lauralee and smiled. I mailed the letter and gave Lauralee a call. I decided that I'd tell her about Liza over dinner that night.

Lauralee still lived in South Austin, just a few miles down the road from UT, with her four cats, Jed, Maple Leaf, Hansel and Gretel. When I came to pick her up, Lauralee was radiant, as always. She preferred to dress in thrift-shop chic, an old T-shirt or blouse with some kind of wildlife-outdoors theme, and well-worn jeans that showed off the elegant contour of her long, athletic legs. I always loved the way she dressed. It reminded me of the 1970s, when we were both younger and wilder and our days were filled with waterfalls and our nights were filled with thunder, and the big, beautiful world seemed to lay at our feet.

But that was then, and this is now. And although we were together again, in my car, driving through Texas, as we had done thousands of time before, the whole fabric of the universe we created together had become unraveled.

The moment was not lost on either of us as we cruised up South First Street in my beat-up old Dodge Aries. But neither of us wanted to get heavy, so we tried to make small talk. We talked about her cats—she just adored her cats—and we talked about her job. I talked a little, just a little, about UT. She hated the University of Texas. She thought it was a school for snobs. She had dropped out of UT in her freshman year back in the mid-1970s, and transferred to another school. She always hated it when I talked about UT.

And so I changed the subject. I told her about Liza, a topic that Lauralee seemed to warm to.

"That's neat that you found someone," Lauralee said. It sounded very sweet and sincere, as everything Lauralee said always sounded. "Where did you meet her?"

"On the Internet. Well, I first saw her on the Internet, then I started writing letters and she wrote me back, and now it looks like we're going to get involved. I'm going over to see her in the Philippines as soon as I can get some free time. She's a real sweet girl, a good kid. I am totally in love."

"Oh!" There was a long pause, and it seemed Lauralee was trying to figure out what to make of this.

"How old is she?" she blurted out after a few moments.

"Well, she's, uh, she's 22, actually."

"Oh!" Lauralee was smiling, trying hard to be positive and non-judgmental, as hippie girls from the 1970s were supposed to be positive and non-judgmental. But I knew there were some 1990s thoughts swirling around in her mind.

"Well, she's quite a bit younger than we are," Lauralee said. Lauralee was 44, the same age as me. "Well, she's half our age, right?"

"Yes, I know." I took my hands off the steering wheel and waved them in the air for effect. "And don't say it because I know—I'm old enough to be her father."

Lauralee giggled at this, but it was a nice giggle. Not a hostile, bitter, sarcastic giggle. A nice giggle.

"Well, so," I stammered, "you don't think I'm an old letch now, do you?"

"No, no. It's just funny."

"Oh, OK, thank you," I said, and I started to address an invisible jury. "Meanwhile, in her mind, the words 'pervert, pervert, pervert' come to the fore, but yes, because she is sunny and nice and enlightened, she is not going to say anything to make her dear old friend feel bad about his pathetic life, but nevertheless, aha!—NEVERTHELESS!—the words ring forth PERVERT, PERVERT, HORNY OLD PERVERT!"

Lauralee was laughing loudly now, laughing so hard that she couldn't speak. She started hitting me on the shoulder: "Stop it, stop it."

I always knew how to make Lauralee laugh. This was how I'd been able to hold her for so long. But lately, there hadn't been much laughter in our lives. This was a good moment. I'd forgotten these kinds of moments. We had a good, hearty laugh over the age gap.

By the time we calmed down, we'd reached the restaurant. It was a fairly new restaurant that was built on land that once was the site of the Armadillo World Headquarters, a legendary concert hall near Town Lake. Lauralee and I had been to the Armadillo once, in 1978, the first time I ever visited her in Texas, to see Todd Rundgren play.

A Todd Rundgren song from that concert started echoing in my head:

*We can't play this game any more, but can we still be friends?*
*Things just can't go on like before, but can we still be friends?*

Sadly appropriate, I thought to myself, that this bittersweet song would be played on this very patch of earth in 1978, and now here we are, my love and I, 20 years later and the words would tell the story of our lives.

But hell, why dwell on it?

Lauralee ordered a breaded oyster plate and I chose a meal of sausage, beans and rice. I knew somehow that the inevitable questions could come, and they did, just as our meals were being served.

"So, why did you decide to go for a Filipino girl?" Lauralee asked while she buttered her cornbread.

"Why? I don't know. Just seemed right."

"You don't seem the type."

"What do you mean? I AM a Filipino, you know."

"Bullshit, you're a Filipino-American, not a Filipino. Two completely different things. And all your girlfriends have been white. You're whiter than me."

Silence for a moment. Two moments. I bit my lip and stopped myself from saying something nasty.

"Yeah, well, it's time for me to go a different way now," I said, keeping it simple.

Silence for a moment. Two moments. Three. Four.

"Maybe I just got tired of fighting wars," I said.

"Wars? What do you mean?"

"Race wars. The psychological wars we have to fight just to get acceptance."

"What?"

"Have you ever noticed, when we're out together, sometimes some people look at us sideways?"

"What?"

"There are a lot of people, more than you think, a lot of people who generally do not approve of a white woman—you!—being with a non-white guy—me!"

"Oh, come on," Lauralee said. "We've been through this before. You're being paranoid again." She went back to buttering her cornbread.

"No, I'm serious. And I'm tired of it. I figure, why fight it? Why fight it? I surrender. I give in. I will follow the master plan. I will do my duty to God and country. I will stay with my own race." I was ranting now with a mouth full of sausage and beans.

"Well," Lauralee said dismissively, "if that's what floats your boat, then go for it."

"I'm just tired of these racist idiots looking at me like they want to kill me because I'm out with you." I was getting worked up.

"Stop it, stop it, will you? I'm trying to eat."

I looked around us. The crowd in the restaurant was generally pretty cool-looking, an assortment of computer yuppies, wannabe rock stars and UT students. There was one muscular, middle-aged man in a corner, wearing his thick gray hair in an Elvis pompadour. He shot a look or two in my direction, and I imagined he might be a member of the local Klan, devising ways of stringing me up and beating me to a pulp.

Over in the other corner was a cheery looking younger man, perhaps early 30s, dressed quite properly in designer polo shirt and pleated khakis. His hair was thinning on top, and he was with two other men who dressed and looked similarly. Every now and then he stole a glance at me, and when he did, he didn't seem so cheery.

As I caught the disapproving glances from Mr. Yuppie, I imagined he had just emerged from his cubicle somewhere in some office, where he was working on some deal to screw some people out of some money while listening to some right-wing, crypto-racist talk show host on the radio. And now he and a couple of his buddies have gone out for a little bite to eat, and now he sees this dark-skinned monkey boy sitting with a beautiful blonde woman, and man, these minorities want goddam everything. Shit, they get the affirmative action advantage, they get into the good schools, they get the good jobs, they get to play football, and what do I have but this measly little shit job working in some office. And I don't make nearly enough money, and now look! Fucking minorities want our women too!

I caught myself in mid-thought. Clearly, I'd been working too hard. I'd become delusional, hysterical. Or had I? Maybe I was just seeing clearly now. I couldn't figure it out, so I went back to my sausage and beans.

"You know what? You've got a point," Lauralee said, startling me. "A lot of people don't like to see interracial couples. It's true."

"Oh? I thought you said I was being paranoid."

"Well, you are. But there's a lot of truth in what you say. For instance, at my work, some of the girls, you know, they talk about men, and one time one girl said that a black guy had asked her out."

"And?"

"And she said that she really hated that."

"Hated what?"

"That a black guy asked her out."

"Why?"

"I don't know. Her family is probably really, really conservative. You know the South."

"The South? I thought this was Austin, Texas, the coolest place on Earth."

"It's still Texas. It's still the South."

"OK, and so?"

"So, we were all talking one day, and she brought it up again, and she said, you know, that white people should stick together. And, well, I thought maybe I should tell them the truth, and so I told them I was living with a Filipino guy."

"Uh, oh."

"Yeah, and they all got real quiet and didn't say anything."

"Yep. Go figger."

"And they never brought up the subject again—at least not while I was with them."

"That sounds about right."

Lauralee looked at me for many moments and I could see the sympathy in her beautiful green eyes. She wouldn't verbalize it, she couldn't, but she was saying to me with that look: "I'm sorry. I know how you feel, and I'm very, very sorry. I've noticed it too over the years—those people looking at us, talking about us behind our backs. I'm sorry we live in such a world. I'm sorry that people can be like that. But if you're tired of fighting it, just imagine how I might feel. I'm tired of it too. Please understand how I feel. Please don't hate me. We can't waste our lives fighting it any more."

After our meal, we had some more small talk and some more laughs. It was getting dark and Lauralee needed to get home and do her laundry, so we drove up South First and I dropped her off at her house.

"Would you like to pet the cats before you go?" she offered.

"What? Oh, sure. Yeah, why not?"

Lauralee brought the cats out and I gave them all a good, vigorous body-pet. They all seemed to like it except for the youngest cat, a calico named Maple Leaf, who always looked at me like she wanted to kill me.

That done, I bade Lauralee and the cats goodbye, and as I drove off I saw Lauralee steal one last glance in my direction as she walked back into the house.

I thought about how much I had loved her once, and I wondered if I would ever be that much in love with anyone again. Would Liza light those fires again within me?

I drove back home in the thinning daylight and thought about that Todd Rundgren song. How did it go again? I'd forgotten how the rest of it went. I couldn't simply pull out the record and play it because all my LPs were in storage back in California.

I stopped at Tower Records on Guadalupe and searched for *Hermit of Mink Hollow,* the old Todd Rundgren album that had that damned song on it. They didn't have it, but they did have a Rhino Records compilation of *The Best of Todd*

*Rundgren,* which had the song, my song, our song, *Can We Still Be Friends,* along with several others.

I got home, unwrapped the disk, put it on the stereo and skipped to track eight.

*We can't play this game anymore, but can we still be friends?*

I sat back on the futon and remembered.

*Things just can't go on like before, but can we still be friends?*

I closed my eyes and thought of Lauralee's funny laugh.

*We had one thing to learn*
*Now it's time for the wheel to turn*
*Don't waste time being hurt*
*We've been through hell together.*

Oh yeah, that's how it went. Now I remember.

*Let's admit we made a mistake, and can we still be friends?*
*Heartbreak's never easy to take, so can we still be friends?*
*We awoke from our dream*
*Things are not always what they seem*
*Memories linger on*
*It's like a sweet, sad, old song.*

That's how it went. I remember. I remember now.

When the song was over, I remembered. The good times with Lauralee washed through my thoughts like waves. And I promised myself at that moment that I would always love Lauralee and remember her fondly.

Then I lay back and thought of the time I'd just had with her and the start of the spring semester and the day I will have tomorrow when I resume work on my dissertation. I thought about the job interviews to come, all the traveling I'd be doing, the next advanced Spanish class I'd have to take, all the beginning reporting papers I'd be grading, and my extra duties as a teaching assistant for a very large media law class.

I took the Rundgren CD off the stereo, and put on Coltrane's *Lush Life*. No words to remember, no words to forget, just Trane's sweet agony.

I lay back and listened and thought and listened some more. I listened to it again and again. As light surrendered to the Texas night, I played that Coltrane CD again and again and again, until I could listen no more.

I walked up the stairs to my loft and fell asleep.

I didn't notice until the next day that there was a message on my answering machine. Colorado State University was looking for a journalism professor and my resume had impressed the search committee. They wanted to fly me up to Fort Collins for an interview.

# 4

## *"Why You Cannot Find?"*

The prospect of working at Colorado State interested me, but being used to the mild weather in California and the heat of Texas, I wasn't too thrilled with the idea of living up in the snow country. I was happy that I'd gotten a nibble on my fishing expedition for a faculty job, though. I was in the throes of a mating dance with America's universities, and this call from Colorado State made me feel attractive and desired.

Meanwhile, life was full of work, and the work continued to define my existence. There were the papers to grade, job-search letters to write, the Spanish homework and that damned dissertation. God, why am I here? The only respite I had was a game or two of pinball every day at the Texas Union, and maybe a side or two of Coltrane. But then it was back to work, or back to sleep so I can get back to work the next day.

The thing that kept me going was the promise of a better day. Liza was the new dawn in my darkness. Her next letter was like a jolt of caffeine.

---

*Feb. 05, 1997*
*Dear George,*

*Thank you very much for your letter and nice picture. You look so healthy and smart. Please send me a photo together with your friends and your relatives. If you send me a photo, I'll send you also, promise.*

*You know, I wish to see you in personal. Please visit here in the Philippines if you have a vacant time. I think your always busy regarding your job there, right? About me, I wish that I can go there in another place. If you need a helper or a house maid, just tell me coz I'll be the one to apply. (I'm just kidding.)*

*I can read your letter you want to find a Filipino girl who is beautiful, thoughtful and honest. Then if you can find that girl you can marry someday. But I might think there are some Filipina girls in your place. Why you cannot find?*

31

*Sorry for this question because I want to know you better. Please tell me the details. Until here my letter and please take good care of yourself and kindly regards to all your relatives and your friends and the most of all to you. I'll be waiting for your response, okey!*

*Yours truly*

*Liza Trujillo*

That paragraph haunted me: "I can read your letter you want to find a Filipino girl who is beautiful, thoughtful and honest. Then if you can find that girl you can marry someday. But I might think there are some Filipino girls in your place. Why you cannot find?"

*Why you cannot find? Why you cannot find?*

Liza's question was a good one. And there really was no easy answer I could give her. Maybe I hadn't been looking for a Filipino girl until now, Liza, until I saw your gleaming image on my computer. Maybe during my whole life I'd been on a journey, a journey to become something I'm not, a journey to become an American. A journey to become as good as any white American. Maybe as part of this journey, I decided to forsake my past. Maybe I was in lifelong denial about who I am. Maybe I craved affirmation in my new culture, seeking to win the spoils of victory that any white American male would have. And maybe that meant I had to have a white girlfriend. Maybe I thought that if I could have a beautiful white girlfriend, then maybe that would wash this brown off my body.

I wanted nothing less than a girl that white men would also lust for. For a while, Lauralee was that white girl. A tall, thin, blonde object of envy. A trophy girlfriend. My reward for having done well in white America. Maybe that's why—with just one exception—all of my girlfriends have been white. Maybe it was my way of becoming something bigger than I was.

Filipino-American girls? I never thought much about them. Maybe because of this, I'd been blind. Maybe I was on an ill-conceived journey all my life, Liza. And now, thanks to your wondrous smile, I have seen the light. Maybe now I'm on the right journey, the journey that I was meant to undertake.

You are my grand quest, Liza. And I WILL come to get you. But it'll have to wait a bit. I have a few more small journeys to take before I come to the Philippines to claim the ultimate prize.

First on the itinerary: Fort Collins, Colorado, and a two-day meeting with the faculty search committee at Colorado State University

At the Austin airport, I boarded a Continental Airlines jet for Houston, where I would catch a flight to Denver. In the Mile High City, I jumped on a passenger van for the brief ride to Fort Collins.

In the van, people were talking about hockey, of all things. The Colorado Avalanche had won the Stanley Cup playoffs last summer and the locals were abuzz about their prospects for a repeat. Some of the passengers were talking about the Rams. I couldn't figure out why Coloradans would be talking about the Rams NFL football team, since they were located in St. Louis. After a while, I discovered they were talking about the Colorado State Rams football team. Oh, I see. Yee-haw! More college football fanatics. I figured I better not say anything about the Texas Longhorns since I was inside a passenger fan full of people who probably hate with a passion the Longhorns and anything associated with Texas.

I tuned out all the sports talk and thought about the possibility of my living and working in Colorado. All I knew about Colorado was the popular myth about the place—wide-open spaces, down-to-earth people, cowboys, would-be anarchists and middle-class radicals in Boulder, cosmopolitan aspirations in Denver, the sappy outdoorsy far-outness of John Denver songs. "Rocky Mountain high, Colorado," started to ring through my brain, but I stopped it before it penetrated too deeply. I was on the highway, after all, not a mountain road. And I was in search of some sort of tangible payoff for my intellectual labors, not spiritual redemption by a campfire.

Well before we got to Fort Collins, I could see snow on the ground. It was also quite cold. I got off the van and sloshed my way to the hotel, called the chairman of the journalism department to let him know I'd arrived, and turned on the TV. After dinner, I wrote a letter to Liza. This time, I decided, I would tell her in no uncertain terms that I love her and that I want her to be mine for all time. I mailed the letter the next morning before the all-day interview session began.

The interviews and guest lecture went well. I spoke to a beginning reporting class about the importance of Associated Press style, and I met with the search committee (comprised of several professors of varying rank). I spoke eloquently, I thought, about my research. I also talked about my professional experience as a journalist. I spoke about the progress of my dissertation. I bragged about the book chapter I'd written a few months earlier with Prof. Maxwell McCombs, the co-creator of the Agenda Setting theory of mass communication and another one of my intellectual mentors at UT. This theory states that media content doesn't tell us what to think, but it does tell us what to think about.

(I didn't know it at the time, but the book chapter, which summarized the 25-year history of Agenda Setting research, would be published a few months later in

*Do the Media Govern?* a compilation by Sage, the academic publisher. The book would be a "hit," used in journalism classes all over the world, and it would enter a fifth printing by 1999.)

After the first day of interviews, I was invited to the home of one of the senior professors. He and his family lived in a hilly area high above the city, in the shadows of an immense mountain. In their front yard, the view was dominated by an expanse of open country, buildings only visible in the distance.

"Wow!" I said, "What an incredible view."

The professor seemed to be tickled by my amazement. "What would a view like this be worth in California?" He knew that I'd grown up in the San Francisco Bay Area.

"A front-yard view like this would not exist in San Francisco," I said. "But if you somehow found it, you could name the price for your home. Ten million, twenty million? I don't know."

The gray-haired professor seemed to be amused by this.

"Well, great," he said. "That's just great. So, come on in and make yourself at home. Dinner will be ready in a few minutes. And by the way, if you need to use the bathroom, I'll show you how to do it."

"Uh, what? I know how to use the bathroom."

"Hah! No, I mean we don't have indoor plumbing as you know it. We have a different system."

It turned out to be manual removal system using a deep pit, buckets, pulleys and friendly chemicals. I was alternately impressed and repulsed by the thought. And I wondered if I was staring at my own waste-management future.

Was the view of the magnificent mountain worth the effort? Was I going to become a professor in this frontier outback of the American West? And what about them Rams?

*Rocky Mountain high, Colorado.*

I came home to Austin exhausted from the trip. But there was no time for rest. I was a teaching assistant for a large media-law class, and I was facing the prospect of having to grade 260 papers. In addition, I was taking an advanced Spanish class, which I needed to pass to fulfill the foreign-language requirement for Ph.D. candidates. Also, my dissertation adviser was expecting more chapters soon.

The phone rang. It was California State University at Northridge, located in the lush and trendy San Fernando Valley of Los Angeles. They liked my resume and they wanted me to come in for an interview.

DUDE!

I was flattered. Another university wanted to check me out for a possible faculty appointment. While I was elated, I also realized that it was another project to prepare for, another trip to take, another thing that kept me from my immediate goal—finishing the dissertation.

Whose idea was this Ph.D. thing, anyway? I needed to get to work. I needed some big inspiration. I needed another letter from Liza.

I wouldn't get one for more than two months.

The trip to LA and the interview at Cal State-Northridge was, shall we say, not an overwhelming success.

On the way to my hotel, I relished the thought of being back in California after a couple of years away. LA really wasn't my home, but just being away from Texas was liberating. Even the crowded Santa Monica freeway gave me a good feeling.

If it felt good being in California, it didn't particularly feel good being at Cal State-Northridge. This was the San Fernando Valley, the Southern California of mega-malls and valley girls and valley dudes and fish tacos and pink flamingoes and rolling earthquakes and disposable culture. This is the kind of place you see caricatured and stereotyped in movies, TV shows and books about LA. It's the land of trendiness bordering on the totalitarian. I didn't know what I hated more, the obsession with the beautiful and new that this place embodied or the fact that all the journalism classes on campus were taught in ugly portable buildings. (A recent earthquake had temporarily displaced the journalism department.)

The day of interviews seemed normal enough, and the students seemed polite and respectful. I visited one particular faculty member who spent almost the entire 45-minute session talking about herself and her career as a reporter at *The Los Angeles Times*. I guess the upside was I didn't have much of an opportunity to say something stupid.

When the day was done, I inquired about a faculty member who did not attend any of my lectures and interview sessions.

"Oh, don't worry about her," a senior professor told me. "She's on, shall we say, extended leave."

The professor went on to tell me that the missing faculty member had been having trouble handling her duties lately, duties that included teaching four classes, editing an academic journal, writing scholarly journal articles, serving as academic advisor to 60 students, serving on various university committees and performing various departmental service functions. Oh yeah, she was expected to do some community service too.

"Yikes!" I said. "That's an awful lot of work."

"Really? That's just a normal workload for a professor here. As an assistant professor, you'd be expected to do even more than that. You'd have to exceed that—if you want tenure."

Great! This is what I needed in my life: another descent into hell.

When I returned to my room in the campus visitors center, I found a note waiting for me. It was a letter from the missing professor, warning me that I'd regret coming to work at CSU-Northridge. She noted that there were "a lot of serious problems" in the department, and she advised me to find a job elsewhere.

I knew at that moment that my future would not be at Cal State-Northridge.

I hopped on board my American Airlines flight back to Austin, discouraged and saddened by what I'd experienced, and depressed because I'd wasted three days and a ton of energy on this fruitless journey. I also had 260 media-law papers to grade. What I needed was another letter from Liza to lift my spirits. It came shortly:

---

*Feb. 28, 1997*
*Dear George,*

*Hello, how are you now? I hope all of your family are doing well and everything will be alright. By the way, how about your recent trip to Colorado? Are you enjoy there? Do you find a teaching job at a college there? I might think it's a nice place coz when I read your letter it was snowing when you went there. You know George, I cannot seen snow ever since only a picture and the movies.*

*Any way, you can say your letter you have a feelings to me but if you think I'm compatible to you and you are willing to accept me of what I am. So, it's up to you to decide if you treated me as one of your very special woman or more than that, and about me it would be up to you and its fine with me. Anyway, what's important is that we get along well, so hopefully there will be no problem.*

*And I would like to ask you a question: here's a couple of questions to you, but don't take this a wrong way. First, do you have some penpals here in the Phil? Lastly, you are interested to marry a woman in the Phil. Why?*

*By the way, you are asking me about my studies. Until now, I have a plan to continue my studies but my work, I work full time daily here in Dept. Store. Now I'm working here in Dept. Store to help my parents. But I continue my studies based on my situation. I will try my very best to continue because I want to success my career and thru the help of our Almighty God.*

*Until my letter here…Regards to all your relatives there and to all your friends. Lastly, to you, my dear George. Bye bye. I'll wait your response together your photos, okey.*

*Liza Trujillo.*

My heart leapt, almost out of my chest. She's intrigued. She wants me. Or more precisely, she's saying in her pigeon English something like, "Yeah, I could like you; and if you like me, then let's have a go." Or something like that. It was impossible to discern the precise meaning through the bad English. My goodness, don't they have any copy editors over there? But the important thing is—she's open to the possibility.

I read that key paragraph over and over. "Any way, you can say your letter you have feelings to me but if you think I'm compatible to you and you are willing to accept me of what am I. So, it's up to you to decide if you treated me as one of your very special woman or more than that, and about me it would be all up to you and its fine with me."

Wow! Wow! Wow!

But what about that other stuff? That stuff about compatibility? Maybe she was saying: "Yes, I'm a simple girl from the Philippine lower class, and you're a big, smart American from the privileged class. And I doubt that we're compatible, but if you think that maybe we could meet and fall in love, then I'm willing to take a chance."

Or something like that.

But wait a minute. What's that weird stuff about "it's up to you to decide if you treated me as one of your very special woman or more than that…"?

What exactly does she mean here? Could it simply be a matter of poor phrasing? Or is she saying something a little bit more complicated? She might be saying: "I could be your wife or I could be your mistress. It's all up to you!"

This thought tickled me, but it also disturbed me. Why did she bring up the idea of being a mistress, a mistress to an American lover? Did she have this kind of an experience before? Is this something she does regularly? Worse, is she a professional at this? Is she a professional mistress? Does she live on the largesse of lonely, well-to-do foreigners? Am I just her latest benefactor-in-waiting?

I was a bit confused. But for the moment, what mattered most was that this beautiful dream girl was telling me that she was ready for me, that she was waiting for me, that she was wide open.

I could feel love blooming. I could feel my hand reaching across the ocean and touching hers. What must it feel like to touch her? What must it feel like to see her smile, to feel her breath on my face, to hold her close?

Liza, forget that silly stuff about being my mistress. I want to find something good and decent and honest and true in my life. I want to find someone who will fulfill an old-fashioned fantasy, who will be perfect and kind and loving and loyal and traditional, someone who will always love me, someone who will marry me and respect me and give me children and honor me for all time.

Girls from the Philippines are like that, right? That's what I've always heard and that's what I have come to know. Filipino girls are traditional and conservative. They marry for life. In the Philippines, there's no divorce. It's a strong cultural taboo, probably coming from the centuries-old Spanish/Catholic influence. And that's why Filipino couples stick together through the hard times, through the impossible times, through the conflicts, through all their troubles, as my mother and father did—just to save their marriage. Americans do not think this way. When their marriages go bad, they seem quite able to dispose of it like an old car. Tired of this Chevy? Well, get rid of it and buy a Ford.

You wouldn't do that to me, would you, Liza? I can see in your face that you're kind and loyal and loving and true. I can tell from your humble words that you are sincere and down-to-earth and open to my love.

I went to work grading the stack of 260 or so media-law papers. It would take me about three full days to finish. I checked the mailbox each day for another letter from Liza. Weeks passed and none came. I looked on the Internet to see if there was any way I could get an email to her at the SM department store. I could find none. I came up with some wild ideas of how to get through to her: I thought of possibly finding someone in Cebu who was wired and who could deliver some emails in person to Liza. Shotgun-style, I sent out some random emails to people living in Cebu (who I found on a Cebu-based Web site) to see if any of them would help me out.

Meanwhile, the mailbox back in my Austin apartment was humming with business. I got a flurry of letters from universities that I had applied to for faculty positions. I received letters of interest from an interesting assortment of schools. The University of North Carolina seemed mildly interested. So did San Diego State. Both said they'd call me soon. I got a call from American University in Cairo; their recruiter wanted me to fly up to New York for an interview. I also got an email from the University of the Philippines. They were intrigued too.

Later, I got a call from Texas A&M University, home of the Aggies and hated rival of the Texas Longhorns. They were mightily impressed with my CV and they wanted me to come in for an interview. The chairman of the journalism department sounded very, very interested. He practically said, without really saying it, that A&M would be ready to hire someone like me. The thought of teaching journalism to a bunch of ultra-conservative, Clinton-hating Aggies from East Texas really, really tickled my funny bone. And I thought that this could also be an interesting cultural experience.

This flood of interest in my intellectual services was exhilarating and my mind was filled with excitement and joy at the prospect of starting a new life somewhere else, somewhere new. This particular mating dance appeared headed for a happy ending—or at least a very interesting one. But there was yet another mating dance afoot, and it made my blood boil and gave me fever like nothing else. I lived every day waiting for words from her, another letter, a call maybe.

And now, looking at my mailbox again, I see no letter from Liza. Again.

And again. And again.

Mad with impatience, I wrote her a couple of letters telling her about my job search, about the progress on my dissertation. I declared emphatically that there's no one else but her, that I'd like to hear from her again, that I need to read sweet words from her again. Soon.

Please make it soon, Liza. I need your love to stop from going mad.

# 5

## *"George Has A Mail Order Bride"*

The funny syndicated columnist Molly Ivins made a guest appearance in a UT journalism class one afternoon, and afterward I had a chance to meet with her.

As we chatted in the ground-floor indoor parking lot of the College of Communication, I chain-smoked Camel Lights nervously and Molly told me a story of how she'd once met my former boss, the late *Oakland Tribune* publisher Robert Maynard, at a journalism conference. We both agreed that he was indeed a visionary. He had done a lot to promote diversity in journalism.

Molly offered her opinions of a number of columnists who I would be profiling and analyzing in my dissertation. She also graciously consented to an extended interview, which I could have in her South Austin home a few weeks later. This interview would turn out to be fascinating, as I somehow knew it would be, and the material I gathered became a key part of my research on the role of columnists in American news culture.

Molly was often invited to appear in journalism classes, and she never failed to entertain. The bane of conservatives, Ivins would not fail to win over even the diehard conservative students in the class with her down-home sense of humor and her insider stories of Texas politics. She also told a lot of dirty jokes and cussed a lot. That helped too.

Before we parted ways on this afternoon, she asked me if I enjoyed college teaching.

"Well," I said. "I teach beginning reporting, which means daily exercises in AP style and writing leads. How much fun could that be?"

Molly let out a full-out, trailer-park belly laugh at that, and I knew that I'd gotten to her. She wouldn't forget me. With that, I went to my office on the fifth floor, a closet-sized space I shared with five other graduate students, and started preparing for my beginning reporting class later that day.

The students in my class had started to wear down under the weight of regular drilling and quizzing. As part of my teaching strategy, my students had to learn and use Associated Press style, which dictates the proper ways to use numerals, state names, street addresses, proper pronouns and other important things when writing news copy.

The students had become quite tired of this.

"What does it matter?" one student cried out in frustration during a particularly long discussion on the proper way to identity congressional subcommittees in news stories. "What does it matter if you capitalize the name of the committee or not? People will know what you're talking about."

I needed a rejoinder. Fast. I stared into the student's eyes, and I looked around at the other students, all finely polished sons and daughters of the Republic of Texas. In their eyes, I found my response.

"I know, young sir, that this is quickly becoming boring to you, this relentless perfectionism, this obsession with detail," I said. I paused a moment, two moments for effect, and made eye contact with each and every student in the room.

"But please remember this: I have been hired by the great State of Texas, in all of its infinite wisdom, to teach you'all the right way to do journalism. And the first step in this process is for all of you to learn AP style."

Silence.

"Now, if you don't learn AP Style, well, if you don't learn AP style, you'd be letting down the great State of Texas, wouldn't you?"

More silence.

"You wouldn't want to let down the great State of Texas, would you?"

One of the students, a tall, slender girl with blond ringlets, snapped up like a soldier.

"No sir," she said. "I would not."

No one else said a thing.

"All right then, let's proceed."

And so it went for the rest of the day. There were no more questions about the usefulness of AP style in journalism education.

I felt like a goddam patriot.

The curly-haired girl came up to me after class.

"I understand now why AP style means so much," she said. "I promise I'll learn it."

"Good," I said to her. "And then you'll have a discipline that will help you get a job later."

"Yes sir," she said.

Now I felt like a goddam drill sergeant.

Another one of my students came by a few minutes later, a smartass who worked as one of the editors at the student newspaper, The Daily Texan.

"That speech you gave in class about AP Style."

"Yeah, what about it?"

"Totally brilliant," he said, "and total bullshit."

"Good observation. You'll make a fine journalist when you grow up. Carry on then," I said, smiling and waving him off.

It had been a long day by this point, and I was ready to go home. But first, I needed to go to the student center and have my ritual game of pinball to unleash my frustrations, then on to Tower Records to check out the John Coltrane CDs.

I closed the computer-lab doors and locked up.

"George has got a mail-order bride."

I heard a voice bellowing from a lab adjacent to mine.

"What? Who's there?"

A woman graduate student who I knew only remotely could hardly contain her glee. She emerged from the open door and confronted me.

"I hear you've got a mail-order bride! Ha ha!"

I reckoned the meaning of the moment instantly. Perhaps embittered by my academic successes, perhaps jealous of the grace with which I'd glided through this doctoral program, she had found her moment to deliver a public comeuppance. She had latched onto a rumor that spoke ill of me and she was making the most of it. It was her moment.

I looked around. Nobody had heard her, it seemed. But she was bellowing loud enough for the entire building to hear.

"George has got a mail-order bride!" She was positively singing it now, like a nasty, taunting little schoolgirl.

"If you'd like to know the truth, I'll explain this to you," I said, rather condescendingly. "If you're speaking about the girl I met on the Internet who I'm now corresponding with," I explained, "the truth of the matter is that I've never met her in person, thus she is hardly my bride."

I continued.

"I will assume for the time being that the person who is the source of this rumor has conveyed to you that I've become smitten with this someone who exists only theoretically, whose glowing image has entranced me, whose promise of eternity has filled a hole in my soul with new hope and new dreams, where before there was only emptiness and despair. This part of your accusation, although you hadn't articulated it in that precise a way, is correct. And I do plan to meet her in person one day soon. This is, in fact, a potential relationship that I hope to initiate through distance communications techniques."

My assailant stopped smiling. She was about to sputter something out, but I kept up the counterattack.

"Now, we need to unpack some of the assumptions built into your choice of terminology, this 'mail-order bride' thing you speak of. Yes, I know that there are men here in America—generally older men—who seek younger women by looking to other countries, like the Philippines, which incidentally, is my home country. Did you know that, by the way? Often, the women these men find are poor and desperate, and they see these men, these older American men, as vehicles for quick and easy immigration tickets to the land of plenty. On the other side, these men see these women perhaps as being easily obtainable—much more easily attainable than their equivalents here in America—and easier to please, as well. All it takes is simple love and affection, and of course, ample financial support. Both parties don't want complicated conversation in their lives. Things are pretty simple and clear-cut to them.

"This is refreshing and new to these men, especially those who have grown weary of the complexities of American mating rituals, who have lost the patience for complicated conversations about what love really is and what love should really be and what equality should be. Your implicit charge then is this: These distance relationships are vacuous. Instead of love, there is convenience. Instead of mutual passion, there is mutual commodification. Instead of caring, there is exploitation. Instead of spontaneous combustion, there is mail order.

"All of these things are bad. They are bad, bad, bad, very bad. And therefore, the parties engaged in such an arrangement are something less than fully formed, fully actualized people. They are bad, bad, bad, bad, pathetic people. Right?"

My attacker stood there speechless.

"Well, have you ever considered other possibilities? Have you ever thought that my situation might be far more complex than your mediocre mind could fathom? Consider for a moment this possibility: Let's say I'm an older American man, let's say in my 40's—which I am—and let's say that I've had a number of satisfying and less-than-satisfying relationships here on American soil with American women. Which I have! Let's also say that my life has reached a point now where my heart yearns for an old-fashioned relationship, where both parties pledge undying love for one another—a forever love—and are willing to stick by it for good, through thick and thin.

"Your remember that thing called undying love? We used to hear about it in books and movies and old wives' tales, in Shakespearean tragedies, in Broadway musicals, in old Beatles songs. In reality, in this time and in this culture, this concept has become antiquated. Love is no longer a forever thing. It exists only as long as it's convenient. When it is no longer convenient, then pfffffffft! It goes away.

"Breaking up is too easy, divorce has become just as easy. All you need is a lawyer to break the spell of undying love. And American morals have canonized the rightness of litigation as a remedy for everything. It's no coincidence that these canons of litigation are writ into law by politicians and lawyers who profit handsomely from litigation. Divorce is good commerce! If it's not a divorce, but a simple breakup you want, all you need do is speak vaguely in terms of freedom, of how rivers must flow, of how suffocated one is feeling, of how one needs to find oneself. And this complexity makes for interesting conversation, but in the course of things, the antiquated, naive little concept of forever-love gets tossed out the window.

"Wait a minute, wait a minute, you're shaking your head. I see I've lost you. Bear with me another moment or two. My point will become clear. In Philippine culture, divorce just doesn't happen. Love is forever. Love might fade, but men and women make serious attempts to stick it through. They don't go running to lawyers at the first sign of trouble, they don't toss their love like Bic lighters that have dried up. I know! I'm a Filipino! Well, a Filipino-American, actually. And I know, from having seen my parents go through it, and from seeing my aunts and uncles, that sustaining a long-term relationship takes guts. It takes fortitude. It takes will power. It takes passion and dedication to make it work.

"This takes a lot of effort then. But we Americans, oh we Americans, we don't have space in our lives for dedication. We live in a disposable society after all, right? When something goes bad, we toss it out into the trash, like a cheap razor that's gone dull. Just buy a new one then, right? Instant gratification. No need for will power, passion and guts. That's messy stuff. Just buy new.

"Well, I'm tired of that. I've done that and I'm tired of it! I want something that'll last. I want something, someone, to believe in forever. And I want someone who will believe in me. Forever! Someone who will stay with me through the bad times as well as the good. Someone who really will live up to those marriage vows, through thickness and thin, til death do us part. And if that someone is only available to me through my own home culture, then so be it.

"The bitter irony is that I came here from the Philippines, and I have become American. This is good. In the past, I have taken up with American women. Ooooh, interracial coupling, this is not so good.

"And now, I've decided to do what is right and find a girl from my home country. And I'm using the Internet to do it. So what? So fucking what? Isn't the Internet supposed to be a tool for empowerment or what? So what do I get from you, supposedly an enlightened scholar? I get grief! I get humiliation. 'George has a mail-order bride,' and all that crap.

"Listen, if you want to depict me as some loser who has ordered a bride through the mail, so be it. I don't care! If it makes you feel better about your pathetic life, go ahead. I don't care!

"When I saw her sweet face smiling at me on my computer screen, I saw beams of eternity, I felt forever love, I felt, I felt God's pleasure. I saw the face that has been in my mind but never in my sight, hidden behind the veil of Americanization that has clouded the truth from me for almost my entire life."

A small crowd of students had gathered around us now. But I was not ashamed.

"She's a poor Filipino girl. She needs me. She needs me because I will love her forever. And she needs me to save her from the clutches of some other man who only wants her because she's young and beautiful and not so complicated. And if that's a bad thing, so be it. If that makes me a pathetic wretch, so be it. At least I'll be a happy, pathetic wretch."

I was done. My attacker gaped at me for a moment, speechless. I looked around at the crowd of students gathered around us. My attacker smiled at me for a moment, and it seemed to be a sweet, apologetic smile. Then she turned to the crowd.

"George has got a mail-order bride. Ha-ha, ha-ha!"

Someone in the crowd stifled a laugh and then the whole lot of them let out a group chuckle.

"Excuse me," my attacker said, walking off. "I'm going to spread the news far and wide. GEORGE HAS A MAIL-ORDER BRIDE! HAWWWW."

The whole crowd erupted in full-out belly laughs as she sashayed down the hall.

Despite my eloquent rant, I had totally, utterly humiliated myself. But somehow, it didn't matter.

I sulked back into my lab and shut the door behind me. I got on a computer and clicked onto the Web site where I knew she would be, waiting for me, smiling at me, welcoming me, shooting beams of eternity in my direction through her lovely, dewy eyes.

"Wait for me, my love," I whispered. "It will take me a little while, but I will be there. And you will be mine, and we will love each other for all time. I swear it, as God is my witness, you will be mine."

Later, I went and played some pinball at the Texas Union recreation center, scoring high enough to win a couple of free games. Then I went to Tower Records and bought another John Coltrane CD.

Then, as the late afternoon sky began to darken the day, I walked down Guadalupe and turned left at the faculty club on 25th Street.

It had been a good day. I had won a battle or two and I had lost a battle or two, and now I was heading home. And I would be alone again, accompanied only by images of a beautiful Filipina girl, whose existence was only theoretical, but whose sweet face and dewy eyes were alive and swirling and tossing in my mind.

It had been a good day, just like all the other good days.

I put on the Coltrane CD and slept.

# 6

## *True West*

Dear George,

*Please smile before you read this letter of mine. Hello, how are you? I received your letter yesterday. When I'm read it, I feel happy because you are very caring and you are very concern to me and thank you very much.*

*I'm sorry for my letter was delayed. I will give you an explanation. I hope you understand me, okey? You know George, my schedule is opening shift 9:00 in the morning, then my off in the evening 7:00 o'clock. When I'm go to the post office to mail my letter its already close and the last month I have no day off then the first week of May I have a day off. Last Monday I will go to post office to mail the response of your first letter. Did you received it? George, don't think a bad way because its not true, okey?*

*You know, even you did not response my letter I will write you again coz I will happy to read your letter. George, I'm not mad to you if you have friends in other places because I'm not selfish and you are free to choose of what you want, right? And sorry if I have mistaken to you, okey?*

*George, you just write here your letter if what can I want to prove your feelings to me. Well, it would be all up to you. The important thing is its from the bottom of your heart, okey? Until here my letter regards to all your relatives and your friends and the most of all to you.*

*Love and care*

*Liza*

It had been a couple of months since I received a letter from Liza, but this one was definitely worth the wait. It was the first time Liza had used the magic word "love." I was absolutely elated by this, totally floored, but also somewhat mystified by a number of other things. First, I wondered about her inability to send a letter to me because she was supposedly too busy at work to go to the post office. Come on! Don't they have mailboxes there? And what is this stuff about friends in other places? Does she think I'm some sort of cad with girlfriends in many places? Where would she get such an idea?

Liza's letter gave me plenty of food for thought, but I couldn't spend too much time pondering the meanings. I was on a runaway train.

We were entering the home stretch for my dissertation. which had now quickly passed the 250-page mark. My advisor, Chuck Whitney, and I agreed that I should finish this thing soon and defend it by July. Meanwhile, he had a few suggestions for revisions. Otherwise, he said, everything looks to be on track.

The dissertation was about the role of newspaper columnists within the traditional newsroom culture, and the ability of some columnists to get progressive/ radical ideas into print in mainstream publications. I focused on the works of Molly Ivins, Alexander Cockburn and Robert Maynard (my former boss at *The Oakland Tribune,* who for several years also wrote a thrice-weekly column).

I'd finished writing my chapters on Maynard, which were relatively easy to write since I'd worked for the man for several years and knew his politics and his written works. I'd also had a couple of great interviews with Molly Ivins and had a chance to observe her at work in her own home. I also had done a thorough analysis of about 100 of her columns. What remained was an interview with Cockburn and analysis of his work. I needed to get to this right away.

I did an Internet search for Cockburn's work, which had appeared regularly in the *Los Angeles Times,* the *Wall Street Journal* and many other mainstream newspapers around the country—a fact that I found quite fascinating since Cockburn is one of the more incendiary radicals in the business. It was interesting to me that his work even found the light of day in the elite publications. Finding out WHY was the key to the dissertation, I figured. It would be the punch line. The grand finale. The fireworks at the end of the game.

I gathered up about 100 of Cockburn's columns from the Lexis/Nexis database, and dug up his home phone number in Petrolia, a small town on the "Lost Coast" of Northern California's redwood country. I also got the names and numbers of key people from newspapers that have published Cockburn's work. I would first read all the columns, then call his editors to find out what they find so valuable in his work, then I would call Alex himself. I had my plan for my dissertation's coup de grace. I was getting ready for my assault on Fortress Cockburn.

In the meantime, I received some more phone calls from universities interested, possibly, in acquiring my services: the University of Southern California,

San Francisco State University and Humboldt State University. They all wanted me to come for a visit. Texas A&M also called again. They wanted to set a time for me to come visit the College Station campus.

Sure, why not? I'm a teaching assistant for a class of 260 undergraduates, I'm supposed to have a finished dissertation ready to defend within six weeks, I'm taking an advanced Spanish class that I'm really struggling with, I haven't heard back yet from the two universities I'd visited, and you'all want me to go on a road trip to audition for faculty gigs?

Why not? WHY NOT? This is the moment of truth, the time of madness! I need a drink! I need some love! I need a letter from Liza—to give me reassurance, to give me strength, to let me know that there was a pot of gold at the end of this rainbow tour. But the letter from Liza did not come. I waited and waited, but it did not come.

I decided to lock myself into a mindset of work for a couple of weeks. Time to be a mule, I figured. Time to lug some heavy loads over the mountain. And so I did. I worked day and night, sleeping no more than four or five hours. I went to the library looking for books about columnists, journalism history, media sociology, critical theory, cultural studies, literary analysis—anything to give me a jolt of scholastic creativity. I wrote and rewrote. I inserted, I deleted, I expounded, I minimized, I proselytized, I theorized, I historicized. And then I footnoted, footnoted and footnoted again. I turned down invitations to go bowling, to go to Longhorns football games, to have any fun of any kind, because I needed to work on my bibliography.

The time quickly came for me to take my trips to East Texas and the West Coast for the job interviews.

The visit to College Station went well. I did notice a lot of military uniforms and buzz cuts around campus, and so I knew all or most of the things they said about Texas A&M were true. This was going to be a descent into Bubba-Land, where only two political philosophies exist. "Son, here in East Texas you're either a conservative or you're a communist," the saying went. And so it was.

Journalism students and professors tend to be liberal, though, so I felt confident that there was going to be an oasis of open-air intellectualism here. I was confident that I would do well. After making the three-hour drive from Austin to College Station, I checked into my hotel, hung up my Italian suit and Perry Ellis dress shirt, and made sure my hard black shoes had a nice military shine. I flopped into bed and didn't sleep. I was thinking about the future, pondering what I'd talk about at the faculty interview the next day, wondering why Liza hadn't written in so long. Had she given up on me, thinking this was all some big farce? Had she found someone younger, handsomer? Had she grown bored with this long-distance, correspondence course in intercultural coupling? Or maybe she just didn't care? What was it? What could it be? What was the problem?

The interview went well. I was asked if I was a traditional scholar or one of these "trendy, young critical guys." I answered that I was open to any manner of scholarly inquisition, as long as the method was suited to the research question. I was asked about my book chapter with Max McCombs. Does it mean that I subscribe totally to the underlying assumptions of Agenda Setting research? Do I think I would ever find myself challenging the findings of Agenda Setting?

I responded, "I would never dare." That got a hearty laugh from the search committee, who knew how much power and influence McCombs and his theory have in the field of mass communication research.

What about critical theory? The foundation of critical studies is the use of ideological analysis, otherwise known as political-economic analysis, also known as Marxist analysis. "Are you a Marxist, Dr. Estrada?"

It was a trap, and we all knew it.

"No sir, I am a capitalist. I invest in the stock market and I hope to retire quite wealthy, thank you." This also received some chortles from the committee.

"We notice, though," a professor on the committee insisted, "that your dissertation advisor is Chuck Whitney."

"Yes, that is correct. And so?"

"And so Dr. Whitney is the editor of the journal Critical Studies in Mass Communication, is he not?"

"Yes, he is."

"Most or all of the work in that journal utilizes one or another form of critical-slash-Marxist analysis, does it not?"

"Why, yes it does. But please don't put Dr. Whitney or myself in such a convenient little pigeonhole, sir. I believe that a true intellectual must be open to all forms of analysis and inquisition, whether they be in the traditional quantitative methods of analysis, like Agenda Setting, or in the more eclectic, critical, cultural, or even post-modern forms. A true intellectual would not be closed to any possibility, including the use of Marxist analysis. It is just one of the available tools in any good intellectual's toolbox. Please don't marginalize me, Dr. Whitney or critical scholars generally because of our choice of analytical methods."

It was a bravura performance, with me saying all the right things, making all the right moves and escaping from all the traps the professors on the search committee were laying out for me. For my finale, I played an audio tape of a phone conversation that President Lyndon Johnson had with Katherine Graham, the publisher of *The Washington Post*, back in 1964. The subject was civil rights, and Johnson was at his finest, prodding, urging, commanding and pleading with Mrs. Graham to give more positive coverage to the issue. I used this tape as a demonstration of what could be done with Agenda Setting research, but I also had another strategic purpose in mind. I knew that Texans love Lyndon Johnson and his legacy, and I figured that if I could use something of his to tip sentiment in my favor during a job search, well doggonit, I'll do it!

And so I did, and so it was. The search committee loved hearing the Johnson tape, and let out a roar when the president started flirting with Graham, calling her "my sweetheart," and threatening to "jump the fence" and come after her some day like a wild bull in heat. It was knee-slapping time at the ranch. Good old Lyndon. He scared the hell out of me when I was draft age and the Vietnam War was raging, but he did well by me this day. All was good in Texas.

In the afternoon, I met with about a dozen Texas A&M journalism students. One of them, obviously a smartass, asked me: "Is it true all you'all people from Austin are communists?"

Laughing and shooting him a wink, I replied: "Well, communists probably wouldn't get tenure, would they?"

From their sly laughs I knew I'd won them over too.

Later on, Randy Sumpter, a young assistant professor at A&M who had gotten his Ph.D. from UT just the year before, sidled up and told me: "You did good. I think they'll be calling you."

"Really? How do you feel about that?"

"Well, I do need a collaborator on some of my research projects." Randy patted me on the back and gave me a grin, and the possibility that I'd be teaching in East Texas in the fall suddenly became a reality. I'd better learn the "Gig 'em, Aggies" hand signal soon.

I had just a few days to catch my breath back in Austin before heading back out on the road for my West Coast appointments. I'd be back in California again, and I welcomed the thought. I checked my mail, which had piled up in the post office, and there was no letter from Liza. When I got home there was a message on my phone machine. The University of Southern California wanted me to visit next week.

At first, I thought no way. I've already got an impossible schedule ahead of me. But after looking more closely at my schedule, and after making some hasty arrangements, I saw that this would be possible. Ridiculous, but possible. Let's do it!. I would fly to LA for an interview with USC, then I would come back to Austin for a few days to do some more writing, attend a couple of Spanish classes, catch up with my TA work and then fly back to California for my interviews with San Francisco State and Humboldt State. That would be it, I decided. No more job trips after these. Come the fall, I'll be working in a fine university, I was sure. No reason to head off to Michigan or North Carolina or Cairo or wherever for some wild joyride. Let's limit this universe right here and now. It's going to be either Texas A&M, Colorado State, Cal State-Northridge, USC or San Francisco State.

I sat back and thought about this for a while.

If it was going to be Texas A&M, I'd be in a very conservative environment, surrounded by bald-headed Aggies jacked up on football, retrograde militarism and Shiner Bock beer.

If it was Humboldt State or San Francisco State, it would be exactly the opposite. Ultra-liberalism, political correctness and California cool would be the rule.

If it was Colorado State, it would be more than cool. It would be freezing. It would be Rocky Mountain High all right, but the only thing that would be high for me would be my heating bills.

USC or Cal-State Northridge would be Hollywood. What more can I say? The thought of wearing my sunglasses on top of my head and calling everybody "babe" didn't really appeal to me.

What a choice!

When I got into this game, all I wanted to do was teach journalism skills: how to write a good news article, how to edit it to make it crisper, how to conform to AP style, how to catch potential libel and invasion of privacy.

When I went looking for a teaching job a few years back, they told me I needed a Ph.D., even though I had 12 years experience as a reporter and columnist for a daily newspaper. And so now, four years later, as I am on the verge of getting that Ph.D., I find out that there is another ritual I have to go through, a sort of mating dance, before I can get that faculty position I so covet.

And, like a single man looking for a perfect wife, search committees seek that perfect partner: someone who knows how to do mass communication research and get it published in proper journals, someone with the professional experience to credibly teach a number of journalism skills classes, someone who gets along well with students and other faculty, someone who will fulfill some sort of diversity-driven hiring need.

These types of candidates are rare. Usually, you get a young pup scholar, late 20s to early 30s, who went straight through grad school and thus doesn't have the requisite professional experience to be teaching undergraduate journalism skills classes. Or, conversely, you get the ham-and-egger veteran journalist who's been in the business 20 years or so, and believes he doesn't need an advanced degree because he knows everything there is to know about journalism.

Both of these types have become clichés to those professors who've served on a few search committees. It is nearly impossible to find someone with both the doctorate and the experience. And so it is refreshing and surprising when someone with my resume shows up. To them, I am almost impossible to resist.

And so it was with Liza too, I figured. Here I come with my Filipino face and my American citizenship and my Ph.D. in waiting and my sweet letters promising love, offering an escape from her dead-end existence. And so, I am impossible to resist. Am I not? So why no letter in more than two months, Liza? Please send me a letter soon. I am going mad not hearing from you. Can't you see that I'm impossible to resist?

Before leaving for LA, I got a phone call from Texas A&M. It's official: They want me! They will be sending me an official job offer soon. They are willing to pay me $40,000 to start—not great, but not bad—and they're willing to give me some research support too. I thank them and tell them I'll give them an answer after I return from a trip to California.

"I need time to sit under a redwood tree and think about my life." They tell me fine, but don't spend too much time pondering the future. The clock is ticking.

I was flying high, knowing that I'd won a position on a prestigious journalism faculty. Rednecks and bulletheads notwithstanding, A&M is known for being a fine university, and I was flattered by their offer.

The interview at USC was incredible. Since it was the University of Southern California, I expected things to be over the top, like their football tradition, like their cheerleaders, like the bleach-blonde coeds with boob jobs, like everything you'd expect from a school that is all Hollywood, all Big Time, all the time. What I found was that USC's salary offer for a new journalism professor would be something in the $30,000 to $35,000 range. I tried to remain calm, but I was aghast. Living in LA on $30,000 or $35,000 would be insane.

"I know it doesn't sound like much," one senior professor said to me, "but all the professors on the journalism faculty work as consultants. That's where you can really do well. USC is a name brand, and you'll find a lot of people wanting to pay you for your opinions."

"Right, the consulting thing. I've heard of this," I said. "But I just want to concentrate on being a good professor for now, you see. I should tell you, though, that Texas A&M has already made me an offer of $40,000."

The gray-haired senior professor looked at me like I was insane.

"You'd rather live in East Texas than LA?"

"Well, A&M seems to be very supportive of me. They've got a lot of money for research. And I've got a lot of friends in Texas. I'd have no problem living in College Station."

I was lying through my teeth.

"OK, if that's what you want. You make it sound real good. I hope it's that good."

He'd called my bluff. Neither one of us blinked. I went on with the rest of the program set for that day. I gave a guest lecture and got a rousing ovation from the audience of undergraduates. I met with a junior-level professor later who told me that the students were impressed with my lecture, and that "there's a lot of support for you on the faculty."

I started feeling good about USC. I met later with the dean. He told me that he was thinking about starting a doctoral program for the journalism department.

"That's why we'd like to have you here. We need to have some Ph.Ds in the department."

"How many do you have now?" I asked.

"Well, none right now."

"None?!"

"That's right. We tend to hire professional journalists, you know, not intellectuals. How many Ph.Ds do we need on the faculty before we can have a Ph.D. program?"

Again, I was aghast. But I tried to keep my composure. "Well, to earn a doctorate, a student should defend his or her dissertation before a committee of at least five professors. At least that's the way it is for me at Texas. So, I'd say you need at least four professors with doctorates. The fifth member of the committee is usually someone from another department."

"Oh? Four? That many, huh?"

The dean seemed to lose interest. "Well, forget it then. I've got another idea I'd like to tell you about…"

I couldn't believe what I was hearing. I felt like I was at a Hollywood pitch meeting, and that this guy was trying to sell me on his latest movie idea. I knew at that moment that I was not going to be teaching at USC.

Back in Austin, there was a ton of stuff to do. I had another stack of 260 papers to grade. I had a meeting with Prof. Whitney to discuss the progress of my dissertation. And I had some overdue Spanish homework to turn in.

I finished grading the papers in a day and a half. The meeting with my advisor went well: "Looks good so far. We're on track." Spanish class was its usual farce.

My Spanish professor's teaching style was called the "immersion" method. For her, this meant addressing students in very fast Spanish, and then staring at you like you were an idiot for not responding immediately. This is what most of the semester was like for me, and the irony of it wasn't lost. Here I was, a Filipino-American, working hard to find my niche in America, but yearning to re-connect with my roots in the Philippines. In the meantime, I was being held back and oppressed by the Spanish language—like the Filipinos who'd been oppressed by the Spanish for almost four centuries. The irony of the situation was irresistible.

I was just fortunate that this professor was merciful, and sensitive to the needs of doctoral students. She knew that our advanced foreign-language requirement was a farce, an artifact of antiquity. And so she was quite liberal with her grading. Were she a different person, she could have flunked me, kept me from getting my doctorate. But she was not that kind of person, thank God. After class she would pepper me with all kinds of questions about my job search, how the interviews were conducted, what kind of materials I sent with my resume, what kinds of questions the search committees asked me, what sorts of job offers I'd received. She was impressed with all the invitations for interviews I'd gotten. It turns out she was just like me, just about to get her Ph.D. and out on the campaign trail doing the dog-and-pony show at different universities all over the country.

I detected empathy from her, a rapport with her. I felt confident that I'd pass the class, no matter how utterly inept I was with the Spanish language. "All I need is a C," I pleaded with her. "Just one little C."

"Don't worry," she said. "Just try your best."

A few days later, I launched the last leg of my quest to find that elusive perfect faculty position. First, I would be going to the Bay Area, where I would do an interview and lecture session at San Francisco State, then I would rent a car and drive 280 miles north on Highway 101 for one last courting dance, this time at Humboldt State University, a small school on the redwood coast.

This trip felt different from the others. It was early May now, and the spring weather couldn't have been more perfect for a homecoming. I'd lived in the Bay Area for almost all my life, and most of my relatives live in San Francisco. In addition, I knew many of the professors and lecturers on the SF State faculty, as many of them had once worked at *The Oakland Tribune*. Also, I had taught beginning reporting classes there before as a part-time lecturer and had gotten to know other faculty members. I'd also gotten an assurance that I'd be in line for a permanent faculty position there after I earned my Ph.D.

I was fully expecting to cash in on this. I expected to get an offer from SF State, and then maneuver into a negotiating position where I'd play A&M and

SF State for the best deal possible. Surely, A&M would come up from its starting offer of $40,000 and I was sure that SF State, with its prestigious, nationally known journalism program, would also make a strong bid.

What happened shouldn't have surprised me. It turned out that I would be just one of three candidates vying for the permanent position on the SF State faculty. I was the only one on the verge of a Ph.D. All the others had master's degrees or less. I should've been the clear choice, right?

Well, no.

It turns out that the Ph.D. is not really held in such high esteem by the majority of the professors in the journalism department of San Francisco State University. A clue to how they regard the Ph.D. lies in the way they bestow honorary Ph.Ds on one another—calling it a doctoral "equivalency"—to honor all the work they've done as professional journalists. No three years of graduate seminars, no dissertation, no defense, no foreign language requirement. None of that. Just, here it is. You deserve a Ph.D. because you've worked in the news business for such a long time. With so many instant doctors running around, it should've been no surprise that they wouldn't appreciate a real Ph.D. coming in and talking about research and Agenda Setting and all this theoretical stuff that sounds like it's straight from Neptune.

The promise that I thought I'd heard turned out only to be only an assurance that I would have a real good chance after I got my Ph.D. I still had to win the majority of votes from the search committee. Nevertheless, I felt good about the audition at SF State. They knew me, they knew what I could do, the students liked me, it felt like home. I imagined it would be good to work there and live in the Bay Area again. I wouldn't mind being a "freak" with a real Ph.D.

After a couple of days of guest lectures and meetings with the search committee, I spent a few more days in the Bay Area, visiting friends and catching an Oakland A's game. Then I high-tailed it up to the little town of Arcata in Humboldt County, way up in Northern California, just 80 miles south of the Oregon border. I'd read a couple of things about Arcata, that it was a politically progressive town, about as far left as it could get in America; that it was not very diverse, the only significant minority being the white kids who wear their hair in dreadlocks. Blond kids wearing dreadlocks. The locals jokingly referred to them as "trust-fund rastas," or "Trustafarians." They are, in fact, middle-class college students joyfully rebelling against the world by wearing their hair in that twisted, matted, Medusa hairstyle sported by reggae stars.

When I met with the Humboldt State search committee, I found the professors to be easygoing and friendly. The interview session was relaxed, compared with the grillings I'd gotten at other universities, and the students seemed to be interested in my guest lectures. One fortunate coincidence was that one of the search committee professors had also been a student of Max McCombs, the co-creator of the Agenda Setting theory, when McCombs was a young professor at UCLA. We traded McCombs stories and laughed, both of us in awe of how prolific a scholar he is.

I met the search committee for lunch and the interview continued. They asked me questions about my academic interests, my research plans, my professional experience. What courses would I want to teach?

"Whatever you've got. Reporting, editing, literary journalism, music criticism, mass comm theory, critical theory, you name it."

Will you finish your dissertation before you move here?

"I think so."

Are you sure?

"Well, my advisor thinks I'm on track. I'm pretty sure it'll get done. It has to! I've given myself no other option but to finish."

How much more do you have to do?

"Just four more chapters."

Four chapters? You can write four chapters in the next three months?

"Like I said, I have to."

How good can they possibly be in that short a time?

"Good enough, I hope. Perfection is not the top priority here. I just want to get it done."

Will you be ready to start teaching full time by late August?

"Absolutely. I've been waiting all my life for an opportunity to be a professor. I'm more than ready. I want this more than anything." Well, I wanted Liza more than anything too, but I left her out of the conversation. No use complicating things at this point. "If you hire me, I promise you, you will not regret it. I pledge to work hard and be the best journalism professor I can possibly be."

Yes, this had regressed into cheesy sales talk, but it was an essential part of the game. What employer wants to hear you vacillate? They want certainty, and so that is what I delivered—certainty in my ability to do the job, certainty that I was the best qualified person for the job, and certainty that I would bring greatness to HSU.

Why not? I was, after all, an articulate minority male with blue-ribbon credentials in professional journalism, I had worked for Robert Maynard, I had a book chapter with Max McCombs, and I was about to receive a Ph.D. from one of the

Top 10 journalism schools in the country. Let's face it—I was impossible to resist.

I said my goodbyes to the Humboldt faculty—without mentioning the offer from Texas A&M—and began the drive back down to the Bay Area, where I'd catch my plane back to Austin. It had been a good campaign stop. I felt real good about my prospects here. I also saw the advantages of living up here in the sticks. Humboldt State was part of the California State University system, the largest public university system in the world. Thus, its faculty made good money, what I'd call big-city wages, equivalent to what CSU faculty make at the big-city campuses—Los Angeles, San Diego, San Francisco, Sacramento. But the cost of living here was definitely more on the rustic side. You could buy a home here for less than half of what it would cost in the San Francisco Bay Area.

It seemed an attractive place, and working here would be good, I figured. But I doubted that little Humboldt State would be able or willing to outbid the big, bad Texas A&M Aggies for my services. A&M, after all, had millions of petrochemical dollars from generous donors in its little trust fund. It was the economics of scale. The bigger university would have more money to spend to hire the person it wanted.

I was resigned to my fate. My future would be at Texas A&M University.

# 7

## *The Divine Wind*

When I came home to Austin, I saw everything laid out in front of me. I needed to pass my advanced Spanish final, I needed to grade one last stack of 260 or more papers for the law class, I needed to finish my dissertation and defend it. Then, if I did all that, I would have a Ph.D. and I could start my new life as a professor of journalism somewhere out there. Then I could leave it all behind, go get Liza and live happily ever after.

A simple, yet elegant blueprint to bliss!

And so I took on this list of tasks one after another methodically, like a man-machine.

I graded all the papers in two days. I started to feel like a search engine, looking for key phrases in the student papers. If the phrases were there, the student would get credit for having understood the assignment. If the key phrases were not there exactly as they should be, the student would get partial credit. If they were not there at all, and the paper seemed to be meandering without some kind of payoff, the student would get little or no credit. It was pretty simple. This assembly-line grading was not necessarily an exercise in profound intellectual exchange—how could it be?—but it was standard practice, a brutal reality, in a big-university environment. Undergraduates in large classes at big universities are treated like cattle. Why should it be any different now? Why should it be different right when I was scheduled to finish my dissertation and get on with my life? Why should it be different now when Liza was waiting for me half a world away, with that luminescent, otherworldly smile?

The papers done, I prepared the best I could for my Spanish final, knowing that I was hopelessly unprepared and thoroughly incompetent in the language. Yes, I could fake my way through a very basic conversation in Spanish, but could I pass a final oral exam at the graduate level? No way—unless the professor was merciful.

59

She was. To my shocked delight, my exam consisted of translating one phrase: "Mil, cuatro cientos, noventa y dos."

The answer was 1492. It is the year that Columbus reputedly "discovered" the American land mass, and launched the European conquest of the western hemisphere.

I gave the year in English, we both laughed, and she congratulated me for passing the course. I was relieved and jubilant at the same time. I couldn't believe what just happened. I had passed the Spanish course, by the mercy of God and a professor with a sense of humor. In addition, I had graded all the law papers with machine-like efficiency; and I had completed a three-state, nine-stop job campaign tour. I was overachieving at supersonic speed. All that was left now was for me to finish the damned dissertation and defend it. With everything else out of the way, this now seemed like a Sunday cruise. Little did I know that there were minefields aplenty waiting for me.

I needed to do a handful of phone interviews for the last part of my dissertation. I needed to interview Alexander Cockburn, then talk to some of his editors. I needed to find out what is was about Cockburn that made his radical polemics so attractive to the *Los Angeles Times*, to the *Wall Street Journal* and other big-time mainstream media institutions. How do I get Cockburn's phone number? I called up directory assistance for Petrolia, California, and asked for Alexander Cockburn's number. The operator gave it to me, just like that. Now that's investigative reporting!

I sat in front of my computer, doing an Internet search for material on Cockburn. In between reading some of his syndicated columns, I checked my email. I noticed there was a letter from Humboldt State, from the journalism chairman, Mark Larson.

They were offering me a job. I had a second job offer. Now I was officially in play.

I responded quickly, saying that I already had a job offer from Texas A&M, and they were offering me $40,000.

Through Larson, Humboldt responded that they'd be willing to top anything A&M was offering, and they threw out a number that was about $4,000 higher than the salary A&M had offered. They also offered to pay my moving expenses from Texas, give me some release time to do research, and install a new Macintosh computer in my office. Also, I knew that the CSU system would pay off my student loans—about $30,000—if I worked there for five years.

This was a monster offer. It changed everything.

I told Humboldt that their offer was very generous, but that the courteous thing for me to do would be to tell A&M and give them a chance to respond.

I stood over the fax machine at the journalism department office at the University of Texas the next day, waiting for Humboldt to fax the dean's official offer sheet. When it finally came in, I couldn't stop grinning.

Prof. Whitney, my dissertation adviser, walked in and I showed him the offer from Humboldt. "Jeez," he said. "I didn't make that kind of money until I was a professor for 10 years."

But this was a new day, and now I was on a roll! Over the next couple of days, I called all the universities that had interviewed me. Northridge said they'd chosen another candidate. So did Colorado State. Just as well, I figured. USC said they didn't want to get into a bidding war. What a bunch of cheapies, I thought. It was now down to SF State, Texas A&M and Humboldt.

San Francisco State surprised me when they said I was not the final choice. I was shocked because just a year earlier I'd been virtually promised a position after I got my Ph.D. When the time arrived, the promise didn't materialize. I was miffed, but it didn't really matter now. I had two other job offers in the bag.

Texas A&M was disappointed, but didn't seem to be terribly surprised, that I had another job offer. The chairman of the journalism department said he'd try and wrest some more money out of the administration so he could give me more incentive to come to College Station. A few days later he called back and reported sadly that he couldn't match Humboldt's offer.

The mating ritual was over. I was going to Humboldt County! I was overjoyed by the prospect of returning to California. This time I'd be living in the redwood country, a part of California far removed culturally and geographically from the Hollywood hustle of LA and the cosmopolitan pomposity of San Francisco. I sent emails to the dean and the journalism chairman at Humboldt State, telling them I was ready to accept their offer. They emailed me back saying that they would be sending me an official contract soon. The deal was done.

All I needed now was a dissertation.

I plugged away at my magnum opus, hour after hour, day after day. It was now more than 300 pages long. As I hacked away, I kept in mind that this didn't have to be perfect, it didn't have to be great, it didn't have to rewrite the laws of physics, it didn't have to change the world, it didn't have to be impossible to resist. All it had to be was Good Enough. And that was me: GE. George Estrada.

Dr. Good Enough, Ph.D.

Days melted into nights, and nights divided the days. Sleep became a memory. I needed to write, write, write, research, revise and write some more. I needed more pages. I needed more citations. I needed to update my bibliography. I needed rest, but I couldn't rest. I needed to continue. I needed to call up Alexander Cockburn, the missing piece. I heard he was not an easy interview. I needed to prepare myself for it. I needed to think up some intelligent questions, and I needed to psyche myself up for it.

As thoughts of being twitted by an Oxford-educated Irish-American radical swam through my head, I sorted through the mail. And there, in between a bill from a credit card company and a piece of advertising from Reader's Digest, was a letter from the Philippines. It was from Liza. My heart pounded and joy filled my soul. My beloved had returned.

---

*Dear George*

*How are you? I hope you are doing fine by this time. You are asking here your letter if I will received your last letter. Yes, I will received your last and 2nd to the last letter. I thought you did not response my letter coz I will waiting for a few week and thank you very much to response and I know you are busy regarding your job, right? I hope you understand me, coz my letter to you was delayed. I'm also busy.*

*George, I try to call you two times but the operator is need the area code of your country but your phone number given to me they don't have area code and also she will not accept the collect call. You know George, I'm excited to see you in personal. I want to hear your voice also, I hope you are a good boy and understanding.*

*Well, until here my letter take care of your self and best regards to your family. And don't forget to pray our Almighty God.*

*Always. W/Love, Liza.*

---

She'd tried to call me! She couldn't get through, but she'd tried. Twice! This must mean something. She's interested. She's definitely interested. She wants to hear my voice. She wants to see me in person. God, her English is horrendous, but that doesn't matter. And my area code WAS in my letter. You see, the first three numbers? That's the area code, Liza. 512. Sorry I didn't explain that in my letter. And why is your letter so short? I wait for more than two months and all I get is three little paragraphs? Yes, I am a good boy, Liza, and very understanding. I understand that you don't know very much English, and that's why your letters are so short and so poorly written. Yes, I understand that you've been busy—I guess too busy to write. Can somebody really be that busy, so busy that you can't get to the post office on time? You want to know busy? You want to hear what I've been doing?

OK, OK, never mind, I understand.

I understand, even though your excuse seems a little flimsy. I understand because just getting a letter from you lifts my spirits and makes me feel alive. I understand—and I forgive you—because you used that word again. That word "love."

"Always, W/Love, Liza."

You used that word in the last letter too. Do you love me, Liza? Really, really love me? I know Filipina girls don't use that word unless they mean it. Unless they really, really mean it. American girls throw that word around casually, unthinkingly, flirtatiously. But I know that Filipinas do not. When they say love, they mean Love, the Big L. Is that what you mean? Love? With a big wet L?

My heart was on fire and my head was lighter than air. I have found love. I am in love. And the girl I love also loves me. And she lives in a magical, faraway land. And I am going to go there and bring her back home, to share my new life in a beautiful, deep green forest near the ocean. It was like a fairy tale. I couldn't believe it. I just couldn't believe it.

Again, I was floating on a cloud, and my mind was swirling with thoughts of love. Meanwhile, the air above central Texas was swirling too. I didn't know it, but Mother Nature was about to send a greeting card that would not be soon forgotten.

My mind was on Liza, and my head was swirling, but the gravity of my dissertation kept me down to earth. I had one last piece of research to do before I could finish this enormous jigsaw puzzle of a dissertation. It was May 28. My dissertation defense was scheduled for July 19. I had to make the call to Cockburn soon. Like now.

And so I did. And so he picked up the phone. And so, all of a sudden, there we were chatting—a former *Oakland Tribune* columnist just trying to finish his dissertation so he can get a faculty job somewhere and marry his dreamgirl, and an angry Irish intellectual with communist roots whose radical commentaries are published and read worldwide. Just chatting, just talking about journalism.

But Alex was not an easy interview, just as the warnings foretold. He was in a hurry. He had columns to write, other calls to take. He was in his usual outraged mood. He wasn't in a mood for small talk, nor for joking around. He probably thought I was a bit of a fool. He just wanted me to get to the point and move on.

In an attempt to establish some rapport, I told him about a conversation I'd had with Molly Ivins while I was doing research for the dissertation. I told him Molly and I had discussed his work, and that Molly had said: "Alex is the last Stalinist."

Molly's criticism was multidimensional. Was she saying that Alex's form of progressive radicalism was self-serving? That it kills ideology, as Stalin killed the memories of ideologues? Was she saying that Cockburn was too cozy with big power, as Stalin was to the U.S. and Britain during WWII, just so his work could get larger forums in the mainstream press, thus enlarging his own personal power? Was she saying that his singular vision of an America under siege tended to erase important points of history—as Stalinist revisionism tended to erase unloyal Soviets from official photographs? Or was Molly just saying that Alex was an egomaniac who most people do not like?

Whatever the case may be, Alexander Cockburn did not take too well to this piece of description from Molly Ivins.

"Tell Molly that Alex says to put all the nice things I've ever said about Stalin on a postcard and send it to me," Cockburn said. "You tell Molly and people like this that they better watch what they say and mind their little act."

Cockburn ended the conversation shortly after, but invited me to call back later. I sensed that he was irked with me, but somewhat fascinated by the thought that someone was doing a dissertation that analyzed him and his work.

And so I rested a bit and called him back. We talked a bit longer, and then he rushed me off again. He was on a deadline. And so in a little while, I called him back again. Like a journalist, I was a persistent. This is not some simpering little student that could be intimidated easily. I called Cockburn back five times that day. Each time he cooperated for a few minutes, then he rushed me off. But by the end of the fifth call, I had the information I needed.

I was done with my interviews. All that was left was a quick analysis of Cockburn's columns and then the writing of the final three chapters. I could do this in three weeks, I decided. Yes, I could. And then I'd turn in the finished draft to Whitney, he'd have some changes for me to make, and then on to the defense before the dissertation committee.

Piece of cake, right? During my career as a journalist, I'd faced many situations where people were angry at me and ready to shred me to bits. This defense shouldn't be a problem, I figured. I'll just prepare as much as possible, and bob and weave and jab and rope-a-dope like Muhammad Ali, and in the end I'll have danced my way to the heavyweight title.

It was now late afternoon, about 4 p.m., but it seemed a little dark. I drew open my curtains and saw that it was quite windy outside, so windy that tall trees across the street from my apartment were bending and swaying and heaving. I looked up and saw big dark clouds moving quickly across the sky, as big dark clouds do in this part of the country when a massive storm is on its way. This could be trouble, I reckoned.

I switched on the TV and saw that the reception was not good. The image was snowy and flickering. A weatherman was speaking quickly, in anxious tones. There were some words on the screen about a tornado alert in the Austin, Travis County, area. And then a video clip of a huge twister—black, otherworldly, god-like—raising debris from houses and farms up, up, up into the dark unknown.

"This is a big one," the weatherman said. "We may be looking at an F5 on the Fujita Scale, the most powerful, most intense, kind of tornado known. If this is true, this would be perhaps the most powerful tornado in the history of central Texas."

I was petrified. I didn't know what to do. I thought of running out of the building, away from the path of this angry beast. But where would I go? What would I do? I thought better of it and went back to the TV. I switched channels to see if I could find better reception. The tornado was on every channel. The wind was getting stronger outside, the trees were bending, the dark clouds seemed to be sprinting past now.

"The best thing to do," the weatherman said, "is to hang onto a post, a bath-tub, anything that is firmly anchored. Do NOT run outside. Repeat: Do not run outside. Just hang on to something solid."

Oh, great. Oh, great. I'm going to die. I'm going to die. Thoughts of death and unfinished business flashed through my mind. I grabbed a stairway post in my living room and hit the floor. Am I going to die here in a small apartment in Austin, Texas? I don't even have a will. I haven't finished my dissertation. I've never even met the girl I love in person. Great, just great!

"The tornado is about 40 miles outside of Austin, in the town of Jarrell, and it seems to be heading in our direction. As you can see from this amazing footage, the twister appears to be causing a significant amount of damage to Jarrell. We are getting reports of entire homes being ripped from their foundations and hurled into the air. In addition, there are reports that this is NOT the only funnel cloud to touch down in our area today. There are at least two, maybe three other tornado sightings in and around the Austin area. We will keep you updated on these, as well as the path of the Jarrell twister as best we can."

As I sat cringing on my living room floor, pathetically hanging onto a post that supported the staircase, I knew instinctively that holding onto this post would certainly not save me from an F5. I thought about divine intervention. I asked God to forgive me of all my sins, and I asked him for rescue—and if physical deliverance was not in the holy cards, then maybe salvation from hell would be OK. It was the Catholic in me, the Filipino Catholic in me, the Spanish-Filipino Catholic in me, the part of me that was created by 400 years of Spanish domination and strict maternal enforcement of dominant Spanish codes. And I couldn't help it, I couldn't resist it, despite being a cynical journalist and "enlightened" scholar. I just couldn't help it. When facing death, I turned to God and His power to save souls.

As the wind continued to swirl, and as the TV weatherman seemed to become more agitated, I felt a calm take over my mind. If this was death, then it might not be such a bad deal. If I die, I wouldn't have to finish this ridiculous dissertation, and I wouldn't have to defend it, and I wouldn't have to worry about packing up all my stuff and moving across the country to my new job. This was a ridiculous thought, of course, and I knew it as soon as I thought it. But for some reason, it gave me comfort. There is some residual benefit to death, I reckoned. It makes painful experience go away, and it allows you to escape your obligations. I could default on all my credit cards and not have to worry about harassing phone calls.

At that moment, I came to see this horrible, evil tornado as a divine wind, fierce and mysterious as the Hand of God.

And then I thought of something a Japanese friend had once told me about the word "kamikaze," that the English translation of this word meant "divine wind." And I thought of my life, and how I'd been somewhat of a kamikaze in the way I conducted the war and peace missions of my life, how I tended to destroy my old self in service of some abstract notion of greater glory. I thought of how I'd quit my job as a columnist with *The Oakland Tribune* and how that destroyed my friendships with the great journalists who had supported me there. I thought of how I'd wrecked my relationship with Lauralee—the greatest love of my life until now—because I had become too much of a self-absorbed graduate student. And then I thought of how my dissertation had harshly critiqued people I respected, how it critiqued the newspaper business, how the game of my dissertation defense would be played—how aggressively I would have to parry and thrust and engage in hostile swordplay with the people on the committee, people who I had come to know and respect, as well.

I knew that when the dust had cleared from my dissertation, there would be a lot of hurt feelings and irreparable rifts in friendships.

Then it occurred to me that the dissertation defense itself could be likened to "a divine wind." Winds would be stirred up by words uttered in the name of intellectual endeavor, beautiful, fancy words that would swirl and twist and fly and turn and lift and create and destroy and conquer.

The whole conversation of graduate school was a terrible and divine wind. It was divine because mastery of this wind would give one the keys to a great kingdom. It was terrible because it entailed an abundance of human effort, effort that could be used in the doing of many good and tangible things. Yet this effort is funneled into the creation of more wind, more destructive force, more twisting and dismantling of earthly things, more sucking of tangible human things up, up and up into a dark death-cloud.

The divine wind of an F5 tornado was upon us now, and the divine wind of my graduate school career was on me now, as well. And the great convergence of these terrible winds was more than my mind could take. I sat helplessly there in my apartment on West 25th Street, in Austin, Texas, clinging to a post, waiting for the inevitable and contemplating the end of everything.

Moments later, it was over. No, not my life. The storm was over. The tornado that had brought hail, rain and extremely fierce winds of up to 300 mph had dissipated mysteriously just as it hit the Austin city limits.

I was alive. I didn't understand what had happened, how this killer tornado had gone away, but it didn't matter. I was alive. Later on, the weatherman said that it had been quite a day in the history of central Texas weather. Not only did we have a visit from an ultra-rare F5 twister, but a total of six tornadoes had touched down in the Austin area.

What a day! The town of Jarrell had been utterly destroyed, and the six twisters annihilated or damaged more than 200 buildings in a four-county area. In all, 27 were killed, their bodies badly mangled and their skin ripped from their bones by the fierce winds. Many were missing or injured. One man in Austin died when a tornado struck his house. Also, an Austin girl drowned in a rain-swollen creek. Dozens of farm animals and house pets were injured and killed. Dismembered cattle were found strewn across the paths of destruction. The weatherman had been right, it was an F5, the rarest and most powerful of tornadoes.

Many innocent people had succumbed to the unearthly power of this wind, and many others had been injured. But I had been spared. I had to face yet another swirling vortex, however. The killer winds that would be stirred up by the holy war of a dissertation defense were rapidly approaching. The day of jihad would soon be here. I pledged that I would write like a Texas tornado for the next few days, I would rustle up waves of windy divinity like nobody's business and dare to call it scholarship. Then I'd be done with this madness once and for all.

Good plan. Let's do it!

# 8

## *Force Majeur*

The coming days and weeks were not quite as exciting as Tornado Day. But a couple of things descended from the sky and spun me around.

First, as I searched through my emails one day in June, I noticed I had a message from the Philippines. It was from Joan, a woman in Cebu City. Joan had read a desperate plea I'd sent out on a Cebu listserve a while back. I was looking for someone to help me get a message to Liza, who had no phone and who apparently didn't know how to use email.

Joan said she'd seen my note and that she'd be willing to help out. Coincidentally, she said, she used to work at SM, where Liza works, and it'd be no problem to take my email messages to her.

My heart leaped again. I wrote a hasty message to Liza saying how much I wanted to hear from her again, how much I'd missed her letters, how much I love her. And then I emailed the note to Joan. I could only imagine what Joan would think when she read it. "Poor lovesick boy!" or something like that.

Joan wrote back immediately, saying she'd bring the note to Liza at Shoe Mart the next morning. How I wish I could be there to see the look on Liza's face when she received the letter from her mysterious admirer in America. How precious that would be!

Then I started to worry about how she would react. Would she think I was crazy? Would she think I was joking? Worse, would she think I was some sort of desperate loser? What would she think of me then? Would she scoff at me? Would she dismiss me with a toss of her hair and a cruel laugh? Would she really spurn me after I'd tried this hard? Could she really reject me after I'd professed such burning love? Could I be, after all, not impossible to resist?

When I checked my email later that evening, there was a letter from Joan, along with a message from Liza. Joan had made contact with Liza at SM—and now, just like that—I had a new letter from my beloved. I was floating on a cloud.

---

*June 11, 1997*
*Dear George,*

*I was so surprised when Joan contacted me, saying I have a letter from you thru email. You know George, it's like magic. You are the lucky man who get the email address of Joan. You can trust her to communicate me thru email because she is very kind. She is working here at Shoe Mart before as Dept. Manager. But the problem is how can you pay Joan?*

*Anyway, George, about your gift that you've sent to me, I received it last week together with your nice postcards, and I'm very happy. I really like your gift, thank you very much to you.*

*Your letter you stated that you will visit here in Phil in December. Do you really have a time in coming here in the Phil? I think you're so busy regarding your job. But you know I'm excited to see you in person. I hope so, you'll be here in December.*

*Well, until here my letter good luck to your new job in California. Take care of your self always, be a good boy and may God blessed you. Bye bye .*

*Love*

*Liza*

---

That word again: Love. it made me mad with joy, it made me stupid with happiness. To have that magical word coming from my beautiful creature of light was almost more than I could bear.

I had made contact with her through the magic of Internet technology, the same technology that first brought her glimmering image to me that fateful day last November, back in the computer lab at school. And now here we were, professing love for one another. What a strange and delightful thing this is. Technology had brought me back to my roots, and had brought me a dream girl.

I hacked out a letter and mailed it back that day:

---

*June 11, 1997*
*Dear Liza:*

*Thank you so very much for the letter. I got it today. You know, I was worried that you had stopped writing to me because maybe you were not interested any more or something. So when I got your letter in the mail, it made me feel very good. I'm glad you're back.*

*Liza, I really missed your letters. I really love getting letters from you, so I felt a bit sad during those two months you didn't write. You said that you were too busy to write. Well, I am busy too, so I understand how life can be sometimes. It's OK. I am just glad that we are communicating again because you know how much I care about you, how much I want you. And you know how much I wish for the day that we finally meet, and we can walk around your city and talk about our dreams, and we can hold each other very tight. That moment, when it finally comes, will be perhaps the greatest moment in my life.*

*Maybe that moment can be in December. I hope so. I think so.*

*Right now though, I must finish my dissertation to complete my doctoral studies. I have to finish it this month and then I have to defend it on July 10. Then I'll be a Doctor of Journalism. How about that? Shortly after this, I'll be moving to California! Yes, the big news is that I got a teaching job at a college in Northern California. (Hurray!!) It's called Humboldt State University, and I will be a professor of journalism there starting in August, teaching three classes per semester. The pay is very good, and the location of the college is magnificent. It's located up in the redwood coastal area, where there are big, lush, redwood forests and a stunning coast line that is so beautiful you'll want to cry. Plenty of fresh air and natural beauty up in Humboldt. A much nicer place to live than San Francisco or Los Angeles. And definitely much better than Texas. You know, Liza, I have many friends and relatives in San Francisco because I grew up there. So, I'm happy to be going back to California because I can visit with all of them often.*

*The town I'll be living in is called Arcata, and it's just a few hours drive north of San Francisco. I will send you my new address after I move there. I will be moving in early August because classes start at Humboldt State University in late August. I have to get a new place to live in Arcata, move all my things there, prepare for classes, and so on. Always busy. Always running. It seems like it never ends.*

*The first time I'll really get some time off is in December during Christmas vacation. I hope that I can come to the Philippines and meet you then. You know, I've been dreaming about you and imagining that moment—the moment we finally meet—for a long time now. Ever since you sent me your first letter last November, I've been dreaming of this moment. Actually, I've been dreaming about you ever since I first saw your picture on that Internet page. I said to myself: "Wow, what a beautiful, gorgeous, lovely girl!" Do you have a copy of that photograph? I'd really like to have a copy if you have one.*

*You know, I'm always looking at that picture and the pictures you sent to me, and I think how wonderful it must be to see your beautiful smile, up close, in person, not just in pictures. I want to see your face, your smile. To see those beautiful eyes of yours when you're smiling. That is what I want. And I want to make you so happy when we are together. I hope that you will smile and laugh and toss back your hair in the wind and reach out to embrace me. Then I can feel the warmth of your soul upon me. I want hold you close, Liza. I want to hear you sigh with delight. And then we will look at each other in wonder, and we will know the magic of the moment. We will realize that a quirk of fate has somehow brought us together. And we will know that somehow, by some miracle, this is real. Not some dream. I want to hold you close and tell you what you mean to me. I want to tell you all of my dreams. I want to tell you how you can be a part of my future. I want to tell you how I will love you and take care of you. My darling Liza, is it possible that I have found the girl of my dreams at last?*

*I think there are probably other boys who want you because you are so beautiful, and they are there in Cebu and they might be trying to win your love right now. Well, I hope you don't fall in love with any of them because I have this feeling that you are the perfect girl for me. I've been waiting such a long time to give all of my love to someone like you, but I've been waiting to find the right girl, someone who is warm and thoughtful and kind and pretty. You seem to be the one. Please wait for me. Please…I promise you won't be sorry.*

*Write to me again soon, my love. I do so love you very deeply.*

*Forever yours (mahal kita)*

*George*

Reading back the letter, I could see that it was a little over-the-top, but the feelings were genuine. I decided to go ahead and send it.

A couple of days before my dissertation defense, one of the committee members who'd be judging my work took me aside in the hallway. "Listen, George, don't forget that the defense is a ritual. You're gonna get roughed up. We all did. Take it like a scholar. Don't take it personally. It's just part of the game. We just want to see how good you are when you're under fire, so we're going to try and shake you up."

Yes, I was going to have to earn that "doctor" title.

On the day of my defense, I was prepared. I sensed that my dissertation would be attacked because I myself was on the attack. I attacked all of media sociology research for its lack of articulation on the special role of columnists in newspaper culture. In my reading of the literature, it seemed that media sociologists viewed journalists as robots, all operating under some sort of nefarious control system devised by elite capitalists. There was no real acknowledgement of individuality, nor much mention of how superior talent can lift a news reporter onto another level, the level of columnist, or critic, or one of the other choice writing positions on a newspaper. Media sociology seemed to be all about mass production being done by faceless masses.

I attacked critical theory for its totalized and crushing view of American media. I attacked cultural studies and post-modernism for being so eclectic and flakey. I attacked Noam Chomsky, perhaps the greatest scholar alive today, for his Propaganda Model's sweeping generalizations about the intimidation and control of journalists.

One member of my dissertation committee said that my opening chapter, in which I talked about my own career and how I'd been inspired by columnists, was "just too precious" for words. I took that to be an insult.

Another committee member said that my attack on Chomsky was weak, that I misunderstood what he was saying in the Propaganda Model, that I should have read it more closely, that Chomsky is perfect in every way and that my analysis was quite vulgar and sophomoric. Another committee member said that one or two chapters need to be completely re-written.

Several of my graduate-student colleagues were sitting in the room, observing the dissertation defense, watching in horror as wave after wave of attacks were hurled at me and my work. Audible grunts and sighs of "oh no" came from the audience with some of the tougher questions. A friendly junior professor who was not on the committee but who came to watch the defense sat on the sidelines and chuckled silently to himself. As each hostile question was thrown at me, he grinned a big toothy grin and nodded at me, as if to say, "Get up off the floor and hit 'em right back."

After all the attacks, one of the professors on the committee addressed me: "I'd like to say that, despite its weaknesses, this was one of the best-written dissertations I've ever read."

That seemed to tilt some sentiment over to my side. When it was over, the committee dismissed me and convened to discuss my fate. I went into my office and batted a nerfball against the wall.

After an agonizing wait of about 45 minutes, I was summoned back into the committee room. My adviser, Prof. Whitney, was the first to greet me.

"Congratulations, Dr. Estrada," he said, offering a handshake.

That was it. I'd done it!

"There were some disagreements about the quality of your work. I, for one, remain unconvinced about your assessments of media sociology. Nevertheless, the committee has decided that with some minor revision, your dissertation will be acceptable. We will give you instructions on what you need to change. If you make these changes and we deem them satisfactory, then you can file your finished dissertation with the university and you will have your doctorate."

Again, I was on a cloud. I got hearty congratulations from my graduate student colleagues and we celebrated later with a couple of cases of cheap beer, Pabst Blue Ribbon and the ubiquitous Shiner Bock. But first, I stopped at the computer lab and sent off an email to Joan in Cebu to deliver to Liza, to share the good news with her.

Later, at the party, I told my colleagues about the job I accepted at Humboldt State, and that news drew an interesting mix of reactions. There were those who chose to comment on the proximity of the marijuana-growing industry. "Hey, did they pass around the bong while they were interviewing you?" one wise guy asked. "Let's hear it for Dope U!" another one screamed. One student seemed shocked when I told her the financial terms of Humboldt's offer: "I'm in awe," she said. Amidst all the merriment, one of the more serious students took me aside and issued a warning:

"You know, the faculty here isn't going to be too terribly pleased with your going to Humboldt State," he said.

"Why?"

"It's not a Carnegie I research university. It's considered a teaching school, where the quality of teaching is emphasized over the amount of research you publish."

"So what? I'm good at teaching. And I know my journalism."

"That's not the point. The Texas journalism faculty doesn't give a damn whether you're a good teacher or not. They want you to produce research, they want you to publish in only the most prestigious journals, they want you to cite their works in your articles. They want you to produce scholarly papers and present them at only the most prestigious academic conferences, to carry on the great tradition of mass communication research."

I started thinking about tornadoes and the high-flying language of academia, and I felt the divine winds swirling around me again.

"Too bad," I told my friend. "I'm going to Humboldt. Right now, I don't care about research. I want to get my new life started."

Bold, desperate words these were. And I said them loud enough so that several people would hear. This pronouncement was perhaps a little too bold, and a little too loud. I heard a few days later that some faculty had gotten wind of my comment and that now there was grumbling amongst them about how brash, young Dr. Estrada had betrayed them.

"It's a disgrace," one influential senior professor was overheard saying about me. "We invested a lot of time and effort on him, and what does he do? He decides to go to a small teaching school and forego his commitment to research."

I could think of only two words to say in response: The first word was "tough," and the second word began with the letter "s." This was my life, and I'm damned well going to do with it what I want. And by the way, while these professors were "investing" their time and effort, they were getting paid pretty damned well. Senior professors made between $70,000 and $100,000 at big universities like UT. Some of the superstars make significantly more. I was the one losing money in the deal, what with tuition, books and the income I was losing by not working. My relationship with Lauralee had collapsed because I'd become such a self-obsessed scholar and an academic workaholic and an asshole at home. And now they wanted me to reject the best offer I had because it was from a "teaching school," and not a research university. Excuse me? Hello? What's wrong with this picture?

I finished editing and revising my dissertation, according to the changes Dr. Whitney wanted me to make. This took me about two days to do. He quickly approved the changes, and now I had to deal with a new threat, "The Lady With the Ruler."

This is the woman who sits in the Office of Graduate Studies and literally uses a ruler to measure the top, bottom, left and right margins of finished doctoral dissertations to make sure the white spaces are exactly the required length. She also has a long list of other technical requirements that must be adhered to before she approves the filing of the paper.

The Lady With the Ruler nailed me on two things. My table of contents was printed using a font that was different from the rest of the dissertation. Also, the table of contents spelled out chapter numbers, "Chapter One, Chapter Two" and so on, while in the chapter headings themselves, I had used the numerals: "Chapter 1, Chapter 2," etc. These were no-nos. Fix these things, and print out the revised copy before you turn it in, she commanded.

I rushed over to the computer lab and hastily made the changes that the Stalinist lady wanted. Then I ran over to Longhorn Copies on Guadalupe Street across from the journalism building, but it was about to close. I told them I'd be in the next morning to print out and copy a revised 350-page dissertation.

I went home, watched TV news for a while, and then Coltraned myself to sleep. The next day I made the copies and delivered the edited work to the Lady With the Ruler.

She looked over my changes and nodded. Then she got out her ruler, meticulously measured the margins on several of my pages and nodded again. I could feel closure within reach. I felt my journey coming to a successful end. But as she leafed through the dissertation, I could see her brows start to furrow. Then I could see her shaking her head. I feared something was terribly wrong.

"The fonts on your page numbers and bibliography," she said.

"What about them?"

"They're different. They're not the same font you used in the text. Your text is Courier, right? Your page number fonts and your bibliography fonts don't appear to be Courier. They're something else."

"And so?"

"And so I can't approve this for filing. Fix those fonts and print it out again. Then you can file it."

I was about to explode. I couldn't believe what I was hearing. Here I had survived four years of graduate school, I had lost a girlfriend, I had written a 350-page tome, I had made it through a hostile dissertation defense, I had evaded a killer super-tornado, and now they're telling me they can't accept my dissertation because my page numbers and bibliography didn't have the correct typeface????!? What the hell kind of madhouse is this!?

The Lady With the Ruler remained calm and steadfast in her resolve. I had to fix the fonts and print the whole damned thing over again. No Ph.D. until I get it done right—right down to a T.

Meanwhile, back at school, I complained to everyone about the runaway bureaucracy that forced me to jump through endless hoops just to file a paper. Some took pity with me, others just howled with merriment at my anguish.

"It's the game, buddy," one professor told me. "Just play the game. Look, you're almost there. Just quit complaining, make the changes, print the thing again, file the damn thing and shut your mouth. No big thing, right? Why fight it?"

He was right. There was no reason at all to fight the Stalinist Lady With the Ruler. Just shut up and go with it. And so I did. I spent the entire next day changing all the page numbers and the bibliography to the proper font and then watching the printing of each page to make sure all the spacings were still correct. As night fell, the 350th page printed. I made a photocopy of the dissertation for my files, and went home. Tomorrow I would do battle again with the Ruler

Lady. It would be a duel to the death this time, I swore to myself. Nothing less than total victory would do.

It turned out to be not a confrontation at all, rather anticlimactic, really. The Ruler Lady recognized me and remembered my problem. She glanced at a few pages and proclaimed the paper now fit for filing. It was over in just a few moments. I now had a dissertation approved and on file at the University of Texas. All roads were clear for the awarding of the doctoral degree. There was nothing left between me and my new title: Dr. George Estrada, Ph.D.

I felt numb. I was glad it was over, but I felt nothing, no tingling feeling, no jubilation, no epiphany. I felt nothing. Just numbness.

Coming home, I put on a Coltrane CD and pondered what I had been through: three years of graduate seminars and one year of dissertation research and writing, an exhausting and confusing job-search campaign spanning three states, an insane Spanish class and a tough dissertation defense—all culminating in a close brush with a lethal super-twister and a bruising wrestling match with the Ruler Lady.

And now I had a Ph.D. and a faculty position at a good university, and now the professional quests were over.

I had reinvented myself before my very eyes, transforming myself from a tired, middle-aged, hack journalist to a glamorous, young journalism professor in just a few short years. And the jigsaw puzzle that was my new life was taking form. There was just one big piece of the puzzle left: my new love affair with the girl of my dreams.

Look out, Humboldt State. Here comes something you've never seen: a Filipino with a Ph.D. and an attitude. Look out, Liza Trujillo. Here comes something you've never seen: a passionate man with a lonely heart and the gift of America, delivered right to your door.

It was now late July, and I was slated to begin teaching classes at Humboldt in late August. I had to get moving. I called a discount moving company, Starving Students, to truck my stuff from Austin to Arcata. Humboldt State picked up the tab for the moving expenses, which amounted to just over $2,000.

Over the next few days, I sold my car, cleaned up the apartment (with the help of a few sympathetic grad students), said my goodbyes to my friends and colleagues at UT, paid one last visit to Lauralee, and hopped a one-way flight on United Airlines that would bring me from Austin to San Francisco, where I would catch a small United shuttle to the Eureka-Arcata airport. I would then rent a car for a week and get situated in my new apartment, which was located on a hill about a four-minute drive away from the HSU campus. I planned to rest, recuperate and check out the area while waiting for Starving Students to arrive with my stuff.

Just a couple of days before I left Austin, I got a letter from Liza.

---

*July 23, 1997*
*George,*

*Hello, my dear. How are you? I hope everything will be okey! Well, I'm here again to write you to let you know about me here. I'm sorry my letter was always delayed because I was transferred another boarding house last week of this month together with my brother and sister and one cousin. Again, I'm so sorry.*

*I will send you a letter last week together a postcards. Did you received it? I hope you like the postcards that I will send you. That's the view here in Cebu City. I will received all your letters and email message thru computer of Joan. You know George, I will feel shy to her when the time she have a letter from you then she came to Shoe Mart to give it to me.*

*George, I'm always thinking if we're compatible to each other. I'm wondering if this is true! I'm always asking myself. But I will be happy because they have a man will care for me and love me. You know George, I will feel in love from you even I will not see you in person. When the time I received your letter because I love to read your letter coz you're so lovely.*

*OK, congratulations to you, Dr. George Estrada, and how about your new job? Did you enjoy it? Good luck and may God blessed you.*

*Love,*

*LIZA*

---

It's funny how every letter I got from Liza elevated my mood, made me feel bigger than I was, made me feel that everything I did was worth the pain and hassle. Even her lame excuses about being too busy to write more often started to seem cute. I could envision my adorable Liza rushing off to the post office clutching a letter, only to find that the post office had closed. I could see those sweet lips forming into a sad, little pout at the disappointment.

Yes, I did get those postcards, Liza. That was very nice of you. But what's this business about whether or not we're compatible? Of course we are! We're Filipino—how can we not be compatible? And you're wondering if this is true, whether this incredible, wonderful thing we've found together is real or make believe. You can't believe it's true. You can't believe this miracle has been delivered to your feet.

Well, my darling, it's real! It's real because we've made it real. Our desire for something better in our lives has made it real. It's real because I searched for you through time and space, and found your gleaming visage smiling at me on my computer screen. Your face, your name, your body—they were electrons given shape and form by a divine wind that we call the Internet. Cyberspace and the divine wind of our desire brought us together. And now, we are no longer abstractions, we are real bodies, hurled together by this force majeur. And now our thoughts are swirling, the foundations of our lives are lifted up and obliterated by the strength of this force, the debris of our loneliness is scattered along the landscape. This is an F5 love affair in the making, my love.

I'll have time off in December, during my Christmas break. I'll be coming to the Philippines to see you. Let the divine wind of air travel fling me across the ocean and deliver me to your arms. I'm coming to get you, girl. Hang on to something sturdy!

# 9

# *The Humboldt Adventure*

Alexander von Humboldt was a German scientist/explorer who came to the Americas in 1799 to map the topography of the New World and to document the different kinds of plants and animals one could find. He climbed mountains in Peru and Ecuador. He mapped over 1,700 miles of the Orinco River in South America. He discovered the first animal that produced electricity, the electric eel. He looked out over the water and discovered the Peruvian Current, which is now also known as the Humboldt Current. Humboldt State University is also named after him.

And so when I came to work at the university named after the esteemed Dr. Von Humboldt almost two centuries later, so too would I find many strange new life forms—including my students.

I sat on my deck outside the bedroom of my new apartment in Arcata and contemplated the deep blue sky and the rich, milky scattering of stars. I also heard the rustling noises of wild beasts. The deck butted right up against a thick, forested area, and I could hear animal noises, grunts, moans, snarls and sniffs amidst the trees and shrubs. There were small, fierce animals around me, I reckoned. I was now in the Northern California wilderness. How cool!

But it was another strange new life form—the students of Humboldt State University—that would give me my most interesting encounters.

I was scheduled to teach beginning reporting, magazine writing and copy editing my first semester on the job. Beginning reporting I could teach without much trouble since I instinctively knew the material, Magazine writing would be a stretch since I never really worked for a magazine. Copy editing, however, would be a bit foreign to me. I reckoned that the grammar, spelling, punctuation and Associated Press style would be straightforward enough, but I had very little experience as an editor—I'm a writer, not a fighter—and I would have to bring myself up to speed very quickly on the nuances of writing headlines and grinding copy.

The students at Humboldt State are the best thing about the place. They are a polymorphous lot, many of them sporting the uniform of early 1990s garage band grunge—tattered clothes, multiple unshaven areas, multiple piercings, multiple tattoos, scraggly hair. This was your Northern California look—bedraggled, defiant of authority, rebelling against the oppression of cosmetics and good grooming. I remember this from my college days at Berkeley, and I noticed that The Look was even more pronounced at Humboldt some three decades later.

Scattered among these Easy Rider/Road Warrior anarchists are normal, run-of-the-mill young adults who look as Middle American as can be. But these are mostly in the physical sciences, not in journalism. The students I had at Texas were more the All American types, respectful of authority and ready to learn. At Humboldt, it seemed to be the opposite: The journalism students here seemed to have an attitude and they definitely told you what THEY wanted to learn. I discovered this during the first week of editing class, when I announced that the first thing we would be doing was mastering grammar, spelling, punctuation and AP style. Audible groans and snorts filled the room.

"That's old school!" said one student.

"What is this? Remedial English?" said another.

I paused, looked around, and gently informed them that editors must be masters of the written language, that perfection is the standard of performance in the newspaper business. If your news articles are filled with bad grammar and bad spelling, you would not last long in the business because you would have no credibility whatsoever. You would be seen as amateurish, childish, undisciplined. Perfection in language is the standard of professional performance, I insisted. Editors must be the masters of order—that is their role, that is what is expected of them—and the first step in achieving that order is absolute mastery of the written language. If students don't want to master the language, they are wasting their time and mine.

I saw a couple of students cringe, a couple of others rolled their eyes, two or three of them turned to their computers in contempt and started surfing the Internet.

"What exactly did you expect to learn in an editing class?" I asked, getting a little agitated

Silence.

"Well?"

"Page design and layout," said one student. "HTML, web-page design."

"How to select pictures, and how to crop pictures. How to manipulate photos with PhotoShop."

"How to critique the media. Like, finding out how they distort things, you know."

And on and on it went. Not a single one of them mentioned the mastery of grammar, spelling and punctuation. Not one mentioned the importance of learning Associated Press Style. Here was a group of students enrolled in an editing class, and they thought they were going to be designing Web pages and manipulating photos using computer software. They thought we'd be spending class time complaining about the local paper. They didn't want to have anything at all to do with mastering words—that was "old school," one of those arcane vocational skills from the fading 20th century. Words aren't any fun. Words are boring. Words suck.

Why should I learn how to spell and punctuate and look things up in the AP Manual of Style? That takes too long. It gives me a headache. It's boring! Here, look, check this out. Watch how I can lay out pages. All I have to do is click on this, drag and drop this, move this text from here to here, write a headline and a caption, hit the spell check, and I'm done. You're still looking stuff up in that dumb book, and I'm DONE. And I'm looking good! I can go home and party now. Forget all that old-school crap, that grammar, spelling and AP style garbage. That sucks!

I was not deterred. I was not about to let a sacred discipline fall into the hands of some high-tech cretins. I told them that we will have conversations about layout and Web design later in the semester, but what matters most is words, and it was their responsibility to master the word skills that all editors must have. So, there would be weekly quizzes in grammar, spelling, punctuation and AP style. Grades would be assigned on a point system. Quiz grades will go down one-third of a grade for each error they fail to catch and fix. What's more, attendance is absolutely required. You lose points if you do not come to class on a quiz day. You lose all of the points for that quiz. You have to learn that newspapers depend on you. You've got to prove that you can be depended on.

Can I depend on you?

Half of the class went along with the program. Among the rest, some chose to stop coming to class, others complained to the journalism faculty that young Dr. Estrada was intolerant and incompetent and should be fired.

I was aghast.

Here I had spent my entire life mastering the language, and finally achieving the highest degree one can earn—and now these young rebels were telling me that everything I know is wrong; that it's a new day; that graphics software is now Lord and Master.

I thought about Liza and others I'd met in the Philippines who wished they could master English because that skill would lift them up to another economic level. And now these Humboldt State students were telling me that the English language was irrelevant. All that mattered was HTML.

This made me want to fight even harder. I told them they had no option. It is time to sink or swim.

Over the next few weeks, and after several grueling quizzes, many of the students came away with a heightened sense of how journalists use language, and many of them actually told me they appreciated the grilling.

"You are the first teacher I've ever had," said one tattooed young man, "who has held me responsible for grammar, spelling and punctuation. Thank you. I needed that."

I couldn't believe my ears. I started wondering what the hell is going on in the public schools these days.

One day after work, I came home to find a letter from the Philippines. It was from Liza.

---

*Oct. 7, 1997*
*My Dear George,*

*Do you received my e-mail letter for you? I send you an e-mail letter a few days. I hope you received it. George, I want to tell you, falling in love with you was a complete surprise for me, even your letters because you are so lovely.*

*You know what? I'm always thinking of you, that you'll be here in December. I'm very excited to see you. I want to talk to you in person. I want very much for you. I really love you a time when I received your letter, but I ashamed you to express my feelings for you. I hope you understand me, okey! You know what George, when I look at your postcard you send me, I'm thinking I hope I can see this nice views in your country.*

*George, don't you worry because there is a love waiting for you too. Well, that's it for now. Take care coz I care for you. Pls. send a photos.*

*Love*

*Liza*

Well, she was true to form—short and sweet. Three paragraphs, and bang, she's out. But it was what was in those three short paragraphs that really floored me.

"George, I want to tell you, falling in love with you was a complete surprise for me…I'm always thinking of you…I really love you…George, don't you worry because there is a love waiting for you too…Take care coz I care for you."

This was the jackpot. There was no getting around it now. She has declared it, SHE LOVES ME, plain and simple.

I was overjoyed, ecstatic, stupidly in love. Could this be real? Could I have really found the one after all these many years?

I swam in this river of unending joy until my brain began dragging me ashore. Wait a minute, wait a minute, I said to myself. OK, OK, this was cool when it was just flirting through the mail. But now she's getting serious. Now she says she loves me. Well, why shouldn't she? You've been telling her you loved her from the git-go. Are we having doubts now? Was I really serious all this time, or was Liza just a distraction, just a temporary amusement to keep my mind off the drudgery of graduate school?

What could I have been thinking? Is it possible that I'd really fallen in love with an image on my computer screen? Is this image now a real, live, flesh-and-blood human who is now declaring her love for me? How is this possible? Isn't this a bit crazy? We've never even met in person. We've only exchanged, what, five or six letters? And now we're talking about love?

We live in different countries half a world away; we come from different cultures; we speak different languages. And then there's that age difference. What would my friends think? What would my colleagues on the faculty think? The words of that cruel, thoughtless woman at the University of Texas resonated through my brain: "George has got a mail-order bride. Hah hah hah!"

Yes, I thought about all this. How it would affect my social standing. How it might affect my career. How it would affect my self-esteem.

Then I read Liza's letters again, and I looked at Liza's picture again. Then I looked at her dewy eyes and warm smile. Then I thought of my late parents and how I never gave them the grandchildren they so wanted. Then I thought of the many years of emptiness that had filled my adult life while I reached for some elusive dreams. Then I thought of the homeland and the culture that I'd abandoned but now wanted to reclaim. Then I thought of Liza and what I could add to her life; and what she could add to mine.

And then the coldness began to leave my body and the hard, cynical analysis began to come apart. I'd been thinking like an American again, dammit. It was time to stop that. Let's pour some mango juice on this and start over. I am in love with Liza, in love with what she represents, in love with her smile, in love with the way she writes—hang the bad grammar!—I am in love with everything about this girl. I want her and I want her now!

I made up my mind. Nothing would keep me from her. No real or imagined social stigmas; no criticism from colleagues; no sarcastic comments from friends. Nothing! Nada! Wala!

Giddy with happiness, I put Liza's picture from the Web site in a nice frame and displayed it in my office at the university. In conversations with students and other professors, I started referring regularly to "my fiancee, Liza," who would be joining me in Arcata soon. My walk acquired somewhat of a pimp swing, and my lectures started getting a little sassy. I was a new man, I had emerged from the darkness with a fine job in a beautiful part of the country and I had found a fabulous new love. What else could a man need?

I sent Liza a letter with some pictures of me walking through the woods near Trinidad, a small, picturesque, seaside town north of Arcata, and set my mind back on "work" mode.

The fun and games continued in my journalism classes, and the whining continued. A handful of students who worked on the Lumberjack newspaper staff were upset because I didn't treat them with any deference, and gave them no special privileges. They too had to deal with grammar, spelling, punctuation and AP style, same as the other students. This infuriated them. A couple of them complained to the department chair, but he just waved them off and told me to keep on doing what I was doing. The other faculty were also behind me on this. It was good to have their support.

The semester wore on, and eventually most everyone mellowed out. My editing students soon found out that I could be a tolerant, forgiving, fun-loving guy—as long as they followed the program. They also soon found out that this grammar, spelling, punctuation and AP style stuff wasn't so hard. It's just that too many of them had had English teachers who were more interested in teaching post-modern literary analysis, and less interested in the nuts and bolts of language use.

"George, I wish I'd taken this class at the beginning of my college career," one young man who was about to graduate told me. "This is the class I needed more than any other."

Yes, the editing class was quickly becoming my favorite of the three classes I was teaching. The reporting and magazine writing classes were to offer me different challenges, however.

In introductory reporting classes, the goal is to teach newspaper reporting, the classic form of journalism. The problem is, journalism is such a fractured discipline that you get students from all corners of the academic world.

For starters, within the journalism/communication major itself, you get students who are interested in newspaper reporting, broadcast reporting, public relations, advertising and mass communication theory. Then, on top of that, you also get a scattering of students from outside the discipline, students from the natural sciences and humanities who are trying to fulfill some writing requirement imposed by their major department.

It becomes then a very difficult task to devise a curriculum that is suited to everyone. If you drive them too hard, you turn off all but the hardcore journalists. If you go too soft to accommodate the non-journalists among them, you bore the hardcores.

So it becomes a bit like improvisational theater. You get a suggestion from the audience and you create some drama from it. You spice it up with some anecdotes from your own real-world experience. You channel the conversation into the lesson for the day and—voila!—you have higher education. When it all clicks, it's wondrous. Sometimes, though, it gets a little bizarre.

I didn't know that the Internet would cause a problem.

One young man in my beginning reporting class, a broadcast news major, turned in an assignment that read pretty well. It was a vast improvement over his past work, which was, frankly, sloppy and unreadable. This particular piece, though, was elegant and well thought-out. It read like professional writing. I found myself nodding my head and raising my eyebrows as I read his piece. I was terribly, terribly impressed by him and by my ability to teach—until I got to the last sentence. It read:

"For more information, click on the following links:"

I was flabbergasted. The guy had obviously copied something from a Web site. Not only had he plagiarized this article, word for word, but he had also been too lazy and too negligent to erase the last sentence, which directed the reader to some hyperlinks that would lead them to other Web sites.

What the hell is this? I thought to myself. What was this guy thinking?

I confronted him the next day and told him I knew he had plagiarized. "Listen, dude, I know what's up. You put off this assignment until the last minute, then you found out that the material you needed for the story was not all that easy to get and you were running out of time, so in desperation you copied something from the Internet. And you were so much in a hurry that you forgot to edit out the giveaway sentence at the end, right?"

"Yeah, that's pretty much it," he said, looking down. "Sorry."

For some reason, I admired the guy's honesty, so I gave him another chance. I told him to write a real story and turn it in as soon as possible, and I'd have to penalize him for tardiness, but I'll forgive him this act of plagiarism if he could just get with the program. I also reminded him that other journalism professors play a little tougher—they would have thrown him out of school for this act of burglary.

He seemed quite repentant, and thanked me profusely for the second chance. It was no big surprise that he turned in a decent story the next week. A little forgiveness goes a long way sometimes, I reckoned.

Our one-week Thanksgiving break was upon us now, and I would have some time to catch my breath. I relished the thought. All that dissertating, moving and teaching had taken a big toll on me. I was losing hair at an alarming rate and gaining a lot of weight. My stomach, which once sported razor-sharp abs, was now protruding like a belly full of Pabst Blue Ribbon.

I spent the break mellowing out, spending time with relatives in Daly City. I also visited my storage space in Alameda and filled up my pickup truck with stuff to bring back up to Humboldt County.

School started back up soon enough, and we all settled in for the fall semester's home stretch. It had been a bit rough, but we all seemed to have our wits about us as we prepared for final exams, final papers and all the other things that come with a term's end. A few days before finals week, I received a letter from Liza.

---

*Nov. 20, 1997*
*Dear George,*

*Hello, my dear. How are you? I hope you are in a good health and condition upon reading this letter of mine. George, I'm sorry if I will not response your letter as soon as possible because I'm always busy too regarding my job here. I'm always overtime, especially this coming Christmas because I have no day-off. I hope you can understand me about my situation. I think in January I have a time off. I will spend all my time to you if you will visit here on January. I hope so. You know, George, I'm always thinking about your visiting here in the Phillipines. I'm very much excited to meet you in person. I love to read your lovely message. You know, when I read your letter I'm always smile. I'm thinking I hope this is true. I hope you are the right guy for me. That's why I'm so in love to you George, because you are so lovely even your letter. I love you very much, and don't worry, there's a love waiting for you here in Cebu.*

*By the way, you are asking about hotels here in Cebu. The Park Place Hotel, it is nice, I think, but more expensive compare to others, the Century Hotel and Mercedes Hotel. Well, that's it for now, my dear George. I just wanted to say hello—and let you know that I'm always thinking about you and I'm imagining the wonderful days that we will have together.*

*Take care and may God bless you always. I love you too.*

*Love,*

*Liza*

Well, there was that magic word again, and there were more magical phrases: "I will spend all my time to you...I'm always thinking about your visiting here...I'm very much excited to meet you in person...When I read your letter, I'm always smile...I hope this is true...I hope you're the right guy for me...I'm so in love to you, George, because you are so lovely...I love you very much, and don't worry, there's a love waiting for you here in Cebu."

I was grinning ear to ear. I couldn't believe I had found someone so wonderful, someone who wanted me this much. Never mind the insanity of it all. I am in love with a wonderful girl, and it feels so good.

Then one night while I was grading papers, more magic happened. The phone rang. It was a collect call from Cebu City, Philippines. It was Liza! I would most definitely accept the charges, operator. Of course! Put her on the line!

"Hello, George?" the voice was shy and unassuming. "This is Liza Trujillo. Do you know who I am?"

"Yes, certainly. Of course I know. You're the girl that I love. How are you? I'm so glad you called."

This brought a snicker from Liza. "How are you, George? I just wanted to hear your voice."

"I'm very excited to see you. I am about to finish the fall semester, and then I'm going to San Francisco to spend Christmas with my family. Then I'll be coming to the Philippines to see you."

"Really? Are you really coming?"

"Yes, darling. I want very much to see you."

She snickered again. "Yes, I want to see you too."

"I really love the letters you sent me. And thanks for the pictures. You are so beautiful."

That brought yet another snicker. "Nga, I'm not beautiful."

"Yes, you are. You are my Filipina dream girl. You are the girl I've waited for my whole life."

"You are funny."

"Why?"

"Because we haven't even met in person yet."

"I don't care. I know already that you're the one for me."

"How? How do you know?"

"I just know."

"Tell me how?"

"Because when I go to bed at night, I think of your face. When I wake up in the morning, I think of your face."

"Nga, I'm not pretty."

"No way! You are the most beautiful woman I've ever seen."

Liza was letting out a full-blown laugh now. "You are blurred," she said. "You better check your eyes."

And so the conversation went, with us joking and laughing and kidding each other, and me telling her how much I loved her. She held back on the declaration of love, though. I figured she was just being prudent, and I was being my usual over-the-top self.

We settled on the dates I would come to Cebu. She promised to take some time off her job to spend with me. She also promised that she would give me a thorough tour of Cebu and all its nicest places.

At the end of the conversation I said it again: "I love you, Liza." She replied, "I like you too." We both laughed at the clumsiness of the moment. But when I hung up the phone, I was blissed out again. I had heard the voice of the woman I love. We were going to have a wonderful time together in the Philippines. This would be the nicest thing to ever happen to me. I just can't wait for the semester to finish so I could wing my way to the island paradise of my soul.

Finals were over soon enough, and grades were turned in soon enough. I was now ready to make the fateful trip to the Philippines to see my fair Liza, the lady of light, the girl of my dreams. Was this finally going to happen? I couldn't believe it. I would be visiting my homeland for the first time in my adult life and I would be seeing Liza in person for the first time. Life could not be any more exciting, more fulfilling, than this, I reckoned.

I called a travel agent who specialized in Philippine air tickets to make a reservation for a post-Christmas flight to Cebu.

"A roundtrip from San Francisco to Manila to Cebu and back will be, umm, $950 plus tax," he said over the phone.

"Nine-fifty?" I was a bit taken aback. "That's a little stiff."

"OK, OK, wait a minute, we have a special today. If you buy it right now, we can do it for $850."

Cool! I'd just saved $100 by complaining a bit. What a great negotiator I was! "OK, that sounds like it could work. Just hold on a minute while I look over my credit cards. I need to figure out which one I want to use."

I stalled for 30 seconds, a minute, while I thought about which credit card would be most advantageous. This one had a reward incentive, this one had frequent-flier miles, this was offered a rebate…hmmm. Before I could make my decision, the agent blurted out: "OK, OK, if you buy right now, I mean right now, I can give you the fare for $800."

This was interesting. The guy had me at $850, and now he dropped the price down to $800 just because I stalled for another minute. This is a new world and a new game, I reckoned. I started falling in love with the Philippines right then and there.

I told this story to my colleagues at the last faculty meeting of the semester, and they were all amused. One professor was startled that you could negotiate airline fares like that. "Probably only with foreign airlines," I said.

"Especially from countries where bartering is a way of life."

They all nodded in agreement. The meeting plodded along, covering all kinds of mundane department business. I was advised that my class evaluations, the surveys done by students at the end of the term, had been reviewed by the senior professors, and they were found to be quite good. I scored very good to excellent overall in all of my classes. My numerical scores were in the mid-4 range on a scale of 1 to 5. That was great news, especially after such a rocky start. I was very happy to hear this. But Mark Larson also had another piece of news to tell me. He said that I would be teaching a theory class in the spring semester, JMC 309 Analyzing Mass Media Messages, a course that would free me from the drudgery of teaching journalism skills classes.

I was elated, of course. This not only freed me from having to grade pile after pile of papers, but it would give me a chance to use the mass communication theoretical training I had in graduate school. I was thrilled by the prospect. Visions of Agenda Setting, Technological Determinism, and Cultivation Theory danced in my head.

Oh, and there was one more thing. Larson had been thinking about the best way to use my professional experience, and he'd come up with a brilliant idea. Beginning in the fall 1998 semester, I would be the new faculty advisor of *Osprey*, the student magazine published by the Humboldt State University journalism department.

Awesome! Now I would be the advisor/publisher of my own magazine. Life is getting more interesting and more fulfilling by the minute. I was on a monster roll. I couldn't believe how well things were going for me.

When I arrived home, I went out on my deck and bowed to the East. I was thankful for this great job that gave me lots of time off and a magazine of my own to publish; I was thankful that I was doing well on the job; I was thankful that I lived in such a peaceful and beautiful place; I was thankful that I had found a new love; and I thanked the gods of discount air travel that I saved $150 by just stalling a bit on the phone.

There were lots of gods out there who were smiling on me, I reckoned. They have given me an interesting, fulfilling and beautiful life.

And now I am about to embark on the most important journey of my life, a journey that even Alexander Von Humboldt himself might find interesting. I bowed again, hoping the gods would continue to smile on me. As I bowed, I smiled. I smiled a contented smile, a grateful smile, a winning smile.

How could I not? How could I not? Everything was coming up roses.

# 10

## *Reflections in Zero Visibility*

Inside a Philippine Airlines jet, New Year's Day, 1998—After 14 or so hours in the air, we are stuck in a holding pattern above Manila. It seems the locals are quite enamored of fireworks. And they managed to shoot off enough play-explosives on New Year's Eve to fill the skies above Ninoy Aquino International Airport with so much smoke that the task of landing this big plane would be very, very tricky.

"We have zero visibility," the pilot said over the PA system. "But there's nothing to worry about. Anyway, the computers will guide us to a safe landing."

Great. Zero visibility caused by fireworks and overexuberance.

What a sorry inconvenience. But then again, what an appropriate metaphor. I'm returning to my homeland in a state of zero visibility. Zero visibility of what life's really like on these tropical shores. Zero visibility of what it is to struggle and suffer under an unforgiving sun. Zero visibility of what it's like to live in a shabby little house with six or seven other people, working at some dead-end job every day, 10 hours, 12 hours, EVERY day, just so I can pay my share of the rent, and my sister's share of the rent, and maybe my cousin's share of the rent too until he can find a job. And maybe I can help out my parents with a little something every week or so, like maybe 200 or 300 pesos. And at the end of the month, there's not enough to pay the rent and pay the bills and buy decent food for everybody and give my parents some money, so what do I do? What do I do?

Well, Liza. I guess you can do what many Filipinas do. You work hard, you make do with what you have, and when you have time off, you go visit your friends, and you sing and dance and tell jokes and laugh, and you all dream about leaving this beautiful island paradise some day. You share fantasies about leaving behind the crushing poverty, leaving behind the squalor, leaving the trap, leaving this beautiful, tropical prison of endless servitude that is your life.

Maybe I should tell you a little more about my life sometime, since I hope to share it with you. And since I'm caught in this holding pattern above Manila, this is as good a time as any, I suppose. Hold it, I'd better write this down.

Dearest Liza,

I've really enjoyed our letters and our brief phone conversations over the past year, and it's hard to believe I'm actually going to be meeting you in person. You know, this trip to the Philippines is especially significant for me because this is my first time back to the islands since my mother and I left, in 1956, to come to America.

Did I cover this stuff in any of the letters I sent to you? Well, maybe I should give you some more detail.

My mother was a beauty queen and a teacher, from Samar, an island north of Cebu. That's right, isn't it? Please correct me if I'm wrong. Philippine geography is not my forte. She spoke Waray-Waray, another one of those Philippine dialects. How many are there, anyway? About 90? That's what I read in a travel guidebook once. Do you speak that one? I know you speak your regional language, Cebuano, and you also speak the national language, Tagalog, but do you also speak Waray-Waray? Not that it matters that much, because I don't know any of the Philippine languages, so we're going to be communicating in English.

My mom was from a large family, something like eight brothers and sisters. She told me the exact number once, but I forgot. Her father, my grandfather, was a photographer and a man of some wealth. He lost all of his wealth gambling and my mother grew up in poverty.

I stopped writing the letter to Liza and thought about my mother for a few minutes.

My mother was determined to succeed and was quite fluent in English, so she earned a teaching credential and landed a job at an elementary school in her hometown of Catarman. Also on the faculty at the time was a bright young teacher named Imelda Romualdez, who would later marry a war hero named Ferdinand Marcos, who would later become the president-cum-dictator of the Philippines. He was toppled in 1986 by Cory Aquino and the so-called "People Power" Revolution, which popular myth tells us, liberated the Philippine nation from the dark forces of dictatorship and ushered in a new era of democracy and freedom.

My mom also practiced a form of "People Power" long before the media coined the term. She was a hardy soul with a fighting spirit. She and her brothers and sisters escaped the invading Japanese during World War II by fleeing to the hills of Leyte. Once, trapped by some Japanese soldiers, she saved her life and the lives of her brothers and sisters by negotiating with the Japanese commander. I don't know exactly what she said to him or what she did, but the fact is, she saved their lives. And I'm alive today because of it. And so are dozens of my aunts, uncles, cousins and children of my cousins.

My mother's name was Milagros. That means "miracles" in English. My mother was a saint, a saint with a diminutive body and a big bag full of miracles. And she had a head full of smarts.

Milagros Moya, all 4 foot 11 inches of her, left the Philippines sometime after World War II in search of something different, perhaps something better in America, something that would make her bigger than she was. America was the land of big buildings, big money and big power, the land of large miracles. She boarded a big boat, disembarked in San Francisco, and gravitated to Oakland, across the bay.

Academics who study immigration patterns would classify her as just one of the "Second Wave" of Filipino immigrants, who came here during and after World War II. The population of Filipinos on the West Coast more than doubled between 1940 and 1960, from 31,408 to 64,459. Here's something I read in a book:

*The Filipinos arrived in California full of hope. During the previous decade, America had emerged as a highly industrialized country, a symbol of the 'impossible dream' for millions around the world.* (From *Filipinos in California* by Lorraine Jacobs Crouchett.)

Milagros Moya's impossible dream began with her working as a waitress in downtown Oakland, at a place called the Manila Cafe, where Filipino immigrants could taste the pork abobo, paksiw (sour fish soup), pansit (thin noodles), and other foods of home. One day, a short, stocky, strutting, hard-drinking man who made a meager wage washing dishes at the Leamington Hotel just up the street walked into the Manila Cafe.

His name was Gregorio Oribado, but he had changed his name to George Estrada. He was an Ilocano, meaning he was a native of Ilocos, the province north of Manila that was the home of war hero Ferdinand Marcos.

Gregorio Oribado/George Estrada was also a veteran of World War II. He served Uncle Sam, as did many Philippine nationals, by enlisting in a branch of the army that provided non-combat support to American troops. He was in the army for all of two months. Then the war ended. America won, and America showered her blessings on all those foreigners who had helped in this glorious victory. George Estrada, for all his two months of service, got full veterans' benefits from the U.S. government. Honorable discharge papers in hand, he boarded the

President Cleveland steamer to America and found work in the Kaiser shipyards in Oakland and Richmond. He later moved up the Pacific Coast, finding work in the canneries of Washington and Alaska. Deciding that canning fish was not to be his life's work, George Estrada brought his 5 foot 2 inch frame back to the Bay Area, and landed a job washing the dishes of the Leamington's affluent clients.

It was a good life, certainly not a bad outcome for a boy from a poor Ilocos province.

He was now in the land of the "impossible dream," and one day during the heady post-war days of mid-century America, when everything seemed possible, when miracles seemed to float in the Technicolor air, he walked into the Manila Cafe and into the life of a small lady of miracles. He was 49 years old. She was 29.

Milagros Moya and George Estrada started living together in a friend's home on Davis Street in the middle-class Fruitvale District of East Oakland and were married in 1952. In late 1952, after Milagros became pregnant, she decided to go back to the Philippines. Why? Because, in a fit of nationalism, she decided that her child was to be born in her homeland. She wanted her child to be enveloped by the lush, sweltering tropical air, to take his first breath in the land of coconuts and mangoes, to have the hot sweetness of the Philippines inside his very soul. And besides, she missed the Philippines. She ached to see her relatives, her sisters, her brothers. She left my father behind temporarily and hopped the President Cleveland for Manila.

I was born in the hospital of the University of Santo Tomas on February 1, 1953, at 4:10 a.m. and for the first three years of my life my mother and I lived in a dilapidated house on the outskirts of Manila. She used to refer to it laughingly as that "rotten house in the Philippines" and she used to tell me about sleeping under mosquito nets and she would show me pictures of those days.

I still have those tattered black-and-white pictures from my childhood. I see a chubby, naked little boy prancing about like a prince while my mom and her relatives smiled and fussed over me. I have in my office today at Humboldt State University a framed picture of my mother and I, a creased sepia-toned photograph with my mother looking prim and elegant, as usual, holding me upright as I stand feebly on a waist-high stool. I have this look of wonder—or is it bewilderment?—as I gaze upon the big world around us. My mother looked proud and filled with peace as she held me up to see this world.

"See what awaits you, child," she might have been thinking. "See all the wonders, the magnificence, the splendor. See what things may be yours. See what dreams await. This is a world of great beauty, of great horror, of gentle winds and killing rains. Bask in the infinite promise of the midday sun, but beware of the danger that lurks in the shadows. Anticipate the miracles of the future, my child, and let them make you something better than what we are."

To this day, that picture serves as an important source of inspiration. I draw energy from it. I feel my mother's spirit emanating from it. I get the strength of will from looking upon the image of the small lady of miracles. Whenever things aren't going right and I feel like giving up, I look at that picture and I remember. I remember what my mother wanted for me, and I think about the things I have now, things that she could only dream of. I remember how she struggled, how she hid in the hills from the Japanese, surviving on grains of rice and not much else. I remember how she suffered with her asthma in her later years, a disease that eventually killed her. And I remember her convulsive coughing fits, her many emergency trips to Kaiser Hospital and how, despite all her struggles, she managed to love me and care for me and teach me English and give me everything I needed to make it in this big, beautiful, horrible world.

I remember how she saved my life not once, but twice, when I was 8 years old. Both times I was choking on a cherry pit. She shoved her forefinger deep inside my throat and I was hacking and biting and flailing and gasping for breath and she grabbed me, held me still, and extracted the killer seed.

I remember how she cried and sobbed when I was hit by a car a year later. It was only a minor injury, a glancing blow, but I remember how she cried and cried and wailed in despair and brought me to the hospital and saw me through the crisis until all was well again.

Yes, mom, you were right. Between cherry pits and onrushing cars, it is indeed a dangerous world. All of those memories from that one old picture. And, if you look for it, you can see the "rotten house in the Philippines" in the background.

We'd left that rotten house behind and arrived in America on the day after Independence Day 1956, accompanied by her sister, my auntie Carmen. It was the middle of the 20th Century and everything was in Technicolor and America ruled the world and we were free from fear and Elvis was on the radio and the air was thick with money and immigrant dreams. Could there be any world more wondrous that this?

My mother and father were reunited in Oakland, with me in tow of course, and we quickly set about with the process of turning ourselves into Americans. I became more American than they could ever have anticipated.

To make a long story short: I was educated and Americanized in the Oakland public schools, and graduated from the University of California at Berkeley in 1975 with a degree in psychology; then I worked in an insurance company for a while but left to pursue my dream of becoming a journalist. I got a job as an errand boy (they called it copy boy or "editorial assistant") at *The Oakland Tribune* and quickly worked my way up the ladder to become a reporter. I was a reporter for about 10 years. I later worked briefly as a columnist before burning out on the newspaper business altogether. I tried becoming a filmmaker and later a musician, but those plans didn't pan out. So I went back to college and got a master's degree and then a Ph.D. in journalism. Now I'm a professor of journalism and I work for the largest public university network in the world, the California State University system, at its smallest campus, the 9,000-student strong Humboldt State University, up in the isolated redwood country of far-northern California.

It's a good life. It's cold and rainy up here. And the students can get a bit sassy. But it's not a bad outcome for a boy who grew up in a rotten house just outside Manila.

I get paid quite well to think and to engage people intellectually. I'm respected and admired in the community. And I get my summers and my Christmases off. What could be better than this?

This is the life I want to share with Liza. And I am returning to the Philippines to taste the sweet mangoes of my youth, and to visit my dream girl in Cebu.

My thoughts continued to drift as we circled smoky Manila. I started thinking about my father and about Robert Maynard, the late publisher of *The Oakland Tribune.*

My father was a nice man. Not a great man, by other people's measures. But to me, he was wonderful and kind and he did most of the things that a father had to do to be a good dad.

He taught me about history, about literature, about being a man. He bought me my first Beatles record, he bought me my first car (a maroon 1964 Mercury Comet), and he told me about baseball. He was a great guy, a good friend. Oh, he had his faults. He drank a little too much whiskey (Old Crow), he hated all Democrats (especially Kennedy), and he tended to scold me for not getting perfect grades in school. The first two things I could have done without; the latter gave me much-needed discipline. I did well enough in school to earn a doctorate, I too hate all Democrats (and all Republicans too, for that matter), and I still have that first Beatles record, though it's a bit scratched and warped now.

When my father died in 1993, I didn't know what to do. All I felt was numbness and an incredible sense of loss. At his funeral, I didn't quite know how to act. Everyone around me—my aunts, uncles, cousins—they were sobbing and weeping and carrying on. I had to put on a false front of man-like strength. Inside I was falling apart. But I knew I had to carry on and be like a rock.

*Goodbye, dad. Rest well. Goodbye, old friend. You were a good man. And I'll miss you every single day of my life.*

My father owned and operated a small printing shop on 10th and Franklin streets in downtown Oakland. He printed business cards, wedding invitations, stuff like that, on large hot-type presses that made deep grinding, rolling noises. I used to take the 14 AC Transit bus and visit him on Saturdays, and he'd give me a couple bucks so I could go around to the used-book stores and buy some amusements for myself. I'd buy all the stuff a dumb kid would buy: old comic books, used *Mad* magazines, pop-music fanzines, sports books. That old stuff is worth a lot of money now, but that's not the point. I learned to read and think and make mental play with those pulp products. The intellect was blooming and my father was there to fund the enterprise. How good of him!

Just down the street, two blocks away on 12th and Franklin, sat the majestic, old Tribune Tower. To my young mind, it was just some monolithic something signifying nothing. I didn't know then what I do now: that *The Oakland Tribune* would be the nexus of my young adult life; that I would become not just a reader, but a writer, a journalist, a creator of texts, a mass communicator of ideas, an official giver of events.

And all because my parents were good people; and because my father invited me to come on Saturdays to his little print shop, where he'd slave over his typesetting slate and his grinding, rolling machines. It lay in the shadow of the mighty Tribune Tower, that humble little storefront, where my father would give me money to buy used books and magazines, where I'd sit for hours and read voraciously through those texts, where I began to imagine that I could be clever enough, smart enough, to create texts like these to make people laugh—maybe grander than these, to make people think. That tiny little shop—since demolished and vanished except in my memory—where my father, fingers stinging and crooked from arthritis, would work like a dog, day in and day out, to provide the things my family needed: food, shelter, clothes, amusements.

I'll never forget the smell of ink and the grinding of the presses in that shop. And I'll never forget what a great man my father was.

Robert C. Maynard was a great man, by many people's standards. He was the first black person ever to cover a national beat (Congress) for a national newspaper (*The Washington Post*). He went on to become the first black person to own and operate a major metropolitan newspaper, *The Oakland Tribune*. There is where I met Bob Maynard.

I watched as he carved a larger-than-life legend, first as a nationally syndicated columnist, then as a regular guest on TV talk shows (the political kind) alongside

David Brinkley, George Will and other power elitists, then as the acknowledged heavyweight champion of racial diversity in journalism. When Bob Maynard went out on the stump to speak about the need for more minorities in journalism, people listened. *The Oakland Tribune* became a model for racial diversity, attaining at one point a 37 percent minority representation, then-highest in the land.

Maynard encouraged his reporters to be aggressive, to hold no cows sacred, to go after whomever needed going after. His columns and editorials openly criticized President Ronald Reagan and his retrograde policies, even at a time when the big and powerful national press was playing patty-cake with the White House.

Things got so frothy that *The Oakland Tribune* was anointed "most liberal newspaper in America" by one of those corporate-sponsored think tanks. Were we shaken by this disgrace? Hell, no. We were proud of it. We wore it like a badge of honor. We were bad boys, and the hell with everyone else. We were the rebel forces and Bob Maynard was our captain. Damn, it felt good.

Maynard was the closest thing I had to a father figure in journalism. He had this regal way about him, in his slow, methodical stride, and in his deep, velvety eloquence. He taught me to respect the institution of journalism, its history and its power. When I was reading Hunter Thompson, he told me to try Upton Sinclair instead. He praised me for my skill, he punished me for my weakness. He acknowledged me for what I was, a hometown boy who had a cute way with words. Yet, he tried to transform me into something bigger—a journalist with an eye on the globe.

I was Oakland. Maynard was Washington. The relationship was uneasy.

Once, when the Oakland Raiders made it to the Super Bowl, I talked the *Tribune* into letting me cover the local color in New Orleans. When I got there, I found out that I didn't have a ticket to the game. It seems that the sports editor had decided to keep all the tickets, and he didn't think I'd need one since my work was going to take place outside the stadium.

I was not pleased by this. I called the home office and voiced my displeasure to a few key people and—wouldn't you know it—a couple hours later Bob Maynard called me up and asked if I would like to have a couple of tickets on the 40 yard-line.

"Well, yes, Bob. That would be fine."

"And what do I get in return?" he inquired sternly.

"Uh," I was thrown for a loop. "My loyalty forever?"

"No, no, don't give me that," Maynard said, chastising my frivolousness. "Tell you what. Just keep on writing those great leads of yours, OK?"

"Great leads? Oh, sure. Yeah, no problem. Thanks, man."

I walked on air the rest of that day.

A couple years later, Bob Maynard decided to give me a column. My first assignment: cover the National Democratic Party Convention in San Francisco.

How did I do? Well, using information I'd gotten from some very exclusive sources, I was the first journalist in the country to identify Geraldine Ferraro as Walter Mondale's vice-presidential nominee to be. Everybody else was a beat late. Young George Estrada of *The Oakland Tribune* had scooped the world. Maynard was impressed. I guess I did good.

Writing a column was fun, and I did it for a little over 18 months. But career burnout was taking its toll. In short, I just didn't want to do it anymore. Every story started to sound the same. Every deadline was just like the last. The faces in the newsroom looked drawn and gray. I could no longer get it up for daily dead-lines; and the whole set of life-values that animate journalism started to seem so hollow, so irrelevant to the things I really wanted. When it stops being fun, it becomes just another job. I had to quit.

Bob Maynard was not happy. He took it personally. The look he gave me when I told him shot a million harpoons through my heart: How could you do this, you little ingrate? How could you abandon the man who taught you every-thing? The man who gave you a set of keys to the kingdom? You insufferable lit-tle shit!

I tried to shake it off, but never did. In my heart, it felt like I'd let down a father.

Bob Maynard died in 1993, shortly after my real father died. It was a painful coincidence. Bob and I never reconciled our bitter parting of ways. After I quit, I'd visit the newsroom every now and then just to say hello to friends or to do a little freelance work. Sometimes I'd run into Maynard there, and all the warmth was gone. He would seem so distant, so aloof, as if we never shared anything in our lives.

Maybe he did harbor resentment, or maybe he was suffering from the effects of the cancer that would later kill him. It was hard to tell because he would always put up such a regal front, even during his dying days.

Maynard's daughter, Dori, compiled a selection of Bob's best columns into a book, *Letters to My Children,* which was published by Andrews and McMeel. Most of the columns feature the old standy Maynard themes: loyalty to family, social compassion, respect for individual differences—and most prominent of them all, the importance of a strong father figure.

Several of the columns speak of how Maynard's own father, a preacher, would discipline him regularly for disrespectful behavior toward family and friends. The lesson learned: appreciate humanity, all humanity, for each person is precious, each life a gift.

When I read those old columns now, I can imagine myself sitting at some dinner table with Bob Maynard as he carves a turkey and dispenses moralisms to me with that deep, velvety voice of his. A father-figure he was, known and cherished around the world.

Then I think of my real father, slaving away at some noisy, churning machine. Printing, cranking, printing, folding, printing, inking, printing, cleaning, printing, hurting, hurting, hurting, hurting.

And I wonder who I miss more. And I wonder who inspired me more. And I wonder if I'll ever meet anyone of their like again.

My contemplation was interrupted by a beep indicating that the captain of the plane was about to address the passengers.

"We are going to attempt a landing in a few minutes, so please fasten your safety belts," he said. "We still have zero visibility, but it's not a problem because anyway the computer is in control. Thank you for flying Philippine Airlines."

And so it was that on my return to my birthplace a computer chip safely guided my plane through the smoke and onto the runway at Ninoy Aquino International Airport. Just as a computer chip in a University of Texas lab had guided me through the fog and brought Liza's gleaming image to me.

And now I was here. I couldn't see a damned thing, but I was coming home.

# 11

## *Meeting of The Spirits*

*An Island in the Pacific...The Queen City of the South...A Showcase of History and Modernity. See Cebu and its zest for life. A people proudly true to their traditions, and ever ready to the challenges of the new millennium. Discover the core of its culture, its distinct identity. The rare sweetness of its mangoes. The cornucopia of its delicious delicacies. The melody of its guitars, the seduction of the sea and its beaches.*
(From a Cebu tourism Web site.)

The landing was smooth, thankfully, but the wait at the Manila airport was long and excruciating, exacerbated as it was by the presence of cheesy shops offering overpriced souvenirs and by the seemingly endless string of customs officials who wanted to see my plane tickets and inspect my money belt. It was probably my fault more than anyone else's that I was subject to multiple inspections, since I was wandering from waiting areas to shop areas and back to waiting areas again just to soak in the atmosphere.

Finally, the plane for Cebu was ready, and I got on (but not before another passport and money-belt inspection) and about two hours later, there I was in Cebu, landing at the Mactan International Airport.

After all that contemplation in zero visibility and after several hours waiting at the Manila airport, I was ready to re-discover the Philippines. I was ready for Liza. I was ready to usher in the rest of my life.

But first, there was customs to deal with. Again.

I'd been told by several friends and relatives that a $10 bill discreetly tucked into my passport would help, uh, expedite things at customs. The common thought was that bribery is such an essential part of the culture in this poor country that it would be regarded as a simple signifier of goodwill. Sort of a "hello" from an American citizen, sort of a way of saying, "Thanks for letting my country exploit all of your people and natural resources for 100 years, and keep up the good work, Pablo, or whatever your name is."

Sort of a tip for good service.

Bullshit, I thought to myself. And I handed over the passport with nary a dollar or a peso inside. I'll take my chances and see what happens.

The customs officer eyed me for a moment, then opened the blue booklet. He leafed through it for a few moments, then without looking up, muttered, "Estrada, hmmm."

I instantly understood this to mean that my family name had some sort of higher meaning to him. And I knew, at this moment, that a thousand calculations were going through the mind of this obscure government employee who was leafing through my U.S. passport at the Mactan International Airport in Cebu City, Philippines, literally just a few miles away from the spot where Chief Lapu Lapu killed Magellan and beat back the first wave of European invaders.

And now, here is someone else from another world, and he looks like one of us. And his last name is the same as our President's. Is this traveler from the U.S. a member of the President's family? His face does have a bit of a resemblance to Joseph Estrada's. Same round cheeks, same flattened nose, same husky musculature. Was there a memo or some kind of notification from above that one of the president's cousins or nephews or illegitimate children or whatever was coming through this terminal today? Should I give this man the VIP treatment? Who IS this man? Why does he have an American passport? He seems to speak with a perfect American accent. Are any of the President's relatives living in America? What should I do? JESUS, MARY, JOSEPH, WHAT SHOULD I DO!?

Despite the thoughts racing through his mind—or so I imagined them to be—the customs official remained outwardly calm. His gleaming black hair remained immaculate, untouched, slicked back and perfect; the brass buttons on his proto-military clothing sat in mute testimony to his officiousness; his countenance was stern. Then a smile broke through his facade of Philippine officialdom. He looked up at me.

"Are you visiting relatives here?"

"Relatives? Not really. I'm visiting my girlfriend and her family, and just sightseeing, generally."

"Oh, you have a girlfriend here!" He seemed pleased to learn this. "How long will you stay?"

"Oh, just a little over a week. Ten days, I think."

"Well, I'm going to stamp 'balikbayan' (Filipino living abroad) in your passport. This means you can stay up to one year. Welcome home, Professor Estrada."

"Oh, well, uh, thanks."

The customs official stamped the booklet and cheerfully handed it back. There seemed to be not a hint of disappointment on his face that there was no American currency in the passport. Or, if he was disappointed or angry, he didn't show it.

That friendly Filipino smile, no matter who's flashing it, is always good at masking the feelings inside. That Filipino tendency to defer to the status of the upper classes—the respectful way he called me "professor"—was also quite endearing. I know. I've been on the other side of this charade. I've used these deference techniques to great effect during my life. They always seemed to work.

That hurdle behind me, I now had to go get my luggage and pass through another customs official. But I kept on thinking about the first customs official's smile.

That same smile was on the lips of my father, whenever he was tending to a customer at his little print shop in downtown Oakland. That same smile was on the lips of my mother, whenever she was working on someone's hair at the Elizabeth Arden salon in San Francisco. That same smile was on my lips as I bestowed respect on an editor, or a senior professor, or any member of the petit bourgeoisie who had power over me; that same "mango smile" that masked my inner feelings of inadequacy, of helplessness, of desperation, of surrender.

The customs man's easygoing, deferential smile, stayed in my head, even as I approached the next obstacle: the luggage checkpoint. I felt little waves of that smile rippling through my veins and into receptors in my cortex. And I felt my mind sending signals to my lips, and I felt the muscles in my face twisting, bending, curling upward into an easygoing, tropical smile. It was so reflexive, it was almost involuntary. The sunny, tropical smile must be encoded into Filipino DNA, I figured. It was a natural defensive response to physical confrontation.

The smile was there even as the luggage inspectors looked at my declaration slip. The smile remained even as one of the inspectors reached over to open my luggage to begin inspection. The smile remained even as the other inspector, noticing my name on the declaration, stopped his colleague and whispered, "Estrada, Estrada." The smile remained even as the first inspector stopped himself, looked at my papers and waved me on.

"*Sige, sige* (continue on)," he said.

The smile remained unchanged. I didn't have to say a word to get past this hurdle. My name was enough. The thought that I might have some presidential bloodlines was enough. How funny this was!

Luggage safely on my handcart, I wheeled toward the taxicab station. But first I had to get some local currency. I headed for the money-changing counters.

An armed guard who looked like a local policeman saw me coming toward the currency exchange counter, and he summoned me over to him. I reckoned there was some sort of formal procedure I had to undergo first.

"You want to exchange dollars?" he asked.

"Yes, sir."

"OK, how much do you want?" The guard pulled out a wad of 500-and 1,000-peso bills, licked his thumb and started counting them off.

"Uh, well, I don't know. Give me a hundred dollars worth."

"OK," he said. "The exchange rate is 42 pesos per dollar."

"OK," I said, never wanting to argue with a man holding a gun. After the exchange, I looked over at the currency counter. The two women there looked at me in dismay and looked at the policeman with disgust. I looked at a letter-board at another counter, and noticed that the official exchange rate was more on the order of 45 to 1. I realized I'd just been punked by a local cop who was taking advantage of unwary tourists.

But that wasn't the only hustle I was going to face on this, my first sweltering day back in the Philippines. Enter the one-toothed cab driver, who saw me outside the airport looking hot, tired and confused. He came rushing to my side and started lifting my baggage into the trunk of his cab.

"Where to, boss?" he said with a very pleasant tone of voice. I was too tired to resist. And so it was that I got into the back seat of his air-conditioned taxi and felt the cool rush of Western technology soothing my overheated soul.

The one-toothed cab driver brought me to my hotel, Eddie's Heritage Hotel, located on a side street off Mango Boulevard near a very large church, Iglesia Ni Cristo. He helped me with my bags, and grinned slyly as a petite young woman walked by.

"You like that girl" he inquired.

"What?"

"I can get for you like that. I can get girl for you like that. Young, pretty."

I gave him a knowing smile and declined, trying my best to be polite. Disappointed for the moment, Mr. One Tooth hoisted all three of my bags and stepped back briskly into the lobby of Eddie's.

It was very clean inside. The lobby was adorned with some sort of faux tropical bamboo-accented décor. It was warm but breezy from the air-con. The receptionists, all adorned in navy-blue jumpsuits with very large bowties, smiled pleasantly.

"Hi, I'm George Estrada from the U.S. I have a room reservation here for 10 days."

The receptionist kept her professional demeanor, but I knew that the surname rang a couple of warning alarms inside her brain. I decided to give her a break.

"No, I'm not a relative of the president," I said with a smile.

We both laughed, and I began to wonder how many times I would have to explain this during my visit. Yes, my name is Estrada, but no, I am not related to the Honorable Joseph "Erap" Estrada, former star of action movies and now president of the Republic of the Philippines. I wondered if people named Clinton or Bush or Kennedy had similar problems back in the U.S.A. Funny, I never thought that a Spanish name like Estrada sounded presidential—but that was my Anglicized mind thinking, wasn't it? This is a different place, and these are different circumstances. An Estrada can be a president, and I could possibly be his relative. I was tickled by the idea.

"Mr. Estrada?" another one of the bow-tied girls called out in my direction.

"Yes."

"You have a call from Miss Liza."

What timing! What a golden moment! She must love me. I just got here a minute ago and she's already calling me on the phone. "She loves me," I proclaimed, just loud enough for the receptionist to hear. Was I stating a fact or just expressing a hope? It didn't matter. This moment mattered, and it was sweet. I took the phone.

"Hello?"

"Hello, George? Have you just arrived?"

It was her. Liza. The voice was gentle and sweet, the English not quite perfect, in the Philippine way that English is rendered imperfectly. "Have you just arrived" came out sounding more like "Hab you juss arybe?" But diction mattered not a bit. Her accent made her sound more childlike, more vulnerable.

"Yes, I got here. Where are you? When can I see you?"

"Umm, I'm at my cousin's house," she said. I could hear excited chattering in the background. "I'm off work today. Shall I visit you at Eddie's tonight?"

That would be fine, of course. Tonight it is then, my love. Tonight, tonight. I was on a cloud. I was floating somewhere above Cebu City with one foot in heaven. In my mind's eye, I could see the face of my beloved, the dewy eyes, the warm smile, the smooth cheeks, the skin with the color of an exotic desert. Back on Earth, with my two eyes, I could see the gnarled face of Mr. One Tooth. I owed him some money. I guess heaven had to wait.

"Yes, right. How much do I owe you?"

"Well, it's up to you," he chuckled.

"What?"

"It's up to you."

Uh, oh, that's right. He hadn't turned on the meter. I'd read about such scams perpetrated by foreign taxi drivers upon unwitting American travelers. Now he's trying to get over on me. But he's leaving it up to me to decide how much to pay him? I was at a loss.

The driver looked at me in anticipation. The receptionists and bellhops all looked at me, wondering what my next move would be, wondering whether I was going to be Mr. Big Stuff or just another discount holiday-maker. What was the Tagalog word for cheap? Kuripot! I certainly didn't want to seem kuripot, not in my first hour of my first day back in the Philippines after a lifetime away.

Quick calculations in my head: a taxi ride from the airport back home usually runs about $20. And the distance was about the same. But this is the Philippines, so let's cut that in half. Yeah, 10 bucks seems about right. Let's give him some American currency too. That'll impress him. The drive was about 30 minutes, I think. Yeah, 10 bucks. OK, that's enough. I pulled a 10 spot out of my wallet and handed it to the driver.

The receptionists and the bellhops raised their eyebrows. Was this not enough? Too much? I couldn't tell.

"Is that enough?" I asked the driver. "Does that cover it?"

He looked astonished for a moment, then he flashed me that toothy grin. "Merry Christmas!" he said.

"What?"

"How about Christmas present?" He wanted more.

One of the receptionists started shouting at the driver, and another one turned to me: "No, no, that's enough. That's plenty already. He's just begging for a tip." Another receptionist did her own calculations out loud: "From the airport, should be only 300 pesos. (About seven dollars.) Ten dollars, my goodness."

Two of the bellhops picked up my luggage and I was scooted upstairs. Meanwhile, behind me, I could hear the receptionists continue to scream and curse at Mr. One Tooth. Strangely, I started to feel sorry for him. OK, so he beat me out of a couple bucks, but so what? What was his life like? What did he come home to every day? What did he wake up to every day? Will a few dollars unfairly taken from me change the permanent economic differential of our lives?

"Is this your first trip to the Philippines?" one of the smiling bellboys asked me. He bore an uncanny resemblance to Keanu Reeves.

"Well, yes," I said. "I was born in Manila, but this is the first time I've been back to the Philippines."

"You're from the U.S.?"

"Yes, yes, California."

"Ah yes, California. Lots of pretty girls."

"Right," I said. "Just like on *Baywatch*."

We all laughed. I wondered if they got the joke or if they actually believed that all American women looked like Pamela Anderson. I remember something I read once in a silly U.S. government guidebook to the Philippines, written for servicemen back in the 1950s.

*Most Filipinos take life as they find it, and they always enjoy a good laugh. They have a keen sense of humor, and when you become well enough acquainted with them, you'll find they delight in funny stories and comical situations. They'll laugh along with you when you subject them to a good-natured ribbing, and poke fun right back at you.* (From *A Pocket Guide to the Philippines*, published by the U.S. Dept. of Defense, 1955, p. 48.)

The bellhops said something to each other in their language, laughed again, and led me into my room. They were either saying, "Wow, I'd love to go to California someday." Or they were saying, "Get a load of this bullshit artist who thinks we're a couple of stupid monkey boys." I couldn't tell.

The room seemed pleasant enough. The bedspread had some sort of multicolored tropical theme, and the headboard was some sort of arched, stained-bamboo thing. There was an adjoining bathroom and shower, a large closet and a long, horizontal mirror above a long, waist-level counter. Not the presidential suite, but not bad for $25 a night, I reckoned.

The shorter of the two bellhops reached up and turned on the air conditioner and the other guy turned on the TV. Some Philippine soap opera was on. A woman with too much makeup on was screaming at a young man in Tagalog. Or was it in Cebuano? I couldn't tell.

"I hope you enjoy your visit in Cebu," the taller bellhop said, smiling very sincerely. Thanking them, I reached into my wallet, pulled out four one-dollar bills, and gave each bellhop two.

"Oh, thank you, sir," the tall one said politely. "Thank you, sir," the other echoed, bowing his head slightly and smiling broadly.

Alone in my room at last, I savored the moment, the place. I was back in my homeland, a magical, mystical homeland, where everything was warm and dreamy, the air was moist and sultry; a place where dreamgirls were waiting, and anything was possible.

Outside my window, I could hear the rumble of street traffic, the coughing of asthmatic jeepneys, the honking of impatient horns. I could hear a cock crowing arrogantly in someone's backyard.

Then I heard some screaming, jubilant whooping, but it wasn't coming from the street below. It was from inside the hotel, from down the hall. It was the two bellhops. They were ecstatic because they'd just been grossly overtipped the sum of two dollars each.

I realized that I was being a little too loose with my money. I smiled, happy that my ignorance had resulted in a windfall for the two young bellboys and a snaggly-toothed cab driver.

I peeked past the curtains to the busy street. I saw a very thin dog walking slowly past the front of the hotel, stopping to look up at the security guard, perhaps hoping to find some scrap of food or charity. I saw a barefoot boy clutching some mangoes, papayas and other fruits to his chest. He was smiling because he had what he needed, and now he was going home to enjoy his feast.

I smiled too, for I knew that feasts would be commonplace in this land of delights. Then I lay on my bed, atop the tropical-motif spread, and watched MTV for a while. Wow, even MTV is different here, I thought to myself. Sleep came, and I welcomed it, knowing that the girl who had only been a dream would be coming to life, and changing my life, in just a few hours.

Her name was Liza, and she was the most beautiful girl in the world. But because I'd never met her in person, because I'd never touched her sweet face, because I'd never kissed her—she was just a theory. Just another theory, unproven, nebulous, disembodied, like all the theories I'd been studying in grad school. Agenda setting. Cultivation theory. Two-step flow. Bullet theory. Critical theory. Post-modern anti-theory.

But this was a theory named Liza—it almost made me cry to whisper her name "lee-sah"—and she had a thin, delicate body I wanted to press against me, and laughing eyes I wanted to swim in, and lush, full lips I wanted to kiss again and again.

Yet, despite my deepest cravings for her, she was just another theory. Just another abstraction. Just another hypothesis, just another idealization, just another imagined state of perfection—who I happened to be in love with. Who also happened to live in the Philippines, half a world away. She was a theory who also happened to be coming to my hotel this very night. This very hour. This very minute. This very second.

The telephone jarred me from my nap. Yes, I was in the Philippines now. Yes, I was lying on my bed at Eddie's Hotel in Cebu City. Yes, a dog was barking outside. Yes, MTV Asia was on the tube. Yes, the rhythmic humm of the air-con whispered through the damp air. Yes, I was awaking from a dream, and Liza was coming soon. I rolled over and picked up the phone.

"Hello, Mr. Estrada? Liza is here now."

Oh, my God. My dreams have come true. My ship has arrived. This is no longer romance fantasy, no longer a flickering Filipina Dream Girl on my computer screen. The theory is being tested here and now. Will I get good data? Will I find significance? Let's get up and find out.

"Tell her I'll be there in about three minutes."

I leapt out of bed, straightened out my blue and white polo shirt, looked in the mirror and fussed with my hair. I was slightly balding on the left side, so I had to fluff my right-side hair slightly westward to give the illusion of young-adult fullness.

I slipped on my big white Avia basketball shoes. Sportswear always tends to give one a more youthful aspect, and it has worked nicely for me during my journey into middle age. Big, thick, lushly upholstered basketball shoes from America were also a prestige item in the Philippines, so these Avias did the trick nicely. I looked sporty, prosperous and American.

Satisfied that it wasn't going to get any better than this, I had one more look in the mirror, took a deep breath and headed out the door. Here we go, I thought to myself. Sometimes all of life comes down to one or two moments.

This is one of those.

I bounded down two flights of stairs, into the lobby, and there she was. I was suddenly looking into the eyes of my Liza. She was no longer a theory. She was no longer made of flickering light. She was really, really here, in the flesh.

She was dressed in white pants and cotton blouse, her shiny black hair falling over her shoulders like a waterfall of black silk. Her face was smooth and luminescent brown, like an exotic desert. Her smile glistened, her eyes danced, as beams of eternity shot out in my direction. Her warm countenance was that of pure welcome, pure acceptance.

Eureka, I thought to myself. I have found the gold.

"Hello, Liza?"

"Hi, George?"

"Yes, it's so good to finally meet you."

"Umm, yes. George, I want you to meet my cousins and my friend."

Liza was accompanied by three young ladies, whom I greeted respectfully. It was customary for a single Filipina to be accompanied by a "chaperone"—in this case, chaperones—on a first date. So this was perfectly normal.

I said it was a pleasure to meet all of them, and they giggled. I don't know if they were pleased to meet me as well, or highly amused at this attempt by an American to connect with them, or generally laughing at me. It occurred to me that they might not understand most of what I was saying. But they seemed friendly enough, so I felt good about this meeting.

I invited everyone to sit, and so we did, on the bamboo-framed couches in the hotel lobby. The young women at the reception desk shot sideways glances at us as we made ourselves comfortable. Liza sat next to me on the smaller of the two couches.

"So, how was your trip?" Liza asked me, making firm eye contact.

"It was good. Nice, smooth ride. I'm a little jet-lagged right now, but I'm happy to see you."

She didn't reply. She shot a glance at her chaperones and giggled. They looked at her and giggled back. One of them said something softly in Tagalog. Or was it Cebuano?

I was unperturbed. I stared at Liza's face for a good long moment. She looked exactly like she did in her *Filipina Dream Girls* photo.

"Wow," I said. "You ARE beautiful."

"Hah?"

"Maganda ka, talaga." ("You are beautiful indeed," I was trying to say.)

"Maganda, nga…" She said this sarcastically, in the self-deprecating way that all Filipinos reply to a compliment. She and her colleagues exchanged glances and laughs. "No, I am not beautiful."

She said this in all sincerity, seemingly. Although I couldn't imagine how this dusky jewel could've ever been considered un-beautiful. And I found it even harder to believe that she was single and available. Was she really available to me? Well, she HAD come to see me at my hotel on my first night in town. She seems eager to meet me, or else she's awfully good at faking it. But if she wasn't serious about me, why did she come here so quickly and why did she drag along her cousins?

These were the things that were running through my head even as we made small talk in the Eddie's Hotel lobby. I also wondered what was going through her head. What were her thoughts now?

*Why did this American guy come all the way here to Cebu? Just to meet me? What's wrong with him, can't he find a girl in America? American girls are so beautiful, and so available. Why can't he find one? Why isn't he married yet? There must be something wrong with him. Why did he pick me to meet? Why me? I'm just a girl from the provinces. Why did he pick me? What are his plans for me? Does he want me to marry him and go to America? Oh, my God! What is America like? Is it like in the movies? Everyone has a nice, big home and nice, big cars and a good job. Everyone is well fed. No one is starving. Everyone has fun in their lives. Not just work, work,*

*work, all the time, work. Work, work, work, for what? Just to pay the rent and buy food? And then your family all comes to live in your house. And they all want to eat too, so by the end of the month you pay out more than you take in and you cannot pay all the bills and you find yourself in debt and then your cousins are asking for some money to buy some school books and then your mother is sick and she needs some vitamins and so you give her some money too and then at the end of the month you have to borrow some pesos from your sister just so you can catch the jeepney to go to work and then and then…oh, my God, it's terrible to be poor. It's terrible to have no other choices in life. It's terrible to live in such a country, where there are so many poor people and so few opportunities.*

She may have been thinking these thoughts. Or I may have been thinking she was thinking these thoughts. Then, on the other hand, she might've been thinking, "Whoa, like, whatever. This is pretty intense," or something like that. I wasn't entirely sure.

I gave her a teddy bear. It was a big, brown stuffed toy that a friend had given me to give to Liza. She seemed genuinely pleased to get it, and hugged it affectionately. I also gave her a Walkman cassette stereo.

"What's that?" she asked, looking mystified.

I explained that it was a personal stereo, with headphones, for listening to music. She really did not know what it was. Incredible, I thought. Her cousins, though, knew exactly what it was, and they explained to her in Tagalog—or was it Cebuano?—what the function of this thing was.

Was Liza such an isolated girl from the provinces that she didn't know what a personal stereo was? I found that incredibly charming, to meet someone who was so unspoiled by late 20th century modernity that she didn't know how to use one of these things. Liza was so unaffected, so vulnerable, it was scary.

We continued to make small talk, and then she had to go. She had a work day ahead of her, and had to get up early. But first, pictures! We've got to have pictures!

I gave my camera to one of Liza's cousins—I've forgotten her name now—and led Liza to a spot against the wall near a large painting. The painting was of some 19th century European scene. "Here," I said. "Let's stand here. All right, big smile." I put my arm around her shoulders and she smiled broadly, that spectral smile of hers, while clutching the stuffed bear to her slender waist.

Her cousin was fumbling with the camera, trying to figure out how to use it. It was not complicated. It was a point-and-shoot camera. All she had to do was look in the viewfinder, frame the shot and push the shutter button.

Of course, she also had to have the camera pointing in the right direction, which was not the case. She was holding it backwards. Her eye was up against the lens and the back of the camera was facing us.

"Uhh, wait a second." I walked over and straightened things out for her. "You want to take a picture of us, not your eyeball."

The pictures were finally taken, and as I look at them today, a number of years later, I see a handsome young Filipino couple caught in the first bloom of affection, smiling at the prospect of a happy future together. How could it be anything else? This was the traditional, conservative, Filipina girl I'd been waiting for all my life. And now I've finally found her. And she's looking for a man like me to provide for her and protect her and love her for all time.

Eureka! Could life be any better than this?

Before they all got up to leave, we made a date for me to come and visit Liza at her job the next day. She'd be at her usual post, wearing her uniform, a yellow top jacket with tight, pressed collars, working in the barong section at Shoe Mart, the large department store in Cebu's mega-mall, selling fancy, festive shirts made of pineapple-leaf fiber to middle-and upper-class Filipino men, shirts that might sell for the equivalent of a week's pay for Liza. Some sell for as much as a month's pay or more.

"Do I get a hug?" I asked Liza as they headed out the door. She seemed amazed by the request.

"Hah?" Her cousins laughed out loud. I didn't wait for an answer. I put my arm around Liza and tried to pull her to me for an embrace. At the last moment she turned away from me, so I ended up hugging her from the back.

A million thoughts raced through my mind. Was this the Philippine social conservatism expressing itself? No hugs or other form of semi-intimate contact on the first date? Or was this an act of personal revulsion? Was this Liza's true feeling for me, the feeling of a beautiful younger woman for an older ordinary man? Was this a naked, instinctive reaction from the gut, stripped of any higher economic calculus? Or was it simply that I was just being too forward with a shy girl?

After we said goodbye, I repeated my promise that I'd come visit her at work the next day. She seemed genuinely pleased to hear this again, and her cousins also repeated their approval of the idea. There didn't seem to be anything fake about this, I thought to myself. She likes me. She wants to see me again. This could be a good thing, I reckoned.

I had a San Miguel beer at the bar, shared some jokes with Robinson, the bartender, and returned to my room about a half hour later. The air outside was sweltering, but my room was cool from the air conditioning.

I watched MTV and ate mangoes. I noticed how incredibly sweet and luscious they were, more so than the mangoes I'd had in America. They also had sort of a sassy, tangy backbite. I looked in the mirror and smiled the mango smile of a man stupidly in love. Life is good in the Philippines, I thought to myself. Things are looking good.

# 12

## *The Dream For Sale*

It was a mall just like any other mega-mall you'd see in America. Except this one was in Cebu City, Philippines. And this was where the lady of light worked, so it was more than your usual mall to me. It was the center of the universe. SM mega-mall was, in fact, a universe onto itself.

Outside, the air was wet and hot, bloodthirsty mosquitoes buzzed about your head, and the jeepneys belched their dirty smoke into the tropical air. But here, inside this oasis of a mega-mall, the air was cool, the melodious tones of bubble-gum dance music lifted your spirits, and the belching noises you heard were from the contented diners inside the food court.

Shopping is a form of escape and transformation, and there were all modes of escape and all kinds of transformations available at SM.

Wanna be cool? Just check out these American sunglasses. Only 25,000 pesos, or about three months' pay for someone from the provincial class. How cool is that?

Or how about this black Nike jacket, with a USA patch on the back. This is on sale, boy-o! Only 500 pesos. The zipper doesn't quite work right, and it's much too hot for the Philippines, but hey! It's Nike! It's American! And it's on sale. For only two days' pay!

Pssst! Want to eat like an American? We have a McDonald's here. We also have a Kentucky Fried Chicken, we have a Texas Chicken and we have a Dunkin' Donuts. Want some ice cream later? We have a Baskin-Robbins too. If you want to eat Philippine food, we have a dozen restaurants in the food court where you can get langonisa (sweet sausage), banggus (fish), dinuguan (cow-blood soup) or whatever you want. There's even Philippine fast food available at Jollibee and Goldilocks. But if you want to go exotic, go to the McDonald's. Try the langonisa happy meal. Super-size it, if you dare.

This fascination with things America seemed an obsession.

One store advertised quite boldly that it carried "Genuine American Clothes." In its front window, displayed like a holy relic, was a pair of black Converse high-top sneakers.

Another store bragged that it offered "Magazines From America." Inside, there were old copies of People and Cosmopolitan wrapped tightly in plastic like they were objects to be protected and cherished.

Outside another store there was a giant cardboard standup display of basketball star Shaquille O'Neal, accurate in height and width. Four pre-teen boys stood before it, gaping and wondering how any person or thing could be so huge.

Watching the people walking around SM on any given day provides enough stimulus for a whole year's worth of imagining.

Schoolgirls walk around in packs, still dressed in their frumpy-modest outfits, looking at clothes and accessories, shopping for CDs, checking out the boys, checking out what other girls are wearing, talking on their cell phones, watching for men who might be looking at them. Foreign men, especially. American men, most especially.

A group of several short, dark-skinned Filipino men wearing dirty clothes, who I imagined to be some low-wage laborers from the provinces, were gathered around a poster that was advertising men's underwear. The men were laughing and joking about the models in the photo, particularly the tall blonde super-model who was lavishing her attentions on a man who evidently had the good sense to purchase this particular brand of underwear. The message, of course, was that any ordinary guy can score a delicious babe, simply if he were to buy this underwear. The short, dark men seemed to find great humor in this ad, and I reckoned that maybe they weren't as dim as I originally thought.

At a currency-conversion counter, I was able to exchange my American dollars for Philippine pesos. The exchange rate greatly favored Americans at this time, with each dollar getting about 47 pesos in return. The prim young woman at the counter asked to see my passport. When I inquired why she needed to see it, she just frowned and held out her hand. "It's policy," she muttered. I handed it over and she photocopied it. She flipped through it and seemed to take great interest in the country stamps of the places I'd visited in the past—Sweden, Denmark, England, the Netherlands, Finland.

While she was satisfying her curiosity, a security guard sidled over and started chatting with me. He was very friendly, and had an easy laugh. He could tell from my accent that I was American, and he wanted to watch the spectacle of me flashing some American greenbacks. As we chatted, I noticed that two salesgirls nearby had stopped what they were doing and were looking dreamily at the wad of cash I had in my hands, about $200 in 20s. I was going to receive several thousand pesos in return. And as the currency girl started counting out 1,000-peso bills, the two salesgirls looked and sighed. They weren't looking at me. They were definitely looking at my hands, and the money that was placed into my hands, and they were dreaming of the day when they would have that much money. One of the girls leaned her head sideways, onto the shoulder of her friend, and she sighed again, an audible, heaving sigh.

I wanted to cry. But I didn't. I wanted to give them the money and tell them to find their dreams. But I didn't. I continued talking to the security guard, who was now asking me questions about America.

"It's nice there in the U.S.?" he asked. "You are balikbayan, no? You like da Philippines? You have a girlfriend here?"

Although he seemed friendly enough—as friendly as you can get while carrying a loaded gun in a holster—I sensed that he was trying to hustle me. Or worse, he might be trying to set me up with his spinster sister. I flashed him the peace sign and dashed off, clutching my handful of 1,000-peso bills close to me.

Inside the SM department store, the ambience seemed to be Macy's, but the selection of goods and the prices seemed to be more of the K-Mart variety. K-Mart with a Philippine twist, that is.

In the Philippine crafts section, shoppers could find beautiful hand-made wood carvings with native themes, mass produced by low-wage laborers and available for just a couple of dollars. In the food section, one could buy packets of dried mango strips, or dried jackfruit or purple candied mangosteen for less than a dollar. In the men's clothing section, one could find brand-name shirts (Hilfiger, Polo, etc.) at deep-discount prices. I started to wonder if these labels were real or faked. I'd heard that counterfeiting of goods was rampant in Asia, and especially in the Philippines. In the shoe department, I found a pair of Air Jordans for only $10. How much did these sneakers sell for in America? $100? $200? Was this $10 pair real or fake? I couldn't tell. I really didn't want to know. I had a pair of what looked to be $200 Air Jordan sneakers for the slim price of $10. In the men's accessories department, I bought a Beatles watch, featuring on its face a scene from the movie *Help!* for only $8. What would this go for in America? 75 bucks or more?

I thought about Liza. Was her love for me real or was she faking it? It had to be real, I reckoned after much contemplation. Filipinas are real. Their words are true, their feelings are pure. They offer real love, everlasting love. Theirs is a deadly loyal love, a love borne of Catholic faith and Catholic fear. Thus, it is real, it is eternal, like salvation is real and eternal, according to Catholic belief. Salvation can't be faked, and neither can love. Thus, Philippine love is real and Philippine love will be your salvation. That was the theory, anyway.

I amused myself with the thought that I had become a tragic cliché, an American man in search of a Filipina bride. I laughed at this as I made my way past the armed security guard at the second-floor entrance to the SM department store, as I turned past a jewelry counter on the left and as I strode confidently into the barong section where Liza worked.

And in just a few steps, just a few moments, there she was, the lady of light, helping a customer, chatting and smiling that spectral smile. We made eye contact and nodded. Her nod said that she was happy to see me and that she would come to me after she was done with her customer. I passed time looking at the barongs displayed on the wall. I wondered why anyone would want to wear such frilly, atrocious shirts.

"Hello, George?" a pleasant young woman with a pageboy haircut walked up and addressed me. She was wearing the yellow jacket and blue skirt outfit that all female SM employees wore. "I'm Jammie, Liza's co-worker."

"Hello, nice to meet you."

"Liza said you should wait just a few minutes, OK? She's helping a customer."

"Sure, sure. No problem. Thanks, Jammie." Jammie? Now, there's a unique name. I wondered where she got it.

Finished with her customer, Liza came by and I almost died with how marvelous she looked. She had the dewy eyes, the pearly smile and the elegant gait of a princess. She was also very happy to see me. She and Jammie said a few things in Cebuano—or was it Tagalog?—and had a few laughs.

"So when shall we go to lunch?" I asked. "When is your lunch break?"

"Um, we can go to lunch at 1," said Liza, looking at her watch. "Is it OK if Jammie comes with us?"

"Of course," I said. "That would be delightful."

"OK then, we'll go at 1. Meet us outside at the employee entrance, OK? It's not allowed for us to be seen walking out the store entrances."

And so in a few moments there I was, leaning on a post at the edge of the parking lot outside the employee entrance at the Shoe Mart Department Store in Cebu City, the ancient capital city of the Philippines, not far from Mactan Island, where the European conquerors first landed more than four and a half centuries before, where Ferdinand Magellan and his lot were defeated by an angry warrior chief and his ragtag crew of angry warriors; where Filipinos showed the outside world that they weren't afraid to fight, that they couldn't be defeated this easily.

Amidst a flurry of activity, I leaned and watched and listened. I looked at all the young boys and girls dressed in their official SM uniforms scurrying out of the employee entrance, chatting away in Cebuano—yes, of course it was Cebuano—gossiping, most likely, about their friends at school. I imagined that most of them attended colleges, night classes, and worked part-time at SM to help pay for tuition. I imagined that some of them worked full time at SM, as Liza does, and that their income partially or fully supported several people, as Liza's does.

Amidst all this lunchtime chatter, amidst this yellow-jacketed whirl, I thought about the death of Magellan and Chief Lapu Lapu's pyrrhic victory. It was just a temporary victory because the Spaniards returned and conquered the Philippines. They gave the natives their names, their God and their culture. "Be Spanish," they were commanded. "Act Spanish." And so it was for 450 years, but then the Spanish empire faded from too much decadence within and too much modernity without, and then the Americans conquered the Spanish and took control of the islands, first with weapons, then with treaties, then with education, then with economic incentives, then with diplomacy, then with persuasion. Then the Americans filled the natives with desire, the desire to be like them, the desire to have the things that Americans have. And so the Filipinos became permanent wannabe Americans.

And now here are all these poor Filipinos, the flower of a generation, all working for low wages in this mall, this vortex of desire, sacrificing their lives by serving capital and serving power, 450 years later. Lapu Lapu killed Magellan for nothing because the power of international capitalism eventually won. And the deep culture of the Philippines gave way to this thing we have here, this mega-mall, where the desire for brand-name clothes, designer sunglasses, colorful underwear, everything we flaunt in America, has replaced the need for community, has supplanted the hunger of memory. This is the conversion plant, where Filipinos turn into Americans, where deep culture is overpowered by deep desire for things, where the past becomes worthless because the present is so shiny and new, so impossible to resist.

As I wallowed in these thoughts, Liza showed up, looking as luminous as she did in her Internet photos. She was accompanied by Jammie. After considering the options, we decided to have lunch at the Texas Chicken restaurant in the mall.

We had to rush through lunch—Liza had only one hour—and so we didn't get much past small talk. But as lunch ended, we agreed to meet the next day, Sunday, at church. She couldn't see me that night because she and her sister had some other commitments. That was fine with me, and so I said my goodbyes, shopped a little bit more, and went back to my hotel to catch up on some sorely needed sleep.

The next morning, I waited for her at the entrance to the Basilica Minore del Santo Niño, which, I learned in my guidebook, was built by Miguel Lopez de Legaspi and a Catholic priest, Father Urdaneta, on the site of the home where a great miracle is said to have occurred some 433 years ago, in the year 1565.

Magellan, the merchant marine from the Old World, did what any would-be suitor-conqueror would do. He brought gifts. One of the gifts he presented to the queen of the island (Queen Juana) was a statue of the child Jesus, known by all here as the Santo Niño (the child saint).

Magellan later fell at the hands of Chief Lapu Lapu, but forty-four years later, in 1565, another conqueror arrived. Miguel Lopez de Legaspi, who would succeed where Magellan failed, brought with him a Spanish priest who was put in charge of Christianizing the Cebuanos. Again, the Cebuanos were not so compliant. In fact, they were downright hostile. So Legaspi set the village on fire and a Spanish soldier later found the image of the Santo Niño unscratched inside the smoldering remains of the house. Since then, the Cebuanos have believed that the Santo Niño image has great powers, God-like powers, and most Cebuano families have a Santo Niño replica or two displayed prominently in their homes. The Santo Niño was adopted by the Cebuanos as their patron saint, and so it has been for almost half a millenium.

It is said that the original Santo Niño image is encased in the Basilica Minore del Santo Niño. And outside the basilica's doors the next day, I waited, a conqueror-suitor from the newest of the great worlds, a man from the West bearing strange gifts, a man who had ridden the divine wind to come to this island to claim the hand of the girl of his dreams.

I was amused by this thought for a moment, but then I saw that the mass was about to commence. Looking up and around me, searching for Liza, I could see the basilica was a grand old church, made of stone and aged wood. I could see that this church was very popular indeed with the local folks. The place was overflowing with activity as the priest began to address the throng over a loudspeaker.

I saw old women and young children walking around selling candles and little Santo Niño statues. Others were selling prayer beads and other religious artifacts. One teenage boy was selling Pokemon cards. I started to fish around in my pocket for loose change, but then I saw a smiling face emerging from the crowd at the entrance to the churchyards.

It was her. She was late and she was beautiful. And she was accompanied by a young woman, maybe 18 or 19 years old, who was smiling even wider than Liza was and who flashed the same slim body, dewy eyes, high cheeks and pearly white teeth.

"Hello, George," Liza said, quickly walking up to me and clutching my hand delicately. She was wearing a denim dress, a dress that I'd seen her wearing in a photograph she sent to me. "Sorry to make you wait. I hope it was not too long."

I wanted to say that I have waited for her for 45 years, but those words didn't come out. All I could see was her smile, her hair, her delicate gait, her frailty. All I could feel was her hand on mine, the little squeeze she gave my hand when she walked up to me, a quick little hint of affection that said, "You are mine. We are finally here together. Please understand who I am and forgive me my imperfections. I trust you. I love you. Please be the man I hope you are."

All of these ideas were conveyed in that one precious squeeze. At least, in my mind they were. After a moment or two, she softly withdrew her hand, knowing that a grasp that was too tight or too long in lingering would indicate far more than mere affection. It wouldn't be proper, after all, for a conservative girl from a fishing village in a distant province to clutch the hand of a virtual stranger, even if that stranger was a rich American who was desperately in love with her.

I felt all these expressions of longing in the little squeeze of her hand. I felt the delicacy and frailty of the lady of light in this touch. It made me feel good and strong, and I knew at that moment that I could love this girl forever. I nodded to Liza, smiled my most loving smile, and looked inquisitively at her companion.

"This is my younger sister, Jessica," she explained.

"Karen," little sister said. "Call me Karen."

"Jessica or Karen? Which is it?"

"Either one," Liza said. "Jessica or Karen."

Their mother was obviously enamored of Anglo-American names. I was somewhat disappointed, although I didn't say so, that Liza and her sister didn't have any of those cheeky names that Filipinos give their daughters, names like Girly, Cherry, Baby Girl or Charmie or Jovie or Menchie or whatever.

We stood in the back of the basilica, in the standing-room section. All the seats had been long taken. The priest gave part of the sermon in English and part in Cebuano—or was it Tagalog? I couldn't tell. When it was time for hymns, an assistant placed the lyrics on an overhead projector so we could all sing along. I tried my best to sing in the foreign language, and I think I saw Liza laughing a bit at my mangled pronunciations.

As I was attempting to sing, I saw a little boy crouching behind me, staring at my feet. When I turned around for a better look, I could see that he was closely inspecting my Nike hiking shoes. The little boy was looking at them adoringly, eyes wide in wonder, as if the shoes were the embodiment of the Santo Niño himself. I pondered the irony of this. These shoes, which I had obtained luckily from the discount bin at a Mervyn's for $10 a few years back, bore the name of a Greek goddess—Nike, the goddess of victory—and they were objects of great desire in the eyes of this child, who was now squatting on the floor of this magnificent church, which was built in tribute to the child-god of the Cebuanos, whose image was given to their queen by the white god from the West, who was later killed by a rebel chieftain, who is regarded as a god-like hero in these islands. The circle of ironies and godhood and strangers bearing gifts and holy relics and holy sites and Nike hiking boots was almost too much to bear. The moment was rich in dramatic irony—but I really didn't care.

All I saw was the face of my beloved next to me, a face with dewy eyes that seemed always on the verge of laughing or crying. Her hair cascaded over her shoulders like waves of black satin.

"What?" she inquired, seeing that I was smiling. I nodded toward the little boy, who was still squatting behind me, adoring my shoes. Liza looked back at him and then at me and raised her eyebrows.

"I guess he likes Nikes," I said. And we both had a giggle about it. I wished for a moment that I could take off the shoes and give them to the little boy, but I knew that this would cause a scene, and I certainly didn't want to do that in my first day in church with my deeply Catholic future wife. As I looked at her again, standing next to me, head bowed, so serene in her devotion to God, so unassuming about her beauty, so uncertain about me, but so welcoming, I knew that I would be proposing marriage to her within the next week.

Maybe within the next few days. Maybe tomorrow. Hell, maybe today.

After church, Liza, Jessica and I went walking in a park nearby and then we went to Fort San Pedro, which my trusty guidebook told me was the oldest tri-bastion fort in the Philippines and the center of the first Spanish settlement.

We walked around within the 2,000 square-meter interior, staring up occasionally at its 8-foot-thick, 20-foot high walls. I imagined what sort of military and commercial activity went on here 450 years ago. I wondered how many Filipinos had been killed or tortured here by Spanish soldiers. As we walked about, an old man came up to us and offered to sell us a guitar. I looked at it curiously and looked at Liza.

"Don't buy that," she said. "I don't want that."

The old man looked at us sadly. I thanked him and bade him adieu.

We continued to walk, and as we did, I pulled one of my old tricks. I slyly took Liza's hand, and asked her if she was my girlfriend now.

"Hah!?" she seemed shocked. She looked at Jessica, who was smiling broadly and giggling. They chattered madly and Liza looked shocked. She made a mild, symbolic attempt to pull her hand out of mine, as if to say, "Sir, you are going much too fast." I started to withdraw it, but Jessica started speaking very quickly to Liza, in an almost scolding manner.

"Sige na, sige na. (Go ahead, go ahead)," she was saying.

Liza was smiling too, knowing that this was one of those defining moments in life. Her admirer from America had just taken her hand and wouldn't let it go. This wasn't a delicate, affectionate finger squeeze—this was a strong, affirmative, in-your-face, you-are-my-girl handhold. Even though she acted as if she wasn't all together comfortable with this, her left hand eventually settled into the determined grip of my right hand, and we were walking like lovers through an old Spanish fort, which once was the nexus of the conquering Western forces. And here I was, a native boy who had become a Westerner, and now I was back in my home country, claiming the native girl of my dreams, and we're walking among the ghosts of the old conquerors, caring not about the sweep of history or the gravitas of the moment. We only cared that we were in love, and we had waited for so long to be with each other, and now we were holding hands and looking in each other's eyes, and seeing our future children in each other's eyes, and knowing that there could be no grander feeling than this. To realize that the one you love also loves you, also wants you, also wants to hold your hand and be with you forever is to realize true happiness, I reckoned.

Hang the Spanish and their brutal ways. We have found love here among the ruins.

After walking for a bit, Liza asked me what exactly it was that I wanted from her. Out of the blue, just like that, as casually as could be. Sensing that this was another was one of those big defining moments, Jessica slipped away from us and sat on a bench. She wanted to give us privacy while we got down to some truth.

"Liza," I said, "I'm not going to waste time because I've wasted a lot of time already in my life. I'm going to tell you exactly what I want from you. I want you to be my wife."

This stopped her in her tracks, her dewy eyes locked mine and I could see more moisture welling up in them.

"I want to bring you to America and marry you. I want you to be with me forever."

We looked at each other in silence for what seemed an eternity, but was actually only about 15 seconds or so. Was I actually saying this? Was I going mad?

"Are you proposing marriage?" she said. "We don't even know each other so well."

"I know," I said. "This is too fast. I just want to let you know exactly what's on my mind. No, this doesn't have to be THE OFFICIAL proposal, if you think it's too fast. But that's what I have in mind. I want so much for us to be together."

She realized then that this was not THE OFFICIAL proposal, but she also knew that it was coming sometime soon. Of course, she knew it. And she also knew there was no reason to rush it. Let's just savor the moment, let's just let the suspense hang in the air like the scent of mangoes at a roadside fruit stand.

"What's the most important thing in your life?" Liza asked me, again startling me with her directness.

"The most important thing? I'd say, my family, my work, my relationship with God. Those are the most important things."

Liza nodded enthusiastically. "Yes, yes."

"What's the most important thing to you, Liza?"

"Me too. My family and God."

We changed the subject to lighter fare, like what we would be doing tomorrow. It was Monday tomorrow, her day off, and she wanted to spend it with me, her American admirer who had come all the way to the Philippines to visit her. We made plans to go to a place called Rock Island Beach and to a Taoist Temple that was a popular landmark in Cebu. She and her sister would come to my hotel at 10 a.m. and we'd be off.

I wanted to ask her if she would spend the night with me, but I thought better of it. That would be way too much for this innocent Catholic girl from the provinces for whom hand-holding in public was daring and bold. There was no way she'd spend the night with me. I didn't ask.

I was happy with the extended, public handhold. This was nice, very sweet. I resigned myself to the notion that this would probably be as far as it would go on this trip. Maybe I could sneak a kiss before I leave, but innocence and reserve would be the watchwords for now.

The three of us caught a cab and the women were dropped off at the carenderia at MJ Cuenco Street, which was really an alley leading to their boarding house. I went on to Eddie's Hotel, had a meal of Beefsteak Tagalog and San Miguel beer and went upstairs for a good night's rest. I took with me a plate of papaya and mango slices to snack on while I watched TV.

As I passed the young woman at the front desk, she looked up at me and said, "Good evening, sir," in a very flirtatious way. When I looked at her, she batted her eyelashes and smiled very prettily. Filipina women are just about the finest women in the world, I thought to myself. I like this place. I really like this place.

I went into my room, turned the television on to the MTV Asia channel and ate the tropical fruit. The air con was humming, the room was cool and comfortable, and somewhere a rooster was crowing. I was in my home country for the first time in my adult life, and hot magic was in the air.

I like this place, I thought to myself. I really, really like it here. Why had I not come here sooner? The things I need most in my life are right here in this place. Why had I avoided it for so long? Why had I been so blind, so unknowing? Why had I been so in denial of where I was from, of what I really was? How could I have been so American?

I went to sleep and dreamed of a girl I knew named Wendy. She was in America, a land far, far away. She was a beautiful blonde and in her early 20s, almost too perfectly beautiful; tall and slender, with long, flowing hair and a sassy manner and a playful laugh. She had about 100 male admirers. I was one of them. I dreamed that she came to my house one day and announced that she wanted to move in with me. In my dream I told her that I couldn't let her move in because I was going to marry a girl from the Philippines. With that, she made some derisive comments about Asian women and mockingly repeated some line she'd heard from an Asian hooker in a movie—"me so horny" or something like that. When I told Wendy I was dead serious about this, she dismissed me curtly and said, "OK, have a good life," and I never heard from her again.

I woke up from this dream and wondered momentarily if it was real. Two years ago, if Wendy would have appeared at my doorstep and expressed such a desire, I would have hesitated for not even a second—she was that impossible to resist.

But I was no longer in the Wendy Zone. I found it possible to resist her. This was a different time and a different place, and I had found the real girl of my dreams. And I would be seeing her tomorrow, so I needed to get back to sleep.

Good night then, Wendy. Good night, America. Hello, Philippines. Hello, all you kind-hearted, family-loving, dark-haired women of my soul. I have returned, and I am yours again.

# 13

## *Proposals, Decent and Otherwise*

Liza and her sister showed up promptly for our day at the beach. Liza was wearing tight blue jeans, and I could see the firmness of her glutes and the sleekness of her legs. Her luminescent smile was on full brightness and her freshly washed hair was like spun black gold.

She was also wearing the University of Texas T-shirt that I'd sent to her a year ago, while we were still getting to know each other through letters. It was the first gift I'd given her, and she regarded it as quite an exotic treasure. It was from America, after all, so in her mind, and in the mind of many Filipinos, it was indeed a thing to be coveted.

To me it was just a drab gray T-shirt on which someone had silk-screened the word TEXAS, a shirt that I'd found on sale for five bucks at a University of Texas bookstore. But Liza didn't have to know all those details. She probably wouldn't want to know them. She was wearing this discount T-shirt proudly because her admirer from America was here with her now, and she wanted to show him how much the boring, gray shirt meant to her, and how much it means to her to be so cared about. That was what mattered.

Jessica also looked hot, wearing blue jeans and a tight, brown, sleeveless blouse. I think she was also wearing some sort of push-up bra because her breasts were fully round and standing, like a supermodel's. Her breasts were rather large compared to Liza's, which were on the small side. On the other hand, if Jessica wasn't wearing a push-up bra, if her breasts really stood up like that, proud and erect, then she was quite gifted physically. She was also barefoot.

I started thinking of friends back home who could be interested in Jessica. Liza would probably love to have her sister in America, so finding a match for her could be a good little side project for me. It wouldn't be too terribly difficult. Right off the bat, I thought of about half a dozen of my friends, single men all, who would be interested without the slightest hesitation.

We found a taxi and asked the driver how much he would charge to take us to Rock Island Beach, which was some distance away, and then wait around for an hour or so before taking us home. We needed to have this kind of special service because the place was somewhat isolated and it wouldn't have been too easy to call for a taxi from there for the ride back. So we needed to have him wait around like a dummy while we had fun in the sun. So, how much?

"Nine hundred," he said. I did the math in my mind. Nine-hundred pesos was roughly equal to 19 bucks. No problem. For a personal chauffeur? No problem! A big score for the driver, a pittance to me. Enough money to feed his family for a week, most likely. An extra-large pizza supreme and a beer for me back home in America.

Jessica sat in the front of the taxi, chatting cheerfully with the driver. Liza and I sat in the back. She looked luscious. I couldn't help myself. I sidled up very close to her and put a hand on her knee, hoping that she wouldn't be too shocked or offended. She didn't seem to mind—at least she didn't say anything—and so I kept my hand on her knee for a minute, two minutes.

I looked in the driver's rear-view mirror and made eye contact with Liza. I saw how beautiful she was. I eyed her lush, full lips and high cheeks, and knew that I was in deep with this girl. I winked at her in the mirror and she smiled. The moment was so perfect I had to do something, anything. I reached up, turned her head toward me and kissed her gently on the forehead. She didn't withdraw even a little bit. She seemed to welcome it, so I boldly moved down and planted another soft little kiss on her cheek. I didn't know what she would do, but I was ready for whatever defensive reaction she might have. This was, after all, a conservative Catholic girl from the provinces, a girl who resisted an innocent little hug the other night, and we were in a taxi with her sister and a stranger.

To my surprise, though, Liza turned squarely and pressed her lips to mine. Moments later, her tongue was in my mouth, furiously lapping my tongue, and soon Liza's body was all over me, rubbing, grinding, heaving like a starving animal. She was on fire with lust, and I was reeling from the heat. I was loving every moment of it, but shocked and somewhat taken aback. What happened to my sweet and innocent little girl from the fishing village? What happened to the Spanish-convent conservatism and Cebuana modesty? And who was this dragon-tongued seductress dry-humping me in the back of a taxi?

Oh my God, what would Jessica say if she saw us? What would the driver say? They said nothing as Liza and I continued to make out sloppily in the back seat. I wondered if they knew what we were doing back there. How could they not? We were kissing and rubbing each other noisily. They continued to pretend that they didn't notice, and I really appreciated it. Liza and I couldn't stop kissing each other, and we continued to kiss and lap and rub as the taxi roared through the smoky streets of Cebu, over the bridge and into Lapu Lapu City, and then onto a thoroughfare that would lead to a long, unpaved road that would take us to Rock Island Beach.

I was in such rhapsody from the kissing, that when we stopped momentarily I said a bunch of dumb-romantic things: "I will always love you and take care of you. I will give you the best of everything. We will have beautiful children."

With each sentence, with each proclamation of undying devotion, with each promise of paradise, Liza nodded and smiled. This was acceptable to her and she was letting me know it. She wanted this. She wanted me. She wanted the life of an American. She wanted to spend her life with me in America.

We got to Rock Island Beach soon enough, and so we all got out of the love-mobile and headed off to the shore. Rock Island Beach turned out to be a little craggy area tucked in behind several shabby houses. There were little cabanas and gazebos built out of bamboo, wood and banana leaves. There was no real beach to speak of, at least none where we were. However, from one of the gazebos, we could see people on speedboats about 70 or 80 yards away. It seemed like there was a resort nearby, and these holiday-makers—they looked like Americans—were roaring across the water in their fast boats, hollering and screaming and having just a good old time.

Jessica squealed in delight as she watched them. I saw in her eyes that she wished she could be on a boat like that, having fun like that. Liza smiled, but didn't seem too terribly impressed. At that moment, I noticed that she had a patch of sticky, white substance on her left arm.

"What's that?" I inquired.

"It's toothpaste," she said. "I burned myself ironing clothes this morning. So I put some toothpaste on it."

Toothpaste?

"Don't you have any burn medicine?"

"Toothpaste is medicine," Liza said, looking puzzled, looking at me as if I didn't know something that was painfully obvious to a lot of people.

I sighed and chalked it up to Filipino folk medicine. Whatever!

We sat in the shade of one of the banana-leaf gazebos and I started nuzzling and kissing her again. I just couldn't stop. I didn't want to stop. This was too nice. But Liza spotted a man lurking around among the gazebos and she withdrew.

"Don't," she whispered. "There's a man there looking at us."

I turned and saw that the man was dressed in shabby clothes and was carrying a plate or basket. He walked right up to us and offered us the basket. It was full of shells. This guy was trying to sell us some Rock Island Beach souvenirs.

"No thanks," I said. The man continued to hold the basket of shells out to us and fixed me with a stony glare. "Really, thanks, no," I insisted.

He continued to stand there and I realized at that moment that he hadn't understood what I'd said. Liza said something quickly in Cebuano, and the shell-hustler nodded politely and walked away.

After hanging out at Rock Island Beach for about an hour, we decided we'd had enough and returned to the cab. The driver was leaning on his door, looking bored and smoking a cigarette. He'd been watching us, to make sure we wouldn't run off and stiff him on the fare. We decided we wanted to go have lunch at the Lighthouse, a stylish restaurant on the main drag, and off we went.

We had a pleasant lunch there. I looked at the bamboo and stained wood decor, all done up in a seafaring theme, and listened to the house band, a quartet of blind musicians performing tropical versions of old American, British and Mexican songs. They did Stevie Wonder's *You are the Sunshine of My Life,* the Beatles' *And I Love Her,* and everyone's favorite, *La Cucaracha.*

Jessica found great delight in the latter, and she asked me what the word "cucaracha" meant. I explained that it meant "cockroach," and she asked me what that was. I said it was a little insect that invaded your home and ate food off the floor, the shelves and any place else it could find it. Jessica didn't quite understand what I said, and so Liza translated in Cebuano.

"Ahhh…," Jessica said, and laughed. She said some Cebuano word, which I took to be the lingual equivalent of "cockroach," and she started singing and laughing, "La cucaracha, la cucaracha." Jessica was a very happy person, I reckoned. She was a lot more outgoing than Liza anyway, backseat behavior notwithstanding.

When we were done at the Lighthouse, we decided to go to the Ayala Center, the other mega-mall in Cebu City. Jessica coveted a job at a women's clothing store there, and she wanted to go schmooze the boss a little bit. Meanwhile, Liza and I took a walk around the mall.

The ambience was the same, except on this day the mall was decorated with multi-colored banners, all sporting some religious slogans. "The Face of Jesus," read one. "God is love," announced another. "Sinulog shirts and souvenirs," pronounced another.

Sinulog, it turned out, was a yearly celebration of the Santo Niño, featuring parades with throngs of colorful costumed dance troupes, all competing to be the best of the Sinulog festival. It was a very big deal here in Cebu province. Liza explained all of this to me in her broken English.

As Liza looked around the Ayala center department store—the equivalent of the SM department store Liza worked in—I watched a group of teenage dancers dressed in black tribal uniforms with gold-colored trim giving a demonstration inside the store in one of the main aisles. Three of the young men in the group were playing some sort of drum instruments strapped over their shoulders. They were marching in very frenetic steps, forward, backward, sideways, as were the young women in the group. The girl at the head of the line was holding a statue of the Santo Niño, repeatedly raising it over her and swinging it in precise patterns above her head. She had her eyes closed and looked like she was in some kind of trance. Religious fervor, I reckoned. The rest of the group was also very much into their dance, except a couple of the boys seemed to be giggling. Then I saw that their girlfriends were on the sidelines in regular clothes watching them and giggling too. Teens will be teens, religious fervor notwithstanding, I supposed.

"Would you like to see Sinulog?" Liza said, sneaking behind me as I watched the teenage dance group "It's on January 18."

"Oh, I wish I could," I replied, genuinely disappointed. "But school starts on the 15th."

School. I hadn't thought of school in a couple of weeks. It seemed like a very distant idea, just a cold abstraction. I was in the sweltering heat of love, and I didn't want to think about grading papers from a beginning reporting class. But I did have to get back to Humboldt in about a week.

I had five days left in the Philippines, and I wanted them to be five of the best days of my new life. Tomorrow, I decided, was going to be the proverbial first day of the rest of my life. I was going to propose to Liza.

On our way out of the store, I heard what sounded like church bells ringing out over the store's public address system. Then the voice of a priest started reciting some sort of prayer to the Santo Niño. As this was sounded, I saw all about me people stopping in their tracks and bowing their heads. A stylish middle-aged woman with heavy makeup stopped looking through silk scarves as the prayer continued. Customers, clerks, managers, tourists who've been there before, they all bowed their head respectfully, some of them mouthing the words to the prayers. In less than two minutes, it was over and people went on their merry way, shopping, cavorting, and lusting for goods.

Liza saw that I was confused by this, and she explained that it was a longstanding tradition in Philippine shopping malls, that prayers would be said at noon and at 3 p.m. I wondered to myself how this ritual would play out in American malls. The sacred would likely not do well next to the profane.

Our last stop of the day was at the Taoist Temple, located in an exclusive area the Cebuanos called "Beverly Hills." In it are preserved the teachings of the Chinese philosopher LaoTse, who lived around 600 BC. The taxi driver waited—they all seemed to be available as personal chauffeurs—as Liza, Jessica and I climbed up the 99 steps leading up to the temple. We walked on a rooftop plaza that featured sculptures of red and gold dragons and a panoramic view of Cebu City.

Liza stood on the edge and looked around her, marveling at the sight of the city below her. I walked up to her with my arms open and she fell into my embrace, her arms spread open like a wild bird. I clutched her to me and spun her around.

She laughed and whooped and I could see that she was feeling free and strong, perhaps freer than she'd ever felt, and more in power of her life than she'd ever felt, and feeling confident and secure in the arms of a man who loves her, spinning joyfully, dizzily, in the thin mountain air while below her all the people of Cebu work and sweat and struggle.

This lady of light was riding a divine wind and the world was something small below her and all the joy that was waiting to be freed from the prison of her life was now screaming from her bones, shouting from her soul, crying out their song of liberation. I am the wind, I am the light, she was crying. I am the sun and the moon. I am in the arms of a strong man who will protect me and love me forever.

As I whirled her about, I saw in her face the delight of a child—and it made me feel good. A somber temple guard eyed us, and we figured that maybe we were acting inappropriately in a deadly serious place. I put her down and we continued our tour of the holy place.

On the way back to the boarding house, I asked Liza if I could see her again the next day. She'd be back at work, of course, but I told her I had a very special gift I wanted to give her.

"What gift? You already gave me too many gifts," she said, referring to a sackful of clothes I had given her, along with a couple of boxes of chocolate, a teddy bear, a bottle of perfume and the personal stereo.

"This is a very special gift," I said as she and Jessica got out of the taxi at MJ Cuenco alley, "and I want to give it to you tomorrow."

That said, we had our goodbyes and I went back to my hotel to watch MTV and eat papaya. Tomorrow would be a big day, so I needed my rest. But first, a celebratory drink! I stopped in the bar and ordered a double shot of Courvoisier.

Robinson the bartender was there, as usual. He measured out a double shot precisely for me and resumed wiping glasses behind the bar.

"So, did you see your girlfriend today?" he inquired.

"Yes, I did. It was wonderful. She really loves me."

"Oh?"

"Yes, I can tell by the way she kisses me."

He laughed. "And so, you're going to take her back to the States?"

"Well, I haven't proposed yet. I'm going to do that tomorrow."

"Oh, really? Tsck, what a lucky girl."

"No, I'm the lucky one," I said. With that I downed the cognac, left a tip and hopped joyfully up the stairs and into my room. I felt like I was 21 years old again, and life seemed brand new and wonderful.

Nothing matters more than this, I said to myself. Not one damned thing.

I got up bright and early, showered and had breakfast brought up to my room. I'd run out of dollar bills to tip the bellhops, so the lucky guy who brought up my breakfast was treated to a tip of 20 nickels. I had to explain to him that these were worth 5 cents each in America, and that all of this equaled one dollar. He seemed sincerely grateful and fondled the handful of Jefferson nickels as he walked out the door.

I imagined what he would do with them. No Philippine bank or exchange counter would take them—too small a deal—and no big store would either. Certainly no black-market currency exchanger would want to bother with such a paltry sum. You need to have $20 bills to get into the currency exchange game, even at the lowest levels. So, my breakfast server probably used my nickels with his friends or kept them as souvenirs. It's just as well. I wondered what new lives those pieces of American nickel and zinc would have here in the Philippine islands.

Then, bizarrely, I began to envy those nickels. I envied them because they would get to stay here while I had to leave and go back to my job and my apartment underneath the big gray skies of Humboldt County.

Shaking off the cobwebs and the crazy thoughts, I got ready for the big moment. My plan was to buy a ring there at the SM mall and then surprise my beloved at her job. Would I get down on my hands and knees? Would I recite a poem? Or have a rehearsed speech at the ready? Naw, too corny. I couldn't bring myself to do that. Besides, I had strongly hinted at my intentions in my letters and we had already broached the subject during our walk at Fort San Pedro, so she knew I wanted to marry her and I was pretty confident she wanted to marry me. So why make a big deal out of it? Why not treat this like it's just a normal thing to do? If I make a big production out of it, it might freak her out. Let's just try and keep it casual, keep it low key, keep it real.

Good plan!

And so it was that I walked up to Liza at the SM department store, in the men's barong section, and casually mentioned that today was the day that I was going to buy an engagement ring for her. She didn't seem to disapprove of the idea.

And so it was that I walked over to the jewelry department right near the barong section and looked at engagement rings. When I found one that seemed nice, I summoned Liza over and asked her casually if she liked this one, and she said OK.

And so it was that I bought it and walked it over to the barong department and presented it to Liza.

"Uh, I can't accept it," she said, frowning.

"WHAT? I thought you wanted it. I thought we are going to get married."

"Yes, but I can't accept it on the job. I'm working right now. I can't accept gifts from anyone while I'm working. It's against the rules."

And so it was that we made an arrangement to meet for lunch, where the official presentation ceremony would take place. Liza, Jammie, Jessica (who also worked at SM in the women's shoe department) and I met at the employee entrance and we walked over to the food court.

And so it was that just outside the Mongolian Barbecue in the food court at the SM department store, which was owned and operated by one of the richest families in the Philippines, a poor boy from the Philippines who had become moderately successful in America presented an engagement ring to a poor young woman from the provinces.

"Liza, will you marry me?"

Quiet. Silence for two beats.

"Liza, what's wrong?" I said.

"I'm thinking," she said.

Thinking? Thinking about what? Was she teasing me again? Jessica was starting to get agitated. "Yes," Jessica whispered across the table to her sister. "Yes," she whispered again to herself, looking down in frustration.

After a few moments of silence, the verdict arrived.

"Yes," Liza said, as if making a pronouncement. "Yes, I will marry you."

Jessica and Jammie yelped and clapped. I breathed a big sigh and put my arm on Liza's shoulder. It was now official, and I couldn't believe that I had found someone so beautiful, so sweet, so wonderful, to be my wife. I couldn't believe that a computer-screen image had come to life and was now in my arms, wearing my engagement ring. I couldn't believe that this all had happened so smoothly, so quickly. I couldn't believe that a lost paradise could be rediscovered so easily.

I felt complete. I felt validated. It seemed I held all the treasure of the world in my hands. This was surely a fine ending for a man who had struggled so much, who had endured so much pain. This was a just reward.

I bought lunch for everybody and we had sort of a mini-fiesta to celebrate this monumental occasion. We were all feeling a bit giddy. Jessica, Jammie and Liza exchanged chitchat excitedly in Cebuano—or was it Tagalog? I couldn't tell. Jammie smiled and looked at us across the table while Liza and I feasted on chicken adobo and rice.

"Are you married, Jammie?" I asked her.

"Yes, my husband is in Taiwan, working. He can make good money there, but not so much here in the Philippines."

"Oh, he's gone all the time then? Aren't you lonely?"

"Yes, a little. But my son keeps me company."

"Oh, you have a boy." I reached into my backpack and found a package of Tootsie Roll Pops I'd brought from America for just such an occasion.

"Here," I said. "Give these to him with my compliments. Tell him they come all the way from America."

Jammie was quite delighted with this gift and thanked me profusely. All during the meal, I noticed that she was looking at Liza and me and smiling broadly.

"Why are you looking at us like that, Jammie?" I asked.

"You are a very good-looking couple," she said to us. "Guwapo and guwapa!"

I couldn't imagine a finer moment than this. It had to be the most wonderful of all the wondrous moments I'd had in the islands in the few days I'd been here. I was here with my dream girl, she had accepted my marriage proposal, and we were celebrating our joy in the company of her sister and her best friend, who both gave their blessings to this union of souls.

Visions of our future in America swirled in our heads. I looked at Liza's face and imagined what our future children would look like—fine-boned, sleek and beautiful, I reckoned. She looked down and smiled shyly, averting my stare out of modesty and reserve.

I stopped and savored these moments, even as we rushed through a short lunch break and ate Filipino fast food in a common food court in a sanitized mega-mall. We were in a hurry, yes, and there was a decided lack of appropriate ambiance. But it didn't matter. The chicken adobo was the sweetest I'd ever had, and the mango ice cream was the most perfect thing I'd ever tasted.

This was a day like no other, this was food like no other, and this was a girl like no other. I had a mouthful of mango ice cream, I was newly engaged to a beautiful girl, and I was stupidly in love.

# 14

## *The Great Divide*

It was a day like all the other days I'd been in Cebu.

Somewhere a rooster was crowing. Somewhere a jeepney needing a tuneup was spewing smoke, signalling its distress.

Me, I was in my room at Eddie's Hotel, digging into my lunch of sweet langonisa, scrambled eggs and rice. A hearty meal, I figured, was called for on this day—for I was going to meet my dream girl's mother, and my future mother-in-law.

MTV Asia was on the tube, and it was offering its usual fare—bland pop for kids. Boy groups were in style this year, big-time. So viewers got a steady stream of 'N Sync, Backstreet Boys, Hansen, the Moffatts and countless other manufactured acts. They all seemed alike. The Moffatts reminded me of the Bee Gees for some reason. They all seemed to have the long faces and droopy eyes of the Gibb brothers. The other boy bands reminded me of the Osmond Brothers. Maybe it was just my imagination.

Liza showed up about 7 p.m. with her brother, a tall, wiry-strong, athletic, silent type named Nelo. He was wearing a Nike baseball cap, a loose black T-shirt and jeans. He didn't speak much English, but he was obviously delighted to meet me.

"Hello, George," he said warmly, as he shook my hand and rubbed my arm. He smiled broadly, flashing a mouth full of perfect teeth, and ran his fingers up and down my right forearm, caressing it and exploring its texture. I thought this a bit unusual, since most American men wouldn't do such a thing on first meeting. But maybe Nelo was merely showing brotherly affection, like a boy from the provinces would, for the man who was going to marry his sister. Or maybe he was feeling up my arm to see what an American arm felt like. Or maybe he wasn't aware that most American men would find his gesture rather effeminate and maybe even gay. American men have such psychic baggage, I thought to myself at that moment. Most people from other countries are not fully aware of it all. How could they know the dark terrain of the American soul? Nelo was a person from another country. Nelo wasn't aware of my psychic baggage. And Nelo didn't speak much English. "Hello, George" seemed the extent of it.

Nelo was to be Liza's chaperone this evening, as well as our dinner companion. I was starting to get a little weary of this Old World notion that single women are not to go out on dates without a third party there to make sure everyone behaved. But I figured I should continue to play along. When in Rome, after all. And besides, I needed to cultivate the good graces of her family. Playing along with this chaperone business also would send a strong signal that I wanted Liza for reasons beyond the carnal ones.

So be it then. Let's go eat.

The taxi dropped us off at a place called the Royal Concourse, which came highly recommended by Joan, the woman who had delivered my emails to Liza back when I was in Texas. We were to meet Joan here. This was going to be one of those minor "magic moments" in an evening that was chock full of "magic moments" in waiting. Joan had helped Liza and me immeasurably by personally delivering these emails to Liza. This evening, I was going to meet her in person for the first time.

The restaurant had a cafeteria-type set up. You slid your tray down a line and checked out the different offerings behind the glass partition. There seemed to be a mixture of Chinese, Japanese and Philippine dishes available.

I loaded up on a healthy portion of beef teriyaki and shrimp tempura, familiar dishes to an American. Nelo and Liza seemed unfamiliar with these dishes, but they were willing to give them a try, as long as there was a lot of plain white rice involved. And indeed there was! Nelo and I had Cokes, but Liza reached reflexively—as she always did—for the mango juice.

Always the mango juice!

Liza and Nelo picked at the tempura and the spicy sweet teriyaki.

"Umm, ma sarap," Liza proclaimed. "Maalat (salty)."

I understood what she said because I had heard such Philippine phrases before, from the mouths of my relatives. "Ummm, delicious, but a bit salty."

Nelo didn't say anything. He picked at the food somewhat reluctantly. I tried to get him to talk.

"Nelo, tell me something. How is it that Liza is still single? She's so beautiful, she probably had many admirers back home, right? How come nobody ever tried to marry her?"

There was a pause, then Liza let out a giggle. Nelo looked at her nervously and then looked at me. He said nothing. Was he simply unable to respond in English? Or was he hiding a secret?

"What's wrong with Nelo?" I asked Liza.

"He's ashamed," Liza said, smiling widely, that spectral smile that shot right to the core of my heart, that dewy smile that dripped with love. "He's ashamed of his English. He does not speak English so good."

As I chewed my teriyaki beef and looked at that face, I fell in love with Liza for the thousandth time. As the scent of her hair teased my senses, as the cute trill of her accent teased my American ears, I fell in love with her for the thousand-and-first time. She touched my arm delicately and said softly, "There were no other admirers who wanted to marry me," and I felt as if she was assuring me, and calling me a very silly boy for even thinking that she was so pretty. And with her touch I fell in love with her for the thousand-and-second time.

Joan appeared at the door a few moments later. We recognized each other from the digital photographs that we'd exchanged through email. And of course she and Liza knew each other from the times Joan brought my emails to the SM department store. She rested her expansive frame next to Nelo, and faced Liza and I at the dinner table.

"Well, I just wanted to see the two of you together," Joan said. "It's a miracle, isn't it?"

We nodded.

"You are both so lucky to find each other."

Liza nodded. So did I. I thought to myself that I was the luckier one.

"Maybe it's just God's will."

Liza and I nodded again. Liza believed it. The Catholic boy inside me wanted to believe it. The American intellectual inside me wanted to assign it to random chance. In reality, I didn't know what to believe. I was just going with the moment.

Joan proceeded to tell us that she was also involved in a long-distance relationship that was fueled by the Internet. Her beau lived in Dubai. She was hoping to move to Dubai soon to be with him.

"There are better opportunities for Filipinos there. I have a business here, but I can't make so much money. I can make more in Dubai."

I brought up the matter of cultural differences, and how it might be difficult for Joan to adapt to an Arab country's ways.

"Oh, but there are cultural differences everywhere, even in America, *di ba?*"

I nodded.

"It depends on how you adapt. Even here in the Philippines, there are big differences in cultures and economic classes. For instance, in normal circumstances, Liza and her brother would not dine at the same table with us."

What?

"It is not considered proper for people from the provinces to dine with people like us. You know, the educated class. People like us."

This took me aback. I didn't know what to say. Was there bigotry and classicism among the Filipinos? Liza simply nodded, looked down and continued to pick at her food.

It was true. Liza and her family would not normally sit at the same table with Joan and her like. Joan was educated, a businesswoman, a person of some worth, a card-carrying member of the elite. Liza was a girl from the provinces, born into a family of fisherpeople, born into crushing poverty, born in a province with no running water, no phones. There were no dreams of transcendence for her, no shining city on a hill, no hope of ever being something better. Her only hope was to move to the big city one day, and maybe find a job in a department store, where she would earn five dollars a day serving the needs of people like Joan. Selling them American CDs, imported perfume, or expensive Philippine clothing—like the barongs Liza sold—all symbols of class division. Either you got it or you ain't, *di ba?*

When you're a girl from the provinces, you will never have these things. You will not dare to dream of owning these things. You will work for low wages, you will live in a slummy boarding house with three or four other people or more, you will barely pay your bills each month because you have to share your meager salary with your siblings and your cousins and anyone else who comes into your family's sphere of need, and you will not even know what it's like to want the things Americans want because that world is so far, far away. So far, far removed from your life. So distant. So impossible.

You will always be a girl from the provinces. And people like Joan would not even look at you, won't even see you when you serve them. That was the manner of people like Joan, who now sat across the table from Liza, who now acknowledged her and feigned friendliness with the girl from the provinces only because there was an American there to legitimize this meeting.

I looked at Joan with a penetrating glare. I wanted her to know that I abhorred this classism of hers. But it only lasted a moment. The mango smile came back and I let her know that I understood. I let her off the hook. She's a victim of her conditioning, a slave too of her own class thinking, after all.

I put my arm delicately around Liza's bowed head to reassure her that I loved her despite our class differences, and she smiled back at me, that dewy, girlish smile of hers. I fell in love for the thousand-and-third time.

After dinner, we all fell into some brief small talk outside the restaurant, and then Joan summoned a cab. She was off into the night. I asked the security guard to take a picture of me, Liza and Nelo, which he did in a very cooperative manner. He seemed to be quite pleased to help out an American. Then we signaled to one of the waiting cab drivers, and it was off to the main event—the meeting with mom.

She would be waiting at Liza's boarding house. And now I would be getting my first look at where my dream girl lived. Getting there would be an adventure in itself.

You can't drive up to it. You have to tell the driver to drop you off at a certain carenderia (restaurant), then you have to walk down a dark, uncertain alley to get to it. You must watch out for potholes in the pavement, loose rocks, puddles of dirty water, small children running wildly about, and the groups of drunken men with lusty eyes and foul mouths.

When you finally get there, you see a shack-like structure that seemed cobbled together with stray pieces of rusted corrugated metal, sheetrock and stone. Is that a distant scent of raw sewage wafting through the air?

This is where Liza lived. My beautiful, dewy Liza lived in this squalor. It was the boarding house she shared with her sister, her cousin and her cousin's husband. Tonight, Liza's mother and aunt were there, as well. And if they were waiting to meet Liza's new boyfriend from America, they certainly didn't seem to be dressed for the occasion.

Mom was wearing a tattered nightgown, and Tita had on a tacky, big dress with a pale pink-and-yellow floral pattern that seemed wrested from some discarded bedsheet. When Liza introduced me, their eyes grew big and they uttered some words of surprise: "Ginoo ko! (My God!)"

I felt like a space alien who had somehow dropped down out of the clouds and into somebody's home.

Liza flashed mom that spectral smile. Mom looked at me, shot a glance at Liza, looked at me again and gave me her own big smile. At that moment, I saw Liza's face in the face of her mom. The dewy eyes; the toothy, friendly, welcoming smile; the delicate, vulnerable cheekbones. I could sense the soul of the family stir from its safe sleep to face the stranger from afar. I could feel the ghost of the lost world meeting the spirit of the New World. I could feel the deep cultural divide that separated us, that indeed made us alien to one another, and I could hear the boards under our feet creak from the enormous irony of the moment.

Mom's smile seemed forced, though. It might be fake, I said to myself. She doesn't trust me. How could she? She doesn't know me. What the hell! Go with it.

I walked up to mom, grabbed her hand, bowed my head, and touched the back of her hand to my forehead. I had seen other young Filipino men and boys do this before to their elders as a sign of respect. I had also seen Latin American males do this. Some old Spanish tradition, I figured. What did it matter? It's just a ritual. It's just a moment, like millions of other cultural moments.

Go with it.

Mom seemed a bit uncomfortable as I took her hand, but smiled through the brief ceremony, nevertheless.

Cool move, I said to myself.

I proceeded to do the same hand-to-forehead bit with Tita. All the others seemed to find some humor in this sight of a highly educated, English-speaking Filipino-American man attempting to find some longlost tie to Filipino culture, attempting in some transparent, clumsy way to acknowledge and respect their traditions. After all, this act was some vestige of the ancient Spaniards, and their Catholic Church. This was old Spain transferred to the American moment. There was an absurd dissonance in the act, a clumsy attempt at re-connection, and everyone felt it.

Young, modern Filipinos hardly ever did this any more, except in very formal family get-togethers. All of the people in this makeshift shack—located at the end of a rocky, drunken alley tucked off a busy street in Cebu City, just a few miles away from where Chief Lapu Lapu killed the invader from the West—all of them seemed to approve of this moment. Liza laughed a little too, perhaps amused by her mother's brief look of discomfort.

I sat on a bench next to Liza. I fixed mom with a look of determined sincerity. She seemed to avert my gaze.

"I love Liza," I announced, taking her hand. "I want to marry her and bring her to America. And she has accepted my proposal."

The room exploded with chatter and surprise; cousins laughed with cousins; cousins addressed Liza in very fast Cebuano, looking alternately concerned and pleased; mom and Tita exchanged amazed looks and said a few things quietly, under the din. Liza seemed quite amused by the scene, smiling that dewy smile and shooting glances at me with her laughing eyes.

The buzz seemed to go on endlessly. No one addressed me. Mom said something to Liza's sister; Liza's sister laughed, looked at me and said something to Liza's cousin; Liza's cousin said something to Tita; Tita said something to mom. I felt like I wasn't there. I felt like they were referring to me in the abstract, like I didn't really exist, like I was some distant theory, not real, a ghost.

"What are they saying?" I turned to Liza.

"Umm, nothing."

"What? Surely they're saying something."

"Wala lang (nothing). They're just discussing."

"But don't they want to ask me something? Don't they want to know more about me?"

Liza's smile seemed to fade. She turned her head, still holding my hand in that delicate way she did, and said something to mom. I couldn't make it out. It was in very fast Cebuano, I figured.

Mom said something back. Then she said something to Tita. With that, Tita pulled back her chair, raised her substantial girth and stood up. She gesticulated in a dramatic way and said something. Everyone stopped their chattering and listened. She was about to make a pronouncement.

I strained hard to listen, to understand her words, but I couldn't make out a thing. Each time Tita finished a sentence, she punctuated her remark with a regal flip of her hand, and each time she did, the room fell even quieter. Was it a dismissive gesture? Was she rejecting out of hand the idea of my marrying Liza? Was she evoking the family's ghosts? Was she giving voice to their protests? The boards beneath us creaked and the rusted metal roof moaned.

Tita sat. She was finished. She looked up sternly, not looking at me, but looking off to the side of me. The look on her face was that of quiet power, almost arrogant. Mom looked down, unable to say anything. Everyone else turned their heads down. No one said a thing. Liza also looked down. Why does everyone look so sad? Oh no, I thought to myself. I'm dead. Tita has forbidden this union.

I turned to Liza and clasped her hands in mine.

"What did she say?"

Liza turned her dewy eyes up at me. She was not smiling.

"Liza, what did your auntie say?"

Liza's sister Jessica broke the grim silence. With her halting English she read me the verdict: "Tita said, at last God has found a man for Liza."

What?

"She said, Liza has been without a man for a long time, and she's been waiting for a good man, and at last God has found one for her."

I wanted to cry. I could see that Liza was on the verge of tears.

"Thank you," I said to Tita, who was now grinning broadly. "Thank you," I said to mom, who was also smiling, though somewhat hesitantly, it seemed. "This is the happiest moment of my life," I said to Liza.

"Me too," she said. "Me too."

She sidled up closer to me and put her head on my shoulder.

The boards beneath us creaked and the roof above us sighed. I held Liza's hand and saw the faces of our children in her loving eyes. We were going to have beautiful children. I felt the cultural distance melt. I felt the joyful irony of the moment: The boy from the slums of Manila goes to America, becomes successful and returns to his homeland to find a girl from the provinces to bring back with him to the New World. I felt like I was living inside a fable; that I was a handsome prince galloping on a gleaming steed, riding back to the provinces and finding a fair young maiden to bring home to his castle. Such a storybook finish, such an Anglo-Saxon fairy-tale ending, such a wonderful myth. How could I not be happy?

Then I remembered I had brought gifts. I had put them in my backpack before we left the hotel.

These were the gifts I had brought from the New World for Liza's family: canned food from America—ham, Vienna sausages, other potted meats and some bags of candy. Hershey's kisses and Brach's jellies. These were everyday items to Americans; treasures from a distant land to a family from the Philippine provinces. I took these from my backpack and presented them to the gathering.

They seemed quite pleased to get them. They chattered and laughed as I pulled each item from my bag.

"Would you like to try these?" I said as I held up the bag of jellied candies. "They're masarap (delicious)." I rubbed my belly.

They tittered at my pathetic attempt at Tagalog, and I was proud of my having achieved yet another multicultural moment. One of them said something about Tagalog, probably my lame attempt to use the Philippine national language, and laughed.

"Jessica, get a plate. Serve the candies."

Jessica dutifully got up from her chair and followed her older sister's orders. She took the candies from me, grabbed a plate from the wash bin near the gray industrial sink, rinsed it, wiped it off and emptied the bag of jellies onto it. She went around the room and each member of the family took a piece or two. Some eyed the jellies suspiciously before tasting. Jessica was thinking beyond the jellies. She was eyeing the bag of Hershey's kisses I had set down next to Liza.

"Ummm," said Liza's cousin's husband. I forget his name. "Cherry, di ba?"

"Yes, cherry," I said.

"Umph, they're very sweet," said Liza's mother, looking a bit shocked, her face twisting as if she'd just bitten into the sourest thing in the universe. I was stunned to hear her speak English. These were the first American words she'd spoken this evening.

"Is this chewing gum?" she asked as her teeth struggled with the sticky consistency of the jellies.

"No, no. You eat them. You swallow it. It's not gum."

She seemed unconvinced as she continued to chew. She furrowed her brow disapprovingly.

"Very sweet."

Too sweet. American candy manufacturers load up their candies with sugar, a cheap commodity in America, a rather expensive one in the Philippines.

The sugar overload is why American kids get addicted to the stuff real easily. Filipino kids don't get much of a chance. Maybe that's why so many of them have such perfect teeth. Maybe that's why mom and Liza and Liza's sister and Liza's brother and Liza's cousins all had perfect teeth. They're not used to this much sweet, this much sugar. And that's why mom had a sensory overload when she tasted the spoils of the Industrial Revolution.

Oh well, I thought. Bad move. Bad call. You can't win 'em all. Just go with it.

Liza's cousins and her brother Nelo reached for more jellies. Jessica made a move for the chocolates. Mom took the jelly out of her mouth and placed it on the table.

"Too sweet," she proclaimed again. "Too sweet for me."

A bit later, after some broken conversation that ranged from the meaningful—"I will love Liza and honor her forever"—to the trivial—"I promise, I will buy her a new car and we will have a big house"—I said my goodbyes to the family. They were all quite pleasant to me as we parted, but I imagined what they might be saying about me after I moved out of earshot.

Taba (fat), bastos (insolent), tanga (dumb), matanda (old), pangit (ugly). Or they could just as easily have said: guwapo (handsome), matalino (smart) and mabait (nice). I simply did not know what they were saying. I didn't know which were Tagalog words and which were Cebuano, anyway, so I was all the more confused.

The truth, of course, was somewhere in the middle, lurking in the darkness, pitching and unstable in the wind. But then again, when has truth ever been fixed? Is truth a universal fixture, like the stars in Orion's belt? Only if you're looking at the sky from the planet Earth. Truth is multiperspectival, multivocal. Truth is what you make it, what you reckon it to be. And those stars in Orion's belt won't be there 10 billion years from now.

Lapu Lapu, the ancient warrior-chief, knew his own truth. And the truth, as he saw it, was that Ferdinand Magellan and his crew of Spanish colonialists were up to no good when they first set foot on the islands back in 1521. The mighty warrior struck a blow for his culture and his people against the intrusion of the New World in the best way he knew how—with a spear through the head.

I would be visiting the Lapu Lapu monument the next day as part of my cultural re-education. And so, after I bid adieu to her sweet-and-sour family, Liza walked me back up the pungent, dark alley; past the group of dirty, drunken, cursing men; back out to busy Mango Street, where I caught a cab and went back to my hotel room. I was going to have a busy day with a warrior-king tomorrow, and I needed a good night's rest.

As the cab departed, I saw Liza turn and walk back into the darkness. She had a casual, almost-routine gait as she negotiated her way across the busy street, around onrushing jeepneys, past the children running wildly, past the drunken men leering at her, on her way back to the shack where the ghosts of her family were creaking and moaning, where her family was chattering endlessly about the incredible future that awaits this beautiful, simple girl from the provinces.

She smiled in my direction—those perfect teeth, those dewy lips. Even her hair seemed to smile as it swayed across her back, in time with her slow, sensuous pace. Could it be any better than this? Can anyone be any more beautiful than this? Can life be any better than this? Can any man be luckier than I? Is the Philippines a wonderful place, or what? Why did it take me so long to re-discover it? How could I have been so blind, so unaware, so American?

# 15

## *Liza's Dream*

It was a day just like every other day in the fishing village of Daanbantayan north of Cebu City. Mother was busy cleaning the family's modest house, waiting for her husband to return home from fishing. What might he bring home today? A nice, succulent lapu lapu fish? A few little crabs? A bucket of clams?

The day was hot and dreamy. The leaves of the palm trees were swaying gracefully in the tropical breeze, the sea lapped up against the beach gently, kissing it affectionately like a lover returning home, then clinging on desperately as it withdraws and rejoins the blue beyond, over and over again. Wet kisses, sad goodbye kisses, passionate hello kisses, over and over again.

Was that the cry of a monkey in the distance? Or a big parrot? Sometimes it was difficult to tell the difference.

Little Liza Trujillo had just emerged from her bath, which consisted of having her mother pour kettles of lukewarm water on her—over and over again—as Liza scrubbed herself while wearing a modest little camasita. Liza started wearing this shirt after her body had started to develop. Mom had seen how some of the neighbor men had snuck peaks over the fence at bathtime, leering at Liza's ripening golden-brown body.

Liza's long black hair was still wet, and it flowed down over her shoulders in lush cascades. The warm air and the gentle breeze made her smile. She knew her father would be home soon with some fresh fish or crab or clams. Feeling happy, secure, clean and frisky, Liza skipped off to the field of tall grass nearby, to her special spot in the middle of the field. There she would hide in the grass, look up to the sky, and imagine what the future would bring to her. She hoped it would be something good. She loved her family; she loved her life in the fishing village; she loved everything about her life in the Philippines. All except the poverty, the crushing poorness, the gnawing hunger, the lack of physical comforts, no machines to do the work, sleeping on the hard floor, the constant work, work, work, the washing, the cooking, the cleaning, the fishing, the commands from

146

mother, the needs of father and sister and brother, the day-to-day repetition of it all, the boredom—Oh God, the boredom!

Surely, there had to be something more for me, she thought. Maybe there was some magic that would deliver me to someplace else. There had been visitors from America—older men with white hair—who had come to the island to court some of the women here. I don't know how they met, but I know the women were exchanging letters with the men for a while before they visited. Often the letters had money in them, sometimes $20 or sometimes as much as $100. These men are so rich!

*One of the women, a friend of my mother's, married a foreigner and is now living in a nice house in Canada. I also heard that another Daanbantayan woman married an American and later divorced him because he was very violent. He would beat her almost every day. She returned to the Philippines and is now a single mother.*

*I hope I can meet a good man, not a bad one. Maybe there is a man—a Filipino man from Cebu or Manila? A Canadian man? An American man? An Arab? An Australian? I don't care—just anyone who could take me to another place and give me something more. Someone who could give me a better life, a more comfortable life, a life free of money problems, a life full of shiny, new things. And if he is a nice man, and handsome, and generous to my family, then I could be very happy. I could have a very good life.*

Liza was pleased with this thought, and it showed in the delighted way she frolicked to the field. A big, happy smile lit her face. She knew that she was pretty. The local boys had always treated her special; and she'd seen how the local men looked at her, even though she was only 12.

"Hoy, Liza!" a voice called out as the happy little girl skipped by. It was Wilson, one of the local boys. He had a major crush on her, obviously, and he was smiling and waving. Liza thought the skinny lad was nice-looking enough, but he was too local, too much a provincial boy, too poor. She waved, flipped her hair, smiled flirtatiously, and continued on. New dreams were waiting, after all, and Wilson would always be there.

Wilson's parents and Liza's folks were good friends, with long family histories. At get-togethers, they often joked about how Liza and Wilson would get married, have children and carry on the family ties. When Liza first heard this, she laughed pleasantly, acknowledging to her family what a cute idea it was. The second and third time she heard it, she laughed a more sardonic laugh, as if to say, "yeah, right." She stopped laughing the fourth, fifth and sixth time she heard it. Her family stopped saying it a couple of years ago, but her mother gets a gleam in her eye whenever she sees the skinny young boy with the neatly combed-back hair whose father, her good friend, had named after U.S. President Woodrow Wilson. What a nice son-in-law he'd be. Hard working, loyal and respectful.

None of these things mattered to the happy young miss bounding at the edge of the field of tall grass. She is here in the moment, and now she disappears from view like a ghost who has faded into a living wave of green. Her delighted laugh is the only clue that she is there.

And now she's sitting in her special spot, the small clearing in the little grass field where she often sits, looking up at the sky. And now the sky is a bright cobalt blue, otherworldly and quiet. The stars are dancing with delight and the full moon is laughing at what a silly thing this little girl is. Is that the sound of bells in the distance? Or is that the hovering of angels? And look! What is this bright white orb doing here next to me? Who put it here? And why is it shining so like a little white sun?

The little girl picks it up and sees that there are some little people inside moving around, like in a scene from a miniature movie.

*Who are they? What could this be? Who is that woman? She looks familiar. Why, it looks like me. It IS me, all grown up. And are those my children, that cute little boy and girl? They look Filipino. Are they mine? My husband, where is he?*

After a few moments, she sees him enter the picture, and she smiles when she sees him holding her tightly as if he never wants to let her go. And Little Liza squeals with pleasure when she sees him kiss her—the future her—on the lips, passionately, like a man very much in love.

*What must it be like to be kissed so sweetly? So forcefully? So nicely? I want to see his face.*

But she cannot see his face. It stays in shadow, as if it were hiding some forbidden secret. But she sees other things, many other things that make her eyes widen and her breath stop and her heart leap. She sees her husband and her and their children entering a big house tucked in between big trees. She sees her children playing happily in a big backyard, playing with a water hose, laughing on a swing. She sees herself serving dinner to her family. She's holding a big platter and on it is a big bird, brown and steaming hot. She's never seen such big chickens. She sees herself driving a big American car, all fast and new and glistening in the sun. She sees row upon row of nice houses, she drives over paved and cleaned streets. And now she's in a store, it looks like a grocery store, with aisle after aisle of food—food in boxes, food in cans, strange fruit on display, freshly cut meat under glass. There is just so much food!

She sees men, white American men. They all stop and look when she walks by. Some of them smile at her. Some wink at her. Some leer at her as if they were starving and want to eat her. She remembers something her mother once told her—that all American men are animals, that they are dangerous, that they are not to be trusted.

Her mother's words echo through her mind and she speeds up now, hurrying past the men, the smiling, winking, leering, dangerous men, and she leaps outside to the safety of her husband's arms. He has appeared there because he somehow knew that she was in danger, and he wanted to protect her with all his strength, all his power. She can see that his body is sturdy—his arms and legs are big and his chest is wide and his shoulders are burly. But she still cannot see his face. It is all darkness where his face should be.

"Are you OK, darling?" her husband asks.

"Yes, dear," Liza responds, smiling. "I am OK because you are here now."

They kiss passionately and they cannot stop kissing and now the sky is getting dark and they're still kissing. And now they are in a hotel room, a nice hotel room, and the air-con is whirring and they are naked, lying in a large bed.

Liza lets out an embarrassed "whoop" when she sees their nakedness, partially shocked, partially fascinated. And now, now she can see his face. She can see that he IS a Filipino man, with brown skin and black hair and the almond eyes of Malayan stock. She can also see that he is an older man, perhaps in his mid to late 30s, or maybe in his early 40s. And now she can hear by the way he talks that he is American. He looks Filipino, but he talks like an American. And this place they are in—this is America. Everyone else looks American, but they do not.

How can this be? Who is this man? What is he? And who am I? What have I become? Where is my mother? Where is my family? Can someone explain this all to me?

As Liza continues to peer inside the glowing white orb, a snake silently wriggles next to her and starts to speak.

"It's your future, child," the serpent says, surprising the girl nearly out of her skin.

"Are you talking to me?" she replies, not knowing what else to say. "And why should I believe this is my future? Why should I believe a talking snake?"

"Because you have nothing else to believe in except the inevitability of your poverty."

"What?"

"Because you want to believe that there is something better for you out there—this is why you should believe me. I am telling you your future. Your dreams will come true. You will have everything you want. You will find a good man who will provide for you, love you, give you beautiful children. He is a man who you won't meet for several years. But you will meet him."

"How will I meet him?"

"A divine wind will blow him here to you."

"A divine wind?"

"The most divine of winds."

"But what is his name? How will he find me?"

"Don't worry. He will find you."

"And bring me to America?"

"That's up to you."

"What do you mean?"

"If you want to go to America, you will go."

"Of course I want to go. Why would I not?" Liza was getting agitated by the talking snake's riddles.

"Child, you will go to The Land of Happiness if you want to; if you truly believe in the thing that is waiting for you there; if the divine winds are at your back; and if you can avoid all of the dangers waiting in the shadows—especially those who want to devour you, those who want to feed on your warm blood."

There is a long pause as Liza contemplates what all this could mean. But before she could ask another question, the snake hisses, "Godspeed, child," and slithers away in the tall grass. Liza looks up at the sky in wonder, then closes her eyes and says a few words to the heavens: "Let this be true. Please, let this be true." Then she peers back into the orb. And there she sees her face, laughing, smiling, glowing, and she sees herself sitting by a fireplace in a big, comfortable house, surrounded by great new things. And she sees a little angel hovering above her, looking down on her, protecting her from harm. And now, outside the house, there are horses, beautiful beasts, running freely in their large backyard, and now there are great, pink birds with large beaks and long necks, each standing on one long leg in a large pond. And now Liza is swimming naked in that pond, and now the pond has turned into an ocean. And now Liza is surrounded by dolphins and now they are all swimming together, laughing and playing and jumping out of the water with utter abandon. And now Liza and the dolphins swim by Liza's father, who is out in the ocean in his fishing boat. Liza waves and shouts delightedly at him and he smiles and waves back. Her father? How did he get to America? Or is she back in the Philippines? It doesn't matter. Liza is now feeling freer and happier than she's ever felt, and she jumps with joy at the vision she sees inside this little white orb glowing in her hands.

Her mother must see this, Liza thinks. I must show this to mother.

She thrashes her way out of the grass field and bounds in the direction of home. She arrives at the moment her father comes home, and she excitedly shows the orb to him.

"What is this?" he asks her in wonder.

"It's magic. It can tell the future. Look, you're in there!"

"Diha ka? (Really?)" Her father always played along with her, always humored her fantasies. "You're just fooling me, huh?"

"No, this is real. Look!"

He looked inside, or pretended to look inside, and said, "Oh yes, I can see."

Little Liza squealed with delight and rushed inside to bring her find to her mother. Mom would be a harder sell. She was the skeptical one in the family.

"Look, mom," Liza said. "Isn't it pretty? It's magic."

"What is this?" mom said, looking at the orb suspiciously. "Where did you get this?"

"In the field. It was in the field. It can tell the future. Look inside!"

Mom looked inside for a few moments and then shook her head. "There's nothing there. You're just imagining."

"No mom, look again, You can see my future, my husband in America. Look!"

"What!?" Mom was surprised by such a wild notion. "What are you saying? Have you lost your mind?" She snatched the orb from Liza's grasp and walked toward a window. "Buang ka. (You are crazy.)"

With that, mom uttered the word "America!" with contempt, and hurled the orb out the window. Liza shrieked "No!" but moments later she could hear the shattering of glass and the tinkling of bouncing/sliding fragments as the orb hit the ground and exploded into hundreds of thousands of pieces.

Liza looked at her mother in stunned silence, and as she looked she saw in her mother's face the image of her own face: the high cheeks, the big perfect teeth, the skin with the color of an exotic desert, the welcoming, loving smile that says "I am here for you forever. You are here for me forever. Trust not these wicked illusions. Trust not these talking snakes. Trust only me and believe only in me."

And it was that face that she saw as she awoke from the dream. It was that face that she saw the many times she had awoken from this dream. What was it now? The 10th time, the 20th time, that she'd had this exact same dream? What does it mean? What does it all mean?

Liza turned her head and looked at the clock on top of her little plastic shelf. It was time to get up and go to work. Time to get dressed in her little yellow-jacket and blue-skirt outfit and report to work at the department store. This was her first big goal, after all, to escape the fishing village, come to the big city and have a decent job in a big department store. And now she had attained her goal; and now there were barongs to sell and rent to pay.

As she looked outside the window of her boarding house, at the end of a dirty alley in Cebu City, she could see that the sky was not the magical cobalt blue of her early-morning dream. And there was no singing of hovering angels—just the collective belching of a million jeepneys in need of a tuneup, and the sight of a few dirty drunks sleeping on someone's porch.

Inside the house, all the others were still in bed—her sister Jessica, her cousin, her cousin's husband, her aunt, her mother. Her mother was awakened by Liza's stirring, and as she opened her eyes, mom's eyes locked Liza's. "I am here for you forever, my child. And you are here for me forever."

Mom didn't need to say it with words. The message was transmitted through her motherly smile and the delicate lifting of her eyebrows. Liza smiled at her mother, then went to the kitchen and started to cook breakfast for the family.

It was a day just like every other day in the Philippine islands; it was a life like every other for a girl from the Philippine provinces.

# 16

## *Fiancee Visas and Other Theories*

After 10 days in Cebu, I had to high-tail it back home to start a new semester. There wasn't time for much more than a few goodbye kisses and a promise that I'd never forget her and that I'd be back soon. I'd had a wondrous, unbelievable trip to the Philippines, the long-forgotten land of my birth. But now it was time to come home and resume my life as a professor at Humboldt State University.

On the flight home, I thought about Liza, I thought about the great times we had together and I thought about the months-long visa application process that we were facing. We would be applying for a K-1 fiancee visa, and this entailed a lot of detail work, as well as my having to disclose a lot of intimate information about my personal life and my current financial state.

I was also anxious to get back to my own home and sleep in my own bed again.

When I deplaned at SFO, I was still a little rocky from the long flight. The scene at the luggage carousel made me even more dizzy. People pushed and shoved to get to their big white "balikbayan" boxes full of clothes, dried foods and souvenirs from the Philippines. I found my big blue trunk and soft blue pullman cases, hoisted them onto a luggage cart and got into one of the customs queues.

A customs agent was making the rounds, doing some preliminary paperwork with some of the people in line. He was a moderately heavy-set black man with an easy laugh and a friendly manner. He seemed determined to put everyone at ease.

When he came to me, he looked at my passport and noticed my address. "Arcata? Where is that?"

"Humboldt County. I live way up north."

That seemed to turn on a lightbulb over his head. "Oh, Humboldt County, eh?" He looked at my blue trunk.

"You don't happen to have any of that fine, fine Humboldt County WEED in there, do you?" he said with a big, broad smile.

Yow! I was shocked at this reference to marijuana, but I played it cool. "No, sir, I wouldn't do that, sir," I said in a most serious tone. While he laughed and wrote something on his pad, I thought for a moment about the ludicrousness of his question. What business would I have bringing Humboldt County marijuana in from the Philippines? That just made no sense at all. But I certainly felt no need to question his logic at this moment. I just wanted to move on. I did realize at that moment that I had momentarily become a cultural stereotype. Just because I was from a reputed marijuana-producing area, this young brother with a badge was insinuating that I might be a smuggler.

"Hah, I'm just messing with you," he said. "It's cool. Here, give this to the agent up ahead and have a nice day." He handed me a piece of paper indicating that I was a returning American citizen. I took it and thought about what a fun-loving guy he was for a customs agent, cultural stereotyping notwithstanding. Maybe it was a San Francisco thing. Or maybe he was from Oakland, and this was just some East Oakland jiving.

After a few minutes, I made my way to a customs inspector sitting at a booth shielded on one side by a thick pane of glass. He looked at my passport, scanned it and checked my records on his computer. After no more than one minute, he handed me back my passport, smiled warmly and said, "Welcome home, Professor Estrada."

Maybe America wasn't as bad as I'd imagined it to be whilst in the fever of the tropical heat and suffering from the delirium of new love. This was my home, after all, and I was glad to be back.

I came home to Arcata a happy man. I'd found a beautiful new love, I was a professor at a fine university, and I was living in the redwood country of Northern California. Could life be better?

I also had a new challenge. I was assigned to teach a mass communication theory class this semester: JMC 309 Analyzing Mass Media Messages.

This would be my chance to show what I'd learned in my doctoral studies. Instead of teaching journalism skills, like how to report and edit simplistic, little news stories, I will now be offering luminous thoughts about media and society.

How media affect society.

How societies affect media.

How media content sets the agenda of public issues and alters public opinion.

How capitalist media shape and perpetuate social inequities.

How reporters and editors are mere pawns in an insidious control game ruled by monopoly capital.

Fun stuff like that.

Professional journalists scorn, hate, marginalize, dismiss and vilify classes like this. They wish classes like this would not exist.

They do so because classes like this challenge the moral authority of what they do. Journalists don't like to have their authority and morality challenged. They want to be praised unconditionally for being brave, self-sacrificing defenders of the First Amendment.

I know. I used to think this way.

Classes like this also have nothing at all to do with the practice of journalism and everything to do with intense, ideological analysis of media content.

Journalists don't like to have their work analyzed by outsiders, especially intellectuals. Journalists who are asked to give guest lectures would rather strut into a classroom and brag about their latest adventures or engage in shameless name-dropping or tell newsroom war stories. Their eyes glaze over when you start talking about embedded ideologies, the culture of newswork, and propaganda models. They turn downright hostile if you even suggest that their work might be an instrument of cultural domination.

It's tough facing the truth.

I know. As a professional journalist, I would often get invited to give guest lectures. I would strut into college classrooms and talk about myself, drop names shamelessly and tell newsroom war stories. And if anyone challenged my moral authority, my eyes would glaze over and I would turn downright nasty.

So now the tables had turned, at least for this class. I was now a media critic, not a media practitioner. I was now challenging journalism myths, not perpetuating newswork folklore. I was now quoting from Adorno and Chomsky and Bagdikian and Parenti, not from Woodward and Bernstein and Cronkite and Rather.

I relished the thought.

The class went well, as I thought it might. The students were an eclectic mix of aspiring journalists, sociology radicals, political science empiricists, postmodern feminists, eco-activists and heavy-metal skaters with dreadlocks. The anti-authoritarian nature of media criticism played well to a Humboldt State crowd.

I started off the class talking about our culture's "way of knowing" and the schools of philosophy that have evolved around this. We discussed Socrates, Plato, Aristotle; we talked about Kant's German idealism; we spoke of Descartes and his "cogito, ergo sum." We moved quickly to Kierkegaard and Sartre and existentialism, and then in the second week, the fun really began.

I told them of the beginnings of mass communication research, of World War II propaganda analysis, of the *Why We Fight* film studies, of the Bullet Theory, the *Invasion From Mars* research, the *Seduction of the Innocent* scare, Paul Lazarsfeld's radio survey work and the two-step flow. I spoke of Adorno and Horkheimer's ideological analysis of the U.S. culture industry, British Cultural Studies and neo-Marxist analysis. I moved on to Agenda Setting, Cultivation Theory, the use of the scientific method in media research. And just to confuse them even more, I threw in Foucault, Baudrillard, Lyotard, and all the joys of postmodernism.

By midterm, they didn't know what hit 'em. They were reeling. They would tell me they were loving the class, but all the theories and conversations that orbited around these theories were making them dizzy.

At one point one of my colleagues on the faculty pulled me aside. He told me that he heard about my theory class, and he congratulated me on teaching the class "the way it's supposed to be taught," but he also advised me to lighten up.

"This isn't graduate school," he said. "You're expecting too much of them. Try and lower the bar a little bit."

I did. I let them watch videos for a couple of weeks.

One of the videos was the six-part *Why We Fight* film series, a masterpiece of wartime propaganda produced by Frank Capra for the U.S. War Department, with animation assistance from the Disney Studios.

Some of the students winced at the bloody wartime footage, some were enthralled by the documentary footage of Hitler and his minions making impassioned speeches—footage that was used by the American government filmmakers to alarm and mobilize American audiences—and some were just relieved to be watching TV instead of listening to lectures.

Later, for a slight change of pace, I had them watch *Dreamworlds*, a scathing video that deconstructs MTV's imagery of women, and charges the rock and roll industry with perpetuating adolescent male fantasies of control and dominance.

The feminists in the class loved *Dreamworlds*. The non-feminists watched, winced and remained quiet, for fear of being shouted down.

We also watched *Manufacturing Consent*, the documentary on media critic Noam Chomsky. I was particularly fond of Chomsky, the celebrated MIT scholar, because I had interviewed him once for an article, and because his views generally enraged professional journalists. William F. Buckley once said of

Chomsky, "I'd like to smash him in the goddam mouth." So, I rightly figured that old Noam was on to something.

In fact, in my dissertation, I had also criticized Chomsky, but for different reasons. I thought his view of newswork was a bit totalizing, his method mostly polemical and lacking in substantial evidence, and his depiction of reporters as being lapdogs to corporate masters a bit too much. Chomsky is right, but he goes too far. Nevertheless, the anarchists, Marxists and skateboard rastas in the class loved the Chomsky video. The political science empiricists grumbled, but didn't speak up much, for fear of being shouted down.

I utterly LOVED this hurly burly of intellectual exchange. This was what being a professor was all about, I figured. Giving students new thoughts, new vistas, different ways of seeing. This was wholly, distinctly different from teaching stilted Associated Press style to beginning reporting students.

When the two weeks of videos were over, the students were to make presentations about their engagements with media. They were to somehow filter their observations through some of the theoretical discussions we'd had.

One of the more unusual presentations sticks in my mind.

One student, an older man, 50ish, with scraggly hair and a long gray beard, walked to the front of the class with a little cassette player and an audio tape.

He proclaimed that he couldn't analyze media credibly because for the past 20 years he'd been living in a little cabin in the wilds of southern Humboldt County, and had no access to radio, TV or newspapers. So, instead, he wanted to play a song for us.

The tape was of *Teach Your Children,* the classic by Crosby, Stills & Nash. As the song played, he stood in front of us with a peaceful smile on his face. The students looked at him, looked at me, and looked at one another in amazement. I just smiled a little mango smile.

The song finished, the old graybeard ejected the tape, unplugged the cassette player and took his seat. He had nothing more to add.

This guy is an eccentric, a minimalist, I reckoned. What the heck. He said his peace. I don't have the vinegar in my stomach to flunk this guy. Not while I'm so much in love with my future. Nice job, dude. Next!

And so it was for the rest of the semester, which was turning out to be quite enjoyable. The students who didn't take to the theoretical material at first quickly jumped onboard when they discovered that all theories led ultimately to scathing critiques of corporate media. What self-respecting radical/progressive student from Humboldt County could resist a good hacking of the media? We were speaking the same language.

One day, as I came home from school, I saw I had a letter from the Philippines waiting for me. It was a greeting card from Liza.

---

*Feb. 18, 1998*
*George,*

*Your thoughtfulness will always be remembered. And your kindness. Hope you never change. Pls. Take care, don't forget to pray our Almighty God always. I missed you and I love you.*

*Busy as always? Asking me, I'm always busy preparing for the super sale for this month. Sorry, I cannot write you soon. Anyway, knowing you for many months now is a challenge me to know you better. I know I'd never reach even halfway of how to adjust a man knowing that again he will be far away from me. You know I'm always thinking of you. I hope you will not change the way you are.*

*Thank you for package. I received all of them. I'm enjoying to heard your tape recording. I like all of them. Where can you get this songs? I'm always listening your tape player and also some pictures. Thank you very much for this.*

*That's it for now coz I'm sleepy. See you next letter.*

*I missed you.*

*Love, Liza*

---

She referred in her letter to a package of cassette tapes I had sent to her, tapes on which I had recorded compilations of some of my favorite songs: *Please, Please Me* and *Strawberry Fields* by the Beatles, *Play With Fire* by the Rolling Stones, *Misty* by Johnny Mathis, *You Really Got Me* by the Kinks, *Kaw-Liga* by Hank Williams, *Let's Go, Baby* by Wang Chung, *Sanitarium* and *Leper Messiah* by Metallica, *Summer Wind* by Frank Sinatra, *London Calling* by the Clash, *Immigrant Song* by Led Zeppelin, *Beautiful Girls* by Van Halen, and *I Honestly Love You* by Olivia Newton-John.

Those kinds of tunes. You know, the classics. I figured she needed to start liking the music I like.

The rains kept on falling and the semester kept on going. I took a little trip to an academic conference in Denver, where I presented three papers. I also caught a Colorado Rockies game versus the Los Angeles Dodgers at Coors Field. Other than that, the semester was not so eventful. I started making plans to visit Liza again during the summer break, but I kept hearing rumors that Philippine Airlines personnel were threatening to go on strike. I started looking into alternative ways to get to the Philippines. Just as finals week began, I received another letter from Liza.

---

*April 22, 1998*
*Hello George,*

*I was going to write a letter to you asking you why you haven't written to me in such a long time. Then I called you, nobody's answer me. Why? I'm wondering what happen to you. My only worry is that maybe I am not good enough for you.*

*Maybe you won't love me. Hope you don't think like this. I really love you. I missed you. I want we are together, do it now. About my passport, don't worry. I'm just process now. And how about my visa? If ever you have time to take my visa pls. do it.*

*Well, that's it for now. Take care, my dear. I always thinking of you and pls. don't ever forget: there's a beautiful lady in Cebu who loves you very much. (It's me!)*

*Love,*

*Liza*

---

The visa! Right, I should start looking into the fiancée visa application procedure. I'd been so caught up in teaching and trying to do well in my theory class that I neglected to start the visa process in earnest. In the back of my mind I was figuring that it would be no big deal, there would be no significant delay. Just apply for it and get it—like a passport. Right?

Uh, no. Not exactly.

I had made a bad miscalculation. In the coming days, I discovered that the process takes at least seven months from start to finish and involves a lot of paperwork.

This was going to be difficult. Not for me, since I was used to filling out U.S. government forms, but it might be a tricky deal for Liza since her comprehension of English was rough at best. It also didn't help that she didn't have a phone. I should have bought her a cellular phone during my visit there last January. Another serious miscalculation on my part.

Because I had been too stupidly in love, and because I was too distracted by my job, I had made some bad judgment calls that had cost us three months time. I should have started this process immediately upon returning to the States last January, and I should have bought her a cell phone when I was there. In other words, I should have done my research before going to the Philippines, and should have anticipated the bureaucratic maze that I would be facing to obtain Liza's fiancée visa. Maybe she'd sensed this, and that's why she seemed a little irked in her letter.

But, to be fair to myself, I hadn't assumed that my trip to the Philippines would result so quickly in an engagement to be married. Everything had happened so quickly, and the long plane ride home made me woozy, and before I knew it the spring semester was upon me, and I was in front of a class talking about mass communication theories, and it was raining a lot, and Liza was now half a world away, and oh my God, I wasn't so sure that I hadn't been hallucinating all of this. By the time I regained my balance, the semester was coming to a close and the reality set in that I hadn't fulfilled my responsibility to her. I was facing the reality that I'd blown it. Three months had gone down the drain and I hadn't even started the visa process yet.

She was doing her part. She had applied for a passport and was attending seminars that the government required for Filipinos who were planning to travel abroad.

In the next few days, I made a mad rush to get up to speed on what we had to do. I obtained the application packet from the INS. I surfed Web sites containing information on K-1 fiancée visas. I bought books on the subject. I talked to people who had gone through the process.

I found out that there would be a lot of questions to answer and that I'd better answer them accurately and succinctly. A stupid answer might send up a red flag that would delay things for another few months.

I also found out that I should include every, I mean EVERY, piece of documentation they asked for. An omission of one checking account statement, for example, might result in a delay.

We also had to provide proof that we had a real relationship, and that we had met in person. The INS asked us to provide photographs, letters, hotel receipts, airplane boarding passes, phone records, anything to substantiate our claim that we were an authentic couple who had actually met in person. Then they wanted to know how we met, where we work, who are parents are, where our parents were born. Then we had to provide information about where each of us had lived for the past five years—with exact addresses, please! Then they wanted to know how much money I had in the bank, what stocks and bonds I owned...and on and on it went.

The semester ended, and summer was upon us now. I had an obligation to attend an American Press Institute conference in Reston, Virginia, and while I was there I spent some time with an old *Oakland Tribune* friend of mine, Eric Newton, who had become one of the executive bigshots at the Newseum. Eric had married Mary Ann Hogan, another Oakland Tribbie, who now was freelancing through her own writers syndicate, and they had two sons. Spending time with them made me want to get my own family started soon.

Returning from the East Coast, I hurriedly made arrangements for my second trip to the Philippines. The pilots and crew of Philippine Airlines indeed went on strike, as threatened, and so I had to find a different way to get to Cebu. I found out that Cathay Pacific flew from Los Angeles to Cebu, by way of Hong Kong. And so I called up a travel agent and booked my flights. There was no haggling this time since tickets were in demand because of the PAL strike. It would cost me a little more than $900 for this flight.

This time, along with my clothes, personal-care products and gifts for Liza, I also packed a large envelope full of visa application documents that Liza and I would fill out together. We'd have to spend some of our quality time together filling out government forms. I didn't relish the thought.

I also packed a plastic bag full of little green apples that I'd bought at the local Safeway. Man doesn't live by mangoes alone, and neither does woman, I reckoned. And so I wanted to give Liza a different tasting fruit—tart little apples grown in the northwestern U.S., sweet enough to tickle your fancy, sour enough to make you feel a little sassy.

I knew that apples like these were not available in the Philippines. The apples there are sort of mushy, not crisp like American apples. So these common little fruits we take for granted here in America would be quite an exotic delicacy there in the Philippines.

When the day came, I threw all of my baggage in the back of my black Nissan pickup and headed south down Highway 101. It would be six hours to San Francisco, where I would stay in a hotel for one night. The next day, I'd leave my truck with my cousin Joyce and her family in Daly City, and then it would be off to the San Francisco Airport for a flight to Los Angeles, where I would catch a Cathay Pacific flight to Hong Kong. There I would have a six-hour layover before my flight to Cebu. What a grueling journey!

But it was all worth it, I reckoned. This is the greatest adventure of my life.

# 17

## *Trouble In Paradise*

The flight to Hong Kong on Cathay Pacific was trouble-free, and the food was foreign and interesting. The stewards and stewardesses were also very friendly. It was somewhat jarring to hear proper British accents coming from their mouths, since my mind was programmed to hear the roller-coaster, sing-song Chinese accent I'd normally hear from the mouths of immigrants back in California. I didn't expect to hear a Chinese person say "Smashing!" with an Oxford accent. I guessed that most of the English teachers in Hong Kong were British.

I had a six-hour layover in the Hong Kong airport, so I browsed the shops for a while, listened to music through headphones and people-watched for a good bit the Chinese, Japanese, Koreans, and everyone else passing through. I was tired and deadly bored from the long flight, and I still had a ways to go before I could settle down and have a good rest.

I finally got into Cebu about midday. I had the customs ritual down now, and everything went smoothly as I passed through the passport checkpoint and the luggage declaration. One of the customs officials might have stolen a glance when he saw my last name, but it didn't register on me. The day was blazing hot. I hailed an air-conditioned cab and arrived at Eddie's Hotel soon enough.

"Mr. Estrada, it's good to see you again," said one of the women behind the counter, smiling charmingly. The other women smiled as well, widening their eyes and flashing their pearly whites. They seemed genuinely pleased to see me again.

I checked in and got the keys to my room—room 303 on the third floor—and this time I brought the luggage up myself.

I dropped off my packs, hung up my shirts, shaved and went down to the hotel bar. Robinson, the friendly bartender, was also surprised and pleased to see me again. He was nattily attired in starched white shirt, tie and slacks, as usual. I ordered a quickie lunch of *gambas a la jilo* (spicey shrimp) with rice, and a Coke.

"No San Miguel this time?" Robinson asked.

"No, not right now. Maybe later."

"Are you here to bring home your fiancée?"

"No, not quite yet. Still waiting on the visa."

"Tsck, it takes a long time, huh?"

"Yeah, you know the government."

"Yes, the government. Tsck."

Robinson wiped off the counter and then left to get silverware and dining linen for me. He returned and whispered, "excuse me," over my shoulder while he set my place on the bar. Then he walked back to the rear of the restaurant, leaned his head into a small window and gave my lunch order to the cooks.

"So, was there a problem with the visa application?" Robinson inquired as he washed glassware at the bar. He seemed keenly interested in all these visa procedures.

"No," I said. "But they ask a lot of questions."

"Oh?"

"And I had to give them details about my past, where I used to live, where I work, how much money I make, what my investments are, and all that."

"Oh?"

"Yeah, they wanted to make sure I could support her, so that she won't go on welfare after coming to the U.S."

"Welfare? What is that?"

"Welfare, you know, when you're desperately poor and the government helps you out with money and food and sometimes helps you pay your rent."

"Really? Tsck, that's very good." Robinson seemed quite surprised and quite impressed.

"We also have unemployment insurance in the States," I said. "If you get laid off, the government gives you money until you can find another job."

Robinson seemed amazed. "We don't have that here. Only in our dreams."

He stared at me, and looked down for a few moments.

"The U.S. government is very kind, very strong," he said. He went on washing and wiping glasses. One of the customers ordered a Bloody Mary, and Robinson rushed off to the refrigerator at the corner of the bar to find some tomato juice and a celery stick.

I sipped my Coke and thought about what Robinson said. It sounded very much like something my mother or father would have said, or something a new immigrant to the U.S. would've said.

Robinson returned momentarily and asked me if I'd ever been on welfare. I told him no, I hadn't. But I was laid off once, and the state of California had given me unemployment compensation.

"Yes, as you said, the government gives you money if you get laid off your job." His eyes opened in wonder. "How much?"

I had to think about it for a few moments. It had been some years ago, back in 1991 or 92 or thereabouts. Then I remembered it had been something like $840 a month. And I remember that was quite helpful, insofar as my apartment rent was only $580 back then. It was also enough to pay for food, gasoline and cable TV—the essentials.

Robinson seemed quite startled by these sums of money, even as small as they were. "My goodness, my goodness," he kept on saying. "The U.S. government! Tsck."

I could see in his eyes that he wished he lived in the U.S. Thus, I didn't have the heart to dispel his fantasy by telling him about the bad stuff in my country: the fact that Asians are often stereotyped, marginalized and viewed suspiciously by the other races; the fact that things are so expensive that a seemingly large salary doesn't seem to buy enough house, enough car, nor enough of anything you covet; the fact that you covet these things because the media convince you that your life is not complete unless you have these things. And so you're trapped in a vicious cycle of consuming and spending and working and lifting your status and spending and consuming and wanting more to lift your status, and so on until you die.

And then what?

And then your children continue the cycle.

I don't think Robinson wanted to hear that. I don't think I really wanted to hear it either, but the thought did swirl about. I started to feel like an affluent American, a rich man. I ordered a cognac.

"Cognac? Uh, I don't know if…Wait a minute!"

Robinson scanned the bottles of fine foreign liquor displayed on the racks behind him. I knew there was cognac there because I had seen a bottle of Remy. And yes, there was a Courvoisier label on the bottle next to it.

The friendly bartender kept on scanning the line of bottles, and I didn't want to tell him where the cognac was because I thought that would embarrass him. Maybe people at this bar didn't order cognac that often, this probably being more or less a San Miguel-type bar with San Miguel-type clients.

He finally found the cognac, and I asked him how much for a shot. He pulled out a price list and, scanning it, discovered that a shot of Remy would run me

100 pesos. Knowing that the exchange rate was about 47 pesos to the dollar, I figured that two dollars or so wouldn't be an unreasonable amount of money to spend on a shot of cognac. Besides, it would impress the hell out of my new friend.

Robinson pulled out a silver shot cup to measure out the right amount, then he poured the orange-brown nectar into a snifter. He watched intently as I cupped the snifter and swirled the cognac around to warm it with the heat of my palm. I explained to him that cognac was a rich man's drink and rich people had certain ways of doing things.

"I have never in my life tasted that," Robinson said, eyeing the booze. "Tell me what is it."

"It's sort of a brandy," I struggled to explain, "but it's a very, very fine brandy, made in a very exclusive region of France."

"Ahh, brandy. I see."

"It's a rich man's drink. I drink it just to feel like I've accomplished something in my life, you see. Cheers."

Robinson nodded and eyed me for a moment, then turned his gaze back down to his glass-washing. I don't know if he was envious of me or thinking what a pompous ass I was. Probably a bit of both.

I decided to have a little walk up Mango Boulevard before heading back to my room, so I excused myself and exited out the glass doors. The security guard saw me coming and helped me with the door.

I walked about 200 feet or so up to the main street and found myself in the bustle of the city. The traffic was thick with cars and jeepneys, zigzagging about, occasionally finding some kind of lane to fall into. The day was quite hot—like any other day in the Philippines—and the smog was very thick. I noticed some of the pedestrians along the sidewalk covering their noses and mouths with tissue or handkerchiefs, to filter the pollution they were breathing in.

I passed the burned-out shell of a jeep parked on the sidewalk, and I wondered what thing could have happened to this poor vehicle. I passed a carenderia, which had a grill out on the sidewalk cooking some meat on skewers. The smoking meat smelled quite delicious, and I wondered what kind of animal it was. I passed a run-down little shack of a house and saw, through its open front door, a young mother giving a bath to two small children. A bright rooster strutted about the front, tethered to a pole. In the front of the house next door, two droopy-eyed young men were taking hits out of a small bottle of liquor. I snuck a look at the label: Tanduay Rum.

I continued to walk a bit, and found my way into a little grocery store. Out of curiosity I scanned the liquor shelves. They didn't seem to have any of the upscale liquor that the hotel bar had, but they offered some interesting choices. Among them was a bottle of cheap Andre champagne from the States, which was offered here in the "Imports" section, and priced at 400 pesos. About $8.50 for a bottle of working-class bubbly that I reckoned would cost about $4 or less at the local Safeway back home.

They also offered candy-flavored liqueurs and various vodkas and whiskeys. Of course, there was a large section for San Miguel beer. And there, tucked on a shelf next to the whiskey, were two rows of Tanduay Rum. Scanning the label, I see that it's a local rum. I reckon this might make a nice little nightcap, so I look at the price—35 pesos.

35 pesos! Less than a dollar?! For a half-pint of rum? Good God, what sort of rot-gut might this be?

"This is a very popular drink," said the young girl at the counter, a bit surprised that I'd not heard of it. "Very popular all over the world. Locally made!"

I decided to pass, and I exited the store and made my way back to the hotel. One of the Tanduay-slurping boys was on his back now, eyes closed, blind-drunk from the rum. His friend sat near him, looking droopy-eyed into the traffic. I heard music coming from a radio nearby:

*My heart goes sha-la la-la-la, sha la-la in the morning.*

Well, this must be their way of having fun, I figured, and maybe they are having a ripping time. Who am I to say? Me, with my cognac pretensions? Maybe they are having fun, blind-drunk in the noonday sun, and maybe I am the one who is in agony, pretending to be something I'm not, searching for something and coming halfway around the world to find it. Who am I to say?

"Long live, Tanduay," I muttered as I walked by.

Back at the hotel, Liza had called. There was a note saying she'd be coming by at 4 p.m., in about two hours. Perfect. I'd have time to relax a bit before my goddess would appear. I flick on the TV, lie down on the bed and have a little rest. It felt good to finally spread my limbs out and diffuse my weight. The queen-sized bed was medium-soft and very comfortable, and I felt like I was floating. The air conditioner whirred and the jeepneys chugged by outside my window. Every now and then, the cock-a-doodle-doo of a rooster would punctuate the symphony of machine noises.

I was in the Philippines again, and I loved it. I loved the thought of being there. I loved the thought that my dream girl would soon be next to me, warm and smiling. I loved who I was at that moment. I loved every second of it.

The room was still pleasantly warm. The air conditioner whirred on, and its rotating fan sent a kiss of cool air in my direction every 15 seconds or so. Can life be any better than this? My thoughts spun away to a distant memory, my tight muscles fell limp, my weight dropped out from under my body, and sleep, blessed sleep, descended like an angel.

About two hours later, the phone rang. It was one of the hotel receptionists.

"Mr. Estrada? Miss Trujillo just called, and said she is on the way now."

"Okay, thanks."

The two-hour nap helped a little, but I was still feeling a bit groggy. I lay on my back a few minutes, imagining what I would say to her, imagining how she might look now, seven months later. Would she still be as dewy and fresh and delicate? Of course, she would. I got up, looked in the mirror, messed with my hair a bit, and put on my shoes.

Waiting in the lobby downstairs, I struck up a conversation with a hefty man from Singapore. He was in Cebu on business, he said. His wife was back home.

"Do you go out at night?" he asked me.

"What?"

"Do you go to clubs at night? You know, the clubs."

"No, not really. My fiancée and I go out to restaurants and such. But she doesn't really like discos."

Mr. Business Singapore laughed at that. He spotted his friend coming down the stairs and excused himself. He said he'd like it if I accompanied them to a club sometime. I said maybe, and he laughed again. I wasn't quite sure what he found so funny.

After a few minutes, Liza arrived. And she was a vision, an immaculate, stunning, breathtaking vision.

She wore a shiny black, form-fitting shirt blouse, tucked into a pair of very tight jeans. Her smallish, delicate derriere nearly burst from beneath the seams. She was carrying that big, black leather bag I had seen her with in the early pictures she'd sent to me. Her black hair was glowing and straight, well down past her bust now. And one of her elfin earlobes poked out from beneath her hair, giving her the look of a sexy brown imp.

As she walked to me, smiling, glowing, I could see there was now a bit of a shake in her walk, a bit more self-confidence, perhaps? With the blackness of her blouse and hair, the immodesty of her jeans and the sassiness of her gait, she reminded me of the sexy Mexican girls I used to know in high school. The kind the white guys lusted over but couldn't have unless they wanted to risk getting knifed in the parking lot one day by some jealous pachuco badass.

Liza was moving in slow motion now, and her brown skin glowed, her teeth shot beams of eternity in all directions as she moved closer.

"Hello, my darling," I said.

She threw her arms around me and kissed me hard.

"I missed you so much," she said softly. I could see it in the moistness of her eyes, in the way she clung on to me, and the way she took my hand, that she really, really meant it. She had missed me terribly. She loves me.

"Good afternoon, ma'am," one of the girls behind the reception desk called out. Liza shot her one of her disarming smiles—unfamiliar with being on the receiving end of a "ma'am"—and we then we headed upstairs, arm in arm.

Safely tucked in my room, we held each other and kissed passionately for what seemed like hours. Still weary from the flight and severely sleep-deprived, and not wanting, of course, to be rude, I backed off her and just stared into her dewy eyes for a few moments.

"God, you are beautiful," I said softly.

"Oh no, not beautiful," she said almost ritualistically. At that moment, I realized that maybe Filipino girls are trained to respond modestly like this when someone declares how pretty they are. It had to be so in Liza's case, because how could she not be aware of how beautiful she was? How could she not know?

"I'm just average," she smiled. "You are the one who is *guwapo*."

I was at a loss for words momentarily, and she laughed at my hesitation. Or maybe the laugh was the result of a private joke she shared with herself. I remember that laugh from before. It wasn't really a full-out laugh. It was more of a soft expulsion of air from the back of her throat that rushed along the upper ridge of her mouth and whooshed past her smiling lips. I remember that laugh from the few times she called me "darling" on the phone, as if she had caught herself saying something strange and alien, or as if that private joke was tickling her again.

"You are my *guwapong tambok nga laki* (handsome, fat man)," she said, laughing hard this time.

"Tambok? I'm not tambok!"

"Not not so tambok, but compared to most Filipinos, you are tambok!"

I grabbed the folds of my belly and shook them defiantly at her. She laughed even more. OK, I was slightly overweight, if 180 pounds was overweight for a man 5-foot-8 inches tall. And I had a couple of layers of skin cushioning an abdomen that just a few years ago was sharp and ripped and chiseled from daily Nautilus workouts.

The daily workouts ended when graduate school had begun. The mind was now chiseled, but the belly was a bit flabby. Liza didn't seem to care, so what difference did it make?

I pulled a can of Coke out of the refrigerator and offered it to her. "Thirsty?"

"No, I cannot drink that. I can't drink Coca Cola. My stomach is sensitive."

"Really?"

"I can't drink tea or coffee either. My stomach..." She rubbed her belly area and laughed.

She hadn't told me this before, or maybe she had but I didn't remember. She was sensitive to caffeine. I said nothing, but I took quick inventory of my own caffeine consumption, which consisted of three cups of coffee at breakfast and several diet Cokes throughout the day.

"Mango," she said.

"What?"

"Maybe you can give me mango juice."

"Oh yes, of course." I remembered how, during my first visit, Liza always reflexively ordered mango juice whenever we went out for a meal. There was a can of mango juice in the refrigerator. I put the Coke back in and took out two cans of juice.

"Good idea, Liza. I think I'll have one too."

She smiled at that, and gladly took a can. I thought back to the mangoes of my youth, and how my mother introduced me to this tropical delight.

Mangoes, shaped like small melons, are the sweetest and most luscious of the fruit of the islands, with a full, deep, flavor that explodes in your mouth. Some say that the creamy yellow-orange flesh of the mango tastes like peach, orange and pineapple combined, but that's not quite right. The texture of a ripe mango is more lush than ripe Georgia peaches, and there is a bit of a sassy-tart backbite that tantalizes the palate, making you crave more. When perfectly ripe, the mango takes on a soft, velvety texture and its juice glides sensuously down your throat with a loving, lingering embrace.

The mango is perhaps the most delicious and most luscious of the world's fruits.

Mangoes were first grown in Asia, and the Philippines is one of the major producers of this delicacy. I had tasted the mangoes in the United States, which are mostly grown in Florida. But somehow, the mangoes of Cebu tasted better. We slaked our thirsts like savages, wiped our faces with our sleeves and laughed.

Oh, how right this was. To be with this girl, at this place, at this time, sipping God's nectar and caring nothing for civility.

I pulled her to me and kissed her mouth, and she kissed me back, our tongues pushing and lapping and probing; then I covered her frail neck with kisses and lost myself in the scent of her hair. I heard her sigh softly and felt her back arch. She rolled her neck and let her head drop backward and sighed again and I kissed her neck more. She was letting me into her world—all the way into her world.

And so it was that I pulled off her clothes, and then slipped out of mine. And as our bodies melted into one, we knew that this was perhaps the most perfect moment of our lives.

Hours later, it had grown dark. We lay in bed, still naked, still locked in a full-body embrace, and listened to the sounds of the city outside. We hadn't left the hotel. We hadn't gotten out of bed, so lost were we in our love.

Every now and then I would plant a kiss on her cheek or her neck. Or I would move further down and she would squeal as if it tickled. Or I would linger at her breasts and lap around her nipples or pull at them playfully with my lips. Liza arched her back and sighed.

"I've been dreaming about these."

"What?" She opened her eyes.

"I've been dreaming about these for a long time. Your breasts. I've been dreaming about them."

"You are crazy."

"No, really. Just last night I was dreaming about your breasts, how beautiful they would be. And they are very beautiful."

"They're small."

"No, no, they're just right. See?" I cupped one in my hand. "Perfect fit!"

Liza laughed. "But American women have big breasts."

"Yeah, but they're too big. Too much. I can't hold it all in one hand, like this."

Liza thought that was hilarious, and she laughed for a full minute. Then I started kissing her nipples again.

"I can't stop kissing them. I've been thinking about them for so long."

"Hmmmm, what do they taste like?"

"What, your breasts?"

"Yes, what's the taste?"

"Mangoes. They taste like mangoes."

Liza laughed her sweet little laugh, and I laughed too, at how clever I was.

I kept on kissing her, and couldn't stop, and as the minutes passed, Liza's sighs blended in with the choking coughs of the jeepneys outside, and the honks of the passing cars, and the whirr of the air-con. And as our bodies pressed closer together, and as I kissed her again and again, on her lips, her neck, her breasts, her stomach, her thighs, her feet, and as I lost myself in the coconut scent of her hair, and as I lingered on the tender softness of all her secret places, I knew that I would never be happier than this.

I remember waking up some time later, and Liza was lying on her back now, the topsheet covering her up to her neck. She stared upward silently, thinking. I wondered if she was hungry. We'd been in bed for almost five hours, and dinnertime had come and passed. I was famished, and I imagined she was too.

"Are you hungry. You want to go have dinner?" I asked.

"No, I'm not too hungry. About you?"

"Yes, I'm very hungry."

"OK, *sige*."

We lay there a few moments more without moving.

"I'm sorry we spent so much time here," I said, breaking the silence. "You probably wanted to go out, and we end up here for five hours."

"Yeah, but we enjoy," she said. She smiled and closed her eyes.

I loved her for saying that, and I felt I should kiss her again. But this time my stomach was the organ ruling my brain, so I bounced out of bed and started to get dressed. Liza got out of bed too, but covered herself modestly with the white sheet. She picked up her clothes, laughed naughtily and headed toward the bathroom.

"Hey, why are you covering yourself?" I kidded her. "I already saw it."

She seemed embarrassed by my little joke, and she shot me a "don't say that" look as she closed the bathroom door.

A $1 cab ride got us to the Lighthouse, about a mile away from the hotel. The Lighthouse was turning out to be our favorite restaurant. The security guard at the front opened the taxi door and politely said, "Good evening, sir; good evening, ma'am," as we walked past. That trained Filipino servility again, I figured. Just another part of the deep culture, so much so that it was part of the ambiance, part of the air. I'd lost count of how many times I'd been called "sir" during my brief visits. Probably double the amount that I'd been called "sir" in the past five years in America.

The blind musicians were still there, and they were onstage performing a forced, Spanish-flavored version of *And I Love Her*. The singer's Filipino accent was charming.

*I gib her all my lub*
*Dat's all I do-oo*

*And ip you saw my lub*
*You'd lub her too*
*I lub her*

Nobody in the room except me noticed his mangling of the words, for all Filipinos speak English like this, turning the F's into P's, softening the V's into B's, crunching This into Dis. It was natural to the ears of all Filipinos to hear English spoken this way. All Filipinos, that is, who are Filipino and not American like me.

I sat at the table and laughed to myself. I thought of my mother and my father, and how after three decades in the U.S., they still talked like this, even up to the days they died. I remember how I, as a school child, used to talk like this until my American teachers humiliated me into correcting my pronunciations.

"Why? What's wrong?" Liza asked. "Why you laugh?"

The way she said "laugh" was more like "lap." I noticed that now as we sat in the Lighthouse, listening to this band of blind musicians, charmingly mangling one of my favorite Beatles ballads.

"Nothing," I said, "It's nothing. I just love the way you speak English."

"Huh? Why? I have a very poor grammar."

"No, I love the way Filipinos speak English. I love it. It's so—adorable!"

"No, my English is very bad."

"No, it's fine. I understand you perfectly."

"I have a very poor grammar." Liza looked down, as if ashamed. She had nothing to be ashamed about. She was beautiful. I loved her creamy brown skin, the way her long straight hair fell over her breasts, her dewy, welcoming eyes, her vulnerable smile. As I looked at her, I fell in love for the 1005th time.

"Don't worry," I said. "After you come to the States, you will pick up English very easily, and it will get better. Just watch TV a lot, maybe take an English class at night school, and we'll be speaking English all the time at home. Don't worry. Your English will improve very quickly."

I reached across the table and patted her shoulder. She looked up at me for a moment, and looked down again. I decided to change the subject.

"How many children shall we have?"

"What?" She perked up and was smiling now.

"How many children? Two, three?"

"You? How many you want. It's up to you."

"No, it should be our decision, not just mine. How many children should we have?"

She was laughing now. "Oh, maybe two or three. That's just right."

"One boy and one girl maybe."

"Yah, I like that. Two kids or three. Or maybe one. What you want?"

I beamed at her across the table. I thought about how beautiful our children would be, and smart. And they would have the best of everything because they would grow up in America.

"I want eight children. How about eight?" I blurted out.

Liza's eyes nearly popped out of their sockets. "Hngh! Eight!?!"

I laughed, letting her know it was just a joke. I wanted eight children as much as I wanted eight Ph.D.s. One would be fine. Two or three and we could have a happy little committee! I laughed to myself. Liza stopped laughing and looked down.

"You know, George, my mother is here."

"Here? Where? In this restaurant?" I whirled around to look at the other diners.

"No, in my home. She came last night and surprised me. I don't know she was coming."

"Oh, she came from the province to visit you?"

"Yah. She's waiting for me."

"She's waiting for you to come home? Doesn't she know that you're with me?"

"Yah, she knows I'm with you."

"Well, why didn't we invite her to join us for dinner?"

Liza looked horrified by that thought. "Oh no, she don't like to go out to restaurants. She's ashamed."

"Why?"

"Too much. Too fancy."

"What?"

"She don't like to be out. She don't like restaurant. She's a simple woman, just a poor woman. You know, she has a lot of pride. She don't want people to look at her and judge her."

I shrugged. "Well, let's at least order some food, so we can take it to her later."

"Yah, OK." Liza liked that idea. She always thought of her mother, always thought of sharing things with her. She is such a sweet daughter, I thought to myself. They have such a close family. Liza will be a great mother one day. "She's just home waiting for me."

Dinner came soon enough. Liza ordered some kind of fish soup, which I sampled and rather liked. It had a zingy tartness to it. I had my usual chicken and pork adobo (meat with tangy-sweet sauce), some barbecued beef thing on a skewer and some ampalaya (bitter melon) salad. There was also a huge bowl of rice, of course, and Liza and I had a wonderful feast.

"Is it good?" I asked Liza when she sipped on the watermelon shakes I ordered.

"Sarap! *(Tasty!)*" She slurped hers down quickly, as if she'd never tasted anything so good, and I ordered a couple more.

Her temporary delight soon passed and Liza started hanging her head again. She fell silent for a long time. I sensed something was bothering her, and I kept on trying to get her to talk about it, but she would insist that nothing was wrong.

The band had stopped playing. And now some happy pop music was playing over the PA system.

*My heart goes sha-la-la-la-la, la-la-la in the morning.*

"I have a problem," Liza finally said something.

"What?" I asked. What could possibly be wrong in the midst of all this happiness?

"My mother," Liza said. "She's always crying."

"What? Why?"

"She don't me to leave. She don't want me to leave the Philippines."

"Ah, so this is the problem. But she knows we're engaged, right? You're going to have a good future with me in America."

"Yes, she knows, but she keeps on crying."

"But you've got other brothers and sisters. They'll still be here…Oh, don't tell me you're her favorite."

"Yes, it's true. I'm her favorite."

Oh great. My dream girl is a mama's girl. We sat and said nothing for a few moments while the band took the stage to start their second set.

"Well, would you like me to talk to her?" I asked. "I can assure her that I'll take good care of you, and everything will be all right. Come on, let's go talk to her."

"No, no," Liza said. "Don't worry about it. I'll take care of it."

"Good," I said, seeing the firm resolve in her eyes. "Good. You make sure you tell her that you've made up your mind and you're coming to America to marry me. You're a grown woman, Liza, and you can make your own decisions."

"Yes, I know. Don't worry. I'll take care of it."

And so it was that while I sat enjoying my watermelon shake and looking into the eyes of my beloved, I started to sense that there was trouble in paradise.

# 18

## *The Voice of America*

Everything had been perfect so far. But now it turns out that Liza's mother is always crying. Great! I needed to trust that Liza would handle this. And I knew she would. She had a whole new world to gain by asserting her will on her mother, who was obviously tunnel-visioned and overly sentimental. Didn't she know that this was best for Liza? Didn't she know what Liza would gain by coming to America and marrying me? It was a can't-lose proposition, and Liza needed to communicate this effectively to her mother.

I also needed to communicate more effectively with Liza. These visits during my school breaks were nice, but we needed to have consistent, regular communication because we had paperwork, crying mothers and other obstacles to overcome before we could realize our goal.

I had been continually frustrated by our lack of consistent contact while I was in America. Liza didn't have a phone in her boarding house and didn't know how to—or didn't want to know how to—use email. I didn't want to keep leaving messages for her at the SM consignor's office, and I didn't want to send emails through third parties. I also couldn't bear the delays of international snail mail.

So here, during my second visit to Cebu, I decided to do something about it. I would buy Liza a phone. Not a regular phone with a land line. I'd heard that it sometimes takes months on a waiting list before the Philippine phone company would install one for you. And I certainly didn't want to have to bribe a phone company official to expedite the installation, which is what some people in Cebu recommended.

The answer, clearly, was a cellular phone. I'd seen them on sale at the SM mall, and I often saw teens sporting designer phones in wild, garish colors. I figured that if teens had them, so should Liza. I figured that I could afford to buy one for Liza and pay her phone bills as long as we limited ourselves.

And so it was that Liza and I went to SM and bought her the first phone she'd ever owned—an AT&T model cell phone and a PhonePal card to activate it and keep it ready for my calls from America.

Liza was beaming as we examined the phone. She caressed it and examined it and held it to her like a cherished object. This was a big day for her, I could see, and she was radiant. She was happy to receive this miraculous thing, this talisman that summoned the divine electronic winds of cellular signals, winds that would deliver Liza's light across the oceans to my lonely home in America; this black glowing thing that could harness these divine winds and carry our voices across the seas, and into our ears, and into our minds, and into our souls, where they would caress each other and never let go. The cellular phone Liza clutched in her hands this day was a bringer of such divinity, I reckoned, and it was just what we needed to keep our dreams on track.

I was happy I could give her this magic, happy that I could now call her and talk with her whenever the need arose, happy that I had the power to deliver miracles to her.

I tried calling her new cell number later from my hotel room. The phone worked perfectly. We both sat in wonder at the prospect that we could actually speak with one another now on the phone anytime we pleased. This simple thing, this convenience that most of us Americans take for granted, was now a miracle that would transform our lives.

I was happy to deliver the modern/postmodern age to this poor girl from the provinces. I felt good about that. It felt good to be financially able to give such gifts of magic to the girl of my dreams. It felt good to be liquid.

After several wonderful days and nights in Cebu, it was time for me to get back to California. Liza and Jessica accompanied me to Cebu-Mactan International for my trip home. As we sat in an airport restaurant waiting for my flight to board, I slipped Liza a roll of pesos—a little over 10,000 pesos, roughly equivalent to $213. I gave Jessica about 4,000 pesos.

"Here's another present for you," I said to them both. "You need some new shoes." I had given them similar amounts at the end of my first visit last January.

"You're too much," Liza said, her eyes getting even more moist than they usually were. "You gave me too much already." Jessica just looked at the rolled-up wad of money in her hand and smiled.

"No, I want you to have this," I said. "I've got plenty of money, and you don't. Besides, Liza, you need this for your trip to Manila for your visa interview at the embassy, right? You've got to pay for airplane flights, taxis, jeepney rides, application fees, all of that. Just put it in the bank. Or buy yourself something nice, or whatever. There's more where that came from. Please take it. You need it more than I do."

I remembered one other thing: "Also, you need it to buy another phone card when the one you have runs out, right?"

"Yah."

"Ahhhh, hah, you better not use your new phone to flirt with boys."

Jessica found this hilarious, but Liza didn't. "No, no," she said. "No flirting. No way." Jessica continued laughing, but put her hand over her mouth to suppress herself.

The flight home again was on Cathay Pacific and again, we stopped at Hong Kong, where I had a layover of several hours. Then it was on to LA and San Francisco.

The flight to LA was rather uneventful. I had the same variety of stewards and stewardesses who looked Chinese, but spoke with British accents. Again, I chalked it up to the longtime British presence in Hong Kong. No matter how many times I heard it, it was still jarring. My mind wanted to hear the sing-song Chinese-American accent, but instead I got British words and phrases like "smashing," "right then" and "straightaway," all inflected in an Oxfordian way. Charming and interesting, but it took some getting used to.

At the LA airport, I waited and waited for my luggage, but it didn't show up. The airline had lost it. I was a bit surly from sleep deprivation and lost luggage, so I was not at all in the mood for the customs agent who picked me out of a moving crowd and demanded that I come to his station for luggage inspection.

"They lost my luggage," I complained to the agent.

"Yeah, yeah, OK," he said. "Let's have a look at your carry-ons."

This customs agent was hard and nasty, not at all like the customs agents I'd encountered in San Francisco. Maybe he wanted to inspect my gear because I looked like the type who would be smuggling some Philippine gold or opium from Hong Kong. Worse, maybe I was a child pornographer bringing home hundreds of videos and pictures from Thailand.

As he eyeballed my passport and emptied the contents of my luggage, he asked me questions about where I live, what kind of job I have, where I'd been on this trip and why I'd been traveling. His tone was harsh and commanding, not at all casual and jovial, like the tone of the San Francisco customs agents.

I got the feeling this LA punk was checking out my accent to see if I was indeed an American or some clever wetback who'd figured out a new scam for getting into the States. He was listening for a slight trill in my r's or maybe soft pronunciations of hard vowels to give away a core of Hispanicized speech patterns. I decided I didn't like this guy very much, but I also figured that it'd be best for me to play along with his officious little bullshit game. I also spoke in perfect English, with perfect pronunciations—just to ruin his day.

He emptied my luggage of all the clothes and delicate souvenirs I'd carefully packed. He suspiciously eyed a bag of candied bananas and asked me to explain precisely what the contents were.

"Well," I said. "Let me read the ingredients list to you. It says here, bananas, sugar, corn syrup…"

"Yeah, yeah, OK, I can read. It just looked a little funny, that's all. So what do you teach?"

"What?"

"You said you were a university professor. What do you teach?"

How was this relevant? How was this germane in any way imaginable to my gaining re-entrance into my home country?

"I teach journalism at Humboldt State University. I can show you a business card, if you'd like, or my faculty ID card."

"No, no, that's fine. So I notice in your passport that you've been to the Philippines twice this year. Any particular reason for that?"

"Yes. I was born there, so it's my ancestral homeland. Also, my fiancée lives there."

"Your fiancée? Did you meet her here or over there?"

This was going way too far. This arrogant little roundhead had no business asking me these questions. I decided to just play it cool, although I figured it appropriate to inject a little attitude in my voice now, a little impatience with this ridiculousness.

"If you want to know the truth, sir, I first met her on the Internet."

"Oh, really? And now you're engaged to be married?"

"Yes."

He laughed a condescending kind of laugh, shrugged and said, "OK, go on." He dismissed me with a wave of his hand, leaving my clothes and souvenirs strewn out on the table, and went back to find another victim to harass.

Welcome to LA, I thought to myself. If all the law officers are like this, I understand perfectly why all those people rioted back in 1992.

I caught my plane flight to San Francisco and after a few days staying at a friend's house in Concord, I finally got my luggage returned to me by an airline baggage courier service. Now it was time to go back home and get ready for the new fall semester, and more classes in beginning reporting, copy editing and magazine writing. But this time, I would have another class to teach—the magazine production workshop that produces the Humboldt State University student magazine, *The Osprey*.

I was about to start my second year at Humboldt State, and this time I wouldn't be teaching a media analysis class like I had the semester before. So it was time for me to take off the invisibility cloak of theory I'd worn and get back to being an in-your-face working journalist. I gave myself a goal: I would turn *The Osprey*, this sleepy little student magazine, into something special, something that mattered. I remembered that the student magazine at the University of Texas had won a number of Robert F. Kennedy Awards for distinguished service, so I decided that *The Osprey* could do the same.

I would give the students a mission—to do important journalism, socially responsible journalism that strikes blows against evil, throws light on dark corners of the world, empowers the powerless, gives voice to the voiceless. And if they could do it, if we could improve the human condition in some small way, and if we were to win an award or two, it's something we all could be proud of. And hey, it looks good on a resume, right?

And so it was that I gave this speech on the first day of class. And so it was that the groaning began.

Not all of them wanted to do socially responsible journalism, it turned out. A couple of staffers wanted to write personal travel stories and publish their travel photos too. Someone wanted to write a light feature piece about a local artist. Someone else wanted to write a fawning profile piece on a rock musician.

And so it was that I repeated the challenge and I told the students to come up with some really serious ideas that we could work with.

One student said she'd like to do a profile piece on a recovering heroin addict. Good! Another said she'd like to do an article about the lack of racial diversity at the university. Another fine idea! Someone else said he'd like to do a piece on students who are single parents, a piece that would describe their struggles and their joys. Another fine idea! More ideas came: a profile of a local church that helps homeless people, a piece about transients who lived on the beach near Arcata, a story about the struggles of minority faculty.

At the end of the day, the staffers who wanted to do fluff pieces got the go-ahead to do them, and the ones who wanted to tackle the more difficult material got the green light too. We had a nice mix of stories, some of them light and airy, but most of them hard and dark.

The important thing was that these were their ideas. The students themselves had come up with them. I had to provide the prodding, of course, and I had to imbue them with a sense of mission. But in the end it would be their stories, their work, their publication. And that's the way it was supposed to be.

The semester flew by, with *Osprey* deadlines, papers to grade from my other classes, and the endless faculty meetings. One night after a particularly grueling day, I needed to relax and get my mind off work for a while, so I popped in a video of the 1989 World Series, to watch the Oakland A's beat the San Francisco Giants again. I'd watched this Game Four tape, oh, about 100 times before, but I needed to watch it again. I turned the sound down to barely audible and lay down on my couch.

Even though I had a lot of work to do, I needed to unwind a bit. I also loved to watch this game because it reminded me of my days in the Bay Area and of the A's and their past glory. The A's hadn't done too well last season, mainly because they had traded Mark McGwire, their great homerun-hitting first baseman, and were trying to rebuild their team. They had some interesting new players, including a young power-hitting first baseman named Jason Giambi. He'll never replace McGwire, I reckoned, but he seemed to have a decent stroke. But it was agonizing watching them lose. On this World Series video, they never lost, and that's why I loved it so much.

Filipinos hate to lose.

I'd been an A's fan ever since they moved to Oakland from Kansas City in 1968. And I became even more of a fan when I nabbed a homerun ball in the left field bleachers that first season, a homer hit by Sal Bando, one of the young players on the team and a clutch hitter who would lead the A's to three consecutive World Series championships in 1972, '73 and '74. I was only 15 years old in 1968, and here I had one of baseball's greatest treasures, a homerun ball, in my sweaty teenage hands.

I've held that ball close to me all my life like a holy relic that brings good fortune. There was magic in that ball, I reckoned. And what a perfect symbol of America—a baseball. A homerun ball yet! Hit by a champion! And hit to me! And now I have it in my life. And it brings all good things to me. And this thing symbolizes who I am. And it symbolizes the force that will bring Liza to me—the force that is America. It brings opportunities, it brings fortune, it brings abundance. You can have all these things too, Liza. All you have to do is plant your feet, see the pitch, swing hard and hit it on the sweet spot. And if you hit it good enough and hard enough, your dreams can come true and you can run around the bases like a young colt that is happy to be alive, happy to breathe the fresh air of new life, and you can run like the wind to your new home, and all your friends and family will be there to greet you and hug you and kiss you. And everyone will love you and cherish you and you will never suffer from want.

Ah, baseball. I love all the cheesy analogies you can draw from it. America is the place where you can hit a homerun, Liza. Let me bring you here! Let it be soon!

My reverie was interrupted by a phone call. It was Liza. What a surprise! She had something important to tell me. Oh, no!

"What is it, Liza?"

"Well, remember I told you that I went to college in Manila for 1 1/2 years?"

"Yes."

"Also, do you remember I told you that I had a boyfriend there? A boy from my home province?"

"Uh-huh."

"And we broke up after he joined the merchant marines."

"Right…and so what are you trying to tell me, Liza?"

"He, he visited me yesterday at work. His name is Wilson. He surprised me at work."

"Oh?" I was getting a little agitated. "What did he want?"

"He wants to get back together with me," Liza said, her voice dropping significantly in volume.

"Oh, he does, does he?" I was now very agitated. "I thought he left you. And you hadn't seen him for what, one year? Two years? And now he appears out of nowhere and he wants you to come back to him?"

"He is my first boyfriend."

"What? Yes, so what? I have very fond recollections of my first girlfriend too. But if she showed up out of the blue, I wouldn't want to get back together with her."

"You don't understand. In the Philippines, a girl's first boyfriend is very special."

Silence.

"And so now what?" I asked. "Did you tell him about me? About us?"

"Yah, I did. Yes, yes. But he won't accept it. He cried when I told him about you, and he said he won't accept it."

"He won't accept it?? What the hell does that mean?"

"It means he won't give up. He won't accept that we are engaged. He proposed marriage to me, and he says he won't give up. I don't know what to do."

Oh, great. Now we have a spurned boyfriend to deal with, along with a crying mother. I was getting more agitated by the minute. Also, I was still facing the prospect of grading a stack of papers.

"Liza, sometimes life comes down to one important moment," I started dramatically, "one critical moment, in which you make a life decision that will affect every moment of the rest of your life; a moment that is so utterly filled with profundity that..."

"Hah?"

"OK, never mind. Listen to this: You have to make a choice. I love you, I've proposed to you and you accepted. I've spent a lot of money and time on our relationship. It's time for you to make up your mind. Is it going to be me or him? Who are you going to marry? It's time to choose."

Pause. Silence. More silence. This was taking a little too long. Nine, ten, eleven. "Well? Liza!? What is your choice?"

"You," Liza declared. "I want you!"

I sighed.

"Are you sure now?"

"Yes, of course," she declared forcefully. "I told you already I love you. I want to marry you."

It felt good to hear those words. It especially felt good to hear her say them with such assuredness. I was happy. I'd won. Filipinos hate to lose.

"OK, you need to tell Wilson that you've made up your mind, and nothing can change it. Tell him to leave you alone. Tell him if he doesn't leave you alone that I've going to personally come to the Philippines and hurt him."

She seemed shocked by my sudden surge of violence, but I told her quickly enough that I was just joking and she calmed down.

"Can you handle it, Liza? Can you tell him this and make him go away? Or do you need some help? I can come help if you'd like."

"No, no," she replied quickly. "I'll take care of it."

"Are you sure?"

"Yes, don't worry. I'll take care of it."

"So, it's Liza and George, right? Not Liza and Wilson?"

She laughed. "Yah, Liza and George forever. Don't worry, I'll take care of it."

I sat for a moment and contemplated the situation. Who is this guy, Wilson? And where does he get the name Wilson? His parents probably named him after the President Woodrow Wilson, I reckoned. That would be so like Filipino parents, to name their son after an American president. I laughed and thought about my father and what he must have felt when he named me George.

My thoughts quickly returned to Liza. Why did she seem to hesitate when I demanded that she declare her choice then and there? Was she put off by my direct and confrontational manner? Or was she stopping to seriously consider her choices? Would she really take him over me?

Maybe she was thinking about her comfortable future, her abundant new life in America, with the new house and the new cars and whatever hubby could buy with a university professor's credit line. And maybe she was thinking about life as the spouse of a Filipino merchant marine who was gone from home several months out of the year, and who might have secret girlfriends in other port towns, and who could provide no more than a meager existence for his family back home.

Maybe she was thinking about what life would be in America, surrounded by aliens, by people who speak English. There would be very little Tagalog in her life, except for visits with my family and watching whatever Philippine videos I could get. And there certainly would be no Cebuano, aside from the occasional, rare encounter with an immigrant from Cebu. There might be one or two Cebuanos in all of Humboldt County.

What a trade she'd have to make. Her home culture, her family, the familiar—for a strange, new land, a new American family, and the mysteries of the New World. Could she make that trade? Could the island natives of 450 years ago trade their land, their deep culture, for Ferdinand Magellan's firesticks, herbs and gimmicks? Could she trade family loyalty for the white god's promises of prosperity and science? Was she that brave and that bold enough? This was the trade that I'd made, when I gave up my frail Filipino self to become a strong, full-bodied, meat-eating American. And this is the trade that a lot of immigrants to America make every day—to abandon the old ways for the new, to escape the darkness of deep culture and the ghosts of the past, to seek the rainbow of fortune. Could she make such a trade? Could a dewy, delicate little creature confront the roaring beast that is this savage land?

Well, I was proud of her because she did. She chose me. She chose America. And God bless her for being smart enough and brave enough and bold enough to do so. Her courage under fire will be rewarded. The lady of light had decided to follow the light.

I tried to visualize what life would be like with Liza here, so I could verbalize these things to her and reinforce the idea that she would be coming to the U.S. I thought about her lying on my big white futon, watching TV with me. Would she like baseball? I thought of the two of us walking hand in hand in the Arcata Community Forest, looking up in wonder at all the big trees. I thought of the two of us walking along the beach in Trinidad, staring out at sea and trying to find the exact southwest compass point at which our sight line would connect with the Philippines.

Maybe she would like to play bingo, so I could take her to the Native American casino up here, Cher-Ae Heights. Would you like that, Liza? Or maybe you'd like to go fishing or camping or kayaking or something in the great outdoors. And there certainly is enough of that up here. If you wanted to go shopping we have one big mall up here. So even though you'll be living in a beautiful rural area, there are a lot of big-city amenities up here to make life comfortable. To help you understand, it would be like living in a province but living in a house with electricity, phones, TVs, VCRs, a washing machine, and all the other things we Americans need to fill our lives.

And if you need a dose of an actual big city, we could drive south for six hours and end up in Oakland, Berkeley or San Francisco. Or we could drive north and end up in Portland or Seattle or even Vancouver, British Columbia.

Liza was fascinated with these ideas, hypnotized by these images. I could sense the resolve in her voice. She would take care of this little problem named Wilson and then we could proceed with the beautiful future that's been laid out before us. As we talked, the 1989 World Series video kept on running on my living room TV.

The A's would win on the World Series video—again—but in real time their fortunes weren't so good. The team hadn't been playing well since they traded Mark McGwire. They were re-building, and they couldn't afford him any more. Loyalty had given way to economic realities. I immediately saw some irony in this.

Was I compelling Liza to be like the A's? Would she sacrifice loyalty to economic realities.

The thought amused me. I thought of Liza wearing an A's cap and I smiled a big smile. Then we started talking about the fiancée visa application and my smile started to fade.

The application was finished and had been submitted to the proper authorities last September, right after my second trip to the Philippines. But, here it was April and the deal still wasn't done. We'd been waiting for months for the final bit of paperwork from the U.S. Embassy, but it had not yet arrived. It was overdue. I knew from my research that the Embassy in Manila, after receiving our application, would send this extra paperwork for Liza to fill out, and then after she returned it, they would send her an appointment time for a medical exam and an interview. But we were stuck waiting for this second batch of forms.

"Maybe it's at the post office," she said. "I'll check tomorrow." I somehow doubted it, but figured it was worth a try.

Liza called me the next evening and told me that, yes indeed, the paperwork had been held up at the post office. The postman had tried to deliver it, but apparently couldn't find Liza's boarding house, tucked away as it was in the back of an alley. Or maybe the postman was scared away by all the disheveled, drunken, cursing men who usually populated the alley. Or maybe someone told the postman that Liza didn't live there. Liza never received mail at her home, only at the Shoe Mart department store office. We should have specifically requested that the Embassy mail this stuff to SM, but they had mailed it to the home address on her bio sheet.

Whatever. In any event, the packet from the Embassy had been sitting in the post office for a month, Liza discovered. That was another month lost, thanks this time to the ineptitude of the Philippine post office and our failure to ask the Embassy to mail the packet to her work address.

Liza said she was terribly confused by some of the questions on the Embassy documents, and we agreed that it would probably be best to wait until I came to Cebu, a month later, to fill out this last bit of paperwork. It was important that we get it done exactly right. That would be ANOTHER month lost, but at this point, I just threw my hands up in the air and figured, what the hell! Let's just get it done right. I was not pleased with the constant delays—it was almost a year since she accepted my proposal and here we were still waiting for a visa—but I was happy that we had averted a major disaster through Liza's persistence. It also helped that I'd bought her a cell phone, so she could keep me immediately informed of all these developments.

*Osprey*, the student magazine, finally came out just after our Thanksgiving break, and it looked good. The cover was foreboding and dark, depicting a homeless man sitting and waiting for a meal at a transient shelter. The centerpiece of the magazine was the article about the recovering heroin addict who lived in Eureka, a shocking, evocative and very touching piece written by staffer Abigail Hudson-Crim, who spent many hours interviewing her subject and doing research about heroin, its history, its biological properties and the assistance programs available to recovering users. It was a complete, fully realized article, and I was so proud of her and the *Osprey* editors for pulling it all together.

The other stories in the magazine showed the type of enterprise and humanity that makes for the best journalism. There was stark reality and uplifting life lessons aplenty in these stories, and the magazine, in my opinion, was better than any other student magazine I'd ever seen.

Most of the students agreed, and so did the faculty, but I did hear some residual grousing from some of the staffers, who felt that I had imposed my will on the students. They wanted to write what THEY wanted to write, and all this stuff about shining lights on dark corners and striking blows against evil was just a bunch of crap. I guess you just can't please everybody, no matter how hard you try.

At the conclusion of the term, I started preparing for my third and, I hoped, final trip to the Philippines. This time, we'd get it right.

A friend of mine knew someone who'd suffered delays in trying to obtain a fiancée visa and had turned to one of the U.S. senators in California to intercede. The tactic had apparently worked because he'd obtained the visa for his fiancée a short time later. And so I decided to send a letter to Senator Barbara Boxer's office to see if I could somehow get our case expedited. I wasn't looking for special treatment. I just wanted to make sure we were not the victims of some unnecessary delays.

Just two days before I left Arcata for my third trip to the Philippines, I got a letter from Boxer's office saying that they'd contacted the U.S. Embassy in Manila, and they were assured that that our case would be handled properly as soon as they received the final bit of paperwork from Liza. That was cool! Nothing like a little nudge to move the machine.

It occurred to me that the key to success was all in the little nudges. I nudged a few professors and got a Ph.D. out of it. I nudged a couple of universities and got a great job out of it. I nudged my students and got a good magazine out of it. Now I nudged a U.S. senator, who nudged the U.S. Embassy in Manila, and VOILA! We have lift off!

That's what life comes down to sometimes, I reckoned. A little nudge-nudge, a little wink-wink, and say no more, say no more.

And so it was that, at this moment, nothing could bother me one bit—not arrogant customs officers, not rebellious student journalists, not crying mothers and spurned suitors, not the bad play of my favorite baseball team. Nothing!

I was wholly, completely satisfied with myself. Not only was I preciously clever, but I also had a beautiful fiancée who was going to join me soon. What could be better than that?

The divine wind blew in over Humboldt Bay and the rains didn't stop. I finished up the last of my school work and got ready for Christmas break, a third visit to the Philippines, and a final mad dash to the visa-paperwork finish line.

# 19

## *Find A Friend For Me*

It was my third visit to the Philippines in 12 months, and the novelty of it all had worn off.

The six-hour drive from Arcata to the San Francisco Bay Area was getting on my nerves. It was getting on my nerves because it took so long and there was nothing much to do except look at trees. My best coping mechanism was to imagine the future with Liza. Also, I learned how to enjoy the solitude. The farther I drove south, the less I thought about my loneliness up in Arcata and the more my mind turned to thoughts of the Philippines.

I rolled past the infamous town of Garberville, and slowed down as I approach the rock-slide area, a narrow stretch of road carved impossibly out of the side of a steep mountainside. Soon, I headed into the shady wilderness known as Richardson Grove. I always remember Richardson Grove as a place where three friends and I camped in the summer of 1971, shortly after high school graduation, and where rangers found a dead man floating in a river.

Another point on this journey to San Francisco is the town of Willits, with its Skunk Train and its Burger King and its Baechtel Creek Inn and its Taco Bell. There would also be the rolling green hills of Mendocino County, the hot-rich vineyards of Sonoma and the wannabe big city of Santa Rosa.

As I drive through these places, I think of Liza again, and I think of the Philippines. What would she make of all this, having never in her life set foot outside the islands? Would the cities scare her? Would the wide-open country and the high greenery of Humboldt remind her of the provinces?

For much of this journey down the spine of Northern California, until I hit Sonoma County, the only radio station I could pick up was a country-western station. Listening to it out of desperate boredom, I couldn't help but think of Texas. And I thought of the three years I spent in Texas before coming to Humboldt. And I thought about how wide-open the Texas topography seems, but how closed its deep culture was. And I thought about Lauralee, and how her deep culture eventually got to her.

And then I thought about how wide-open the progressive politics seemed to be in green Humboldt County. But I realized how closed off Humboldt seems from the rest of the world—trapped under a canopy of majestic redwoods and gray, damp skies.

And then I thought about the Philippines, and how wide-open its horizon is, the Pacific stretching unto eternity, reaching for everything and nothing at once, reaching deep into the mind of God. But I think of how closed off the Filipino people are, trapped beneath their servitude to power, trapped by the empty promises of Western pop culture, trapped inside the 16th century Spanish convent mentality housing their deepest, deepest culture.

In the Bay Area, I left my pickup truck with a friend in Concord (a suburb northeast of Berkeley). He then gave me a ride to the San Francisco International Airport. He dropped me off at the Philippine Airlines terminal, and I checked in and showed my passport. The counter clerk smile pleasantly because she saw my last name and thought that maybe I was related to President Joseph Estrada. How many times had I been through this routine? I was getting tired of it too. I remained silent and smiled that mango smile. Just let her think what she wants to think, I decided.

I'd chosen a flight that departed near midnight because it would get me to Manila at 5 a.m. or so, Philippine time. Then I'd catch a plane for Cebu a couple of hours later and arrive at a perfectly reasonable 10 a.m.

The trick was to try and get some sleep on the plane. So, once on board, I would make my way to the smoking section in the back, where not too many people wanted to sit. There, I could find a row of three unoccupied seats and stretch out for a nice nap. Of course, I'd be breathing second-hand smoke for several hours, but what the hell! If I was able to sleep for three or four hours or maybe more, I'd feel OK when I arrived in the Philippines.

I hoped this third visit would be my final one. I had the last bit of visa paperwork for Liza and me to fill out. The INS wanted to know where I'd lived in America, so I had to try and remember all of the addresses I'd had since I moved out of my parents' house at the age of 21. Liza also had to report all of the addresses she'd had as an adult. She easily remembered her two addresses in Cebu City, but she had a hard time remembering her address in Manila, where she had gone to college for 1 1/2 years before moving back to Cebu. It was during that time in Manila that she had a brief romance with Wilson, the guy she knew from her province.

There was also a bio sheet that asked her ridiculous questions, like whether she'd been a communist or a terrorist or a prostitute. We both laughed at the prospect of checking the "yes" box on all of them. After finishing the paperwork, we needed to get some photos done for her visa. The INS had some very specific instructions for these photos—they had to be an exact size down to an eighth of an inch, Liza had to be in 3/4 profile, the background had to be a solid color (preferably white or off-white), and the photo had to be printed on special paper stock. Then, for some reason, I also had to have the same thing done for me since I was the official petitioner for the fiancée visa. Finally, when the photos were done, we had to write our names in pencil on the back.

These very specific instructions were all about control. The U.S. government wants to know if you are able to read and understand English, and if you are able and willing to follow ludicrous instructions. Such control is what empires are made of, I explained to Liza.

"Hah?"

Never mind.

While we were at the photo studio, I asked the photographer to go ahead and take some portrait shots with the two of us. You know, "the lovers in love" type of shot that can be enlarged and displayed for all time in a fancy frame. We could make copies and give them all to our friends and relatives.

Corny, yes. But hey, I was really getting into this romance thing. And Liza, of course, thought it was a fine thing to do. Anyway, I was totally in love with this fine young woman from the Philippines and I wanted all the world to see her.

Liza showed up that afternoon with three friends—two young women and one guy—all of whom worked at the mall. They wanted to meet Liza's Fil-Am fiancée they'd heard so much about. They wanted to see what a Fil-Am looked like, what I sounded like, what I smelled like. Would I have a big horn growing out of my forehead? Would I have long green fingers and long blue hair? Would I be violent like they see in the movies? Would I be arrogant and powerful like most American tourists they meet? One fat American man was in the lobby screaming about some service he hadn't received properly. Was I like him? What sort of demon was Liza engaged to?

Again, I felt like I was about to be put on display. I felt like a museum piece. This was becoming a recurring theme.

They looked me over, giggled and chattered to each other in Tagalog. Or was it Cebuano? Or was it some other Philippine dialect? I couldn't keep track any more. I was more than happy to meet with Liza's friends, however, and I graciously invited them to dine with us. On cue, they acted out the Filipino ritual of pretending to be embarrassed at such an offer, and I acted out the ritual of insisting that they join us, and then after more prodding by me and by Liza and after the appropriate amount of hesitation, they finally agreed, and we went into the hotel restaurant at Eddie's Hotel, the Beverly Room.

The waiters made a fuss over us, as they normally did for me, and they sat us down at a long table near the bar. I ordered for us a plate of crispy patas (pork knuckles) and rice for five. As we waited for the food, the excited chatter continued among the friends. And I noticed that the friend of Liza's who was seated directly to my left was eyeing me up and down, really checking me out. Her name was Nancy, she worked at the Ace Hardware in the mall. She was tall for a Filipina—about 5-feet-5—and when she smiled she revealed two long rows of gleaming metal in her mouth. Braces! She must be from a well-off family, I figured, since your average Filipino couldn't afford such a luxury.

We started talking about Americans, specifically about American men who come to the Philippines looking for women.

"Liza is very lucky to find a nice guy like you," said Nancy. "We can't find someone like you here, a Fil-Am who is successful and young and very nice."

"I'm not that young," I said. "I'm 46."

Pause.

"Oh, but you don't look 46. You look maybe 32," said Nancy, her mouth glittering. "And age does not matter. What matters is what is inside your heart, and if you love each other."

This was probably the 100th time I'd heard this—this was the chant, the mantra, the ritual for young Filipina women faced with the prospect of an older foreign man. "Age does not matter," as long as I'm a good guy. Whenever I heard it, it sounded like rationalizing, like something you say to convince yourself that you're doing the right thing. In her calculus, though, I was better than the others because I am a Filipino-American. The Philippines is the only place on Earth I could hear such an assessment, I reckoned. I decided I liked Nancy very much.

Sitting to her left was a young man named Rumel and to his left a young woman named Marites, who also seemed to find me very interesting. Whenever we made eye contact, Marites flashed me a toothy smile.

"Can you find one for me?" Nancy asked.

"What?"

"An American guy like you. You know, a professional, a Fil-Am, a nice guy."

I didn't want to tell her that I didn't know anybody like that who was currently looking for a girl from the Philippines. I didn't want to tell her that successful Fil-Am guys tend to find their mates in the U.S. I didn't want to tell her that many successful Fil-Am guys often went for white American women. I didn't want to tell her that I was once like that too.

"Well, I can try," I told Nancy, knowing full well that the odds were pretty long. She smiled that heavy-metal smile of hers and started to write down her mailing address.

Rumel said something in Tagalog—or was it Cebuano?—and everyone at the table laughed. I assumed that he too was looking for an American friend.

"Yes Rumel, I'll try to see if I can find an American girl for you," I offered, knowing again that this would be extremely difficult. Everyone then laughed again, even more heartily. Liza tugged at my shirt sleeve.

"Rumel just got married," she explained.

"Oh, sorry. Sorry, Rumel." He smiled and nodded and looked away. Moments later Rumel looked at me again, this time with a face that said, well, if you find someone anyway, let me know.

This was another recurring pattern with many of Liza's friends. They all seemed to want to meet an American. They seemed to think that Americans held all the answers to their prayers. They prayed that one day they would escape poverty. An American can help them to do that. An American can remedy their poverty and change their lives almost overnight with two bold strokes—a marriage proposal and a fiancée visa.

Liza's friends are not alone in their search for well-to-do foreigners. I remember reading a study by the U.S. Immigration and Naturalization Service, which noted that there were more than 200 international matchmaking services offering as many as 150,000 women annually from all over the world in newsletters, magazines and Internet-based penpal clubs. According to the study, a great majority of these women are from Southeast Asia and the former Soviet Union.

One of these services, Cherry Blossoms, lists more than 6,000 women at any given moment—and more than half of them are from the Philippines.

The government study analyzed five popular catalogs featuring 14,000 Asian women, and found that 70 percent were from the Philippines. Of these Filipinas, 20 percent were 16 to 20 years old; 41 percent were 21 to 25; and 24 percent were 26 to 30. Cumulatively then, 61 percent were 25 or younger, and 85 percent were 30 or younger.

The study found that these Filipina women "come from places in which jobs and educational opportunities for women are scarce and wages are low." Further, the women say they are attracted to American men because "they look like movie stars" and because they "make good husbands," while Filipino men do not.

"Americans are thought to be faithful to their wives, while the native men are cruel and run around with other women. True or not, this is the perception."

Among American men seeking Filipino brides, it was found that 94 percent were white, most were highly educated (about 6 percent had a Ph.D. or an M.D.) and professionally successful, and most were politically conservative. Their median age was 37.

Why do these highly educated, professionally accomplished Americans want a girl from the Philippines? According to the INS study, "Most of the personal reports from American men who have married women through these agencies talk about 'traditional values.' That is, American women are thought not content to be wives and mothers but seek personal satisfaction through their own careers and interests, while the foreign woman is happy to be the homemaker and asks for nothing more than husband, home, and family. Again, true or not, this is the perception."

How successful are these matchmaking services overall? About 10 percent of these women find and marry a foreign man through the services. That means there are between 10,000 and 15,000 international penpal marriages per year, according to the study's estimates. Of these, approximately 4,000 to 6,000 are marriages to U.S. men.

So, of the 100,000 to 150,000 women who list annually in these services, 4 to 6 percent will wind up marrying a man from the United States. Any way you look at it, it's a longshot.

I was Liza's longshot. And now her friends wanted to catch a winning horse too.

As I sat and ate crispy patas with Liza and her hungry friends in the Beverly Room of Eddie's Hotel in Cebu City, Philippines, I pondered their fascination with Americans, their dreams of transcendence and their appreciation of my feelings for Liza.

Then I thought about some of my "liberal" and "progressive" friends back home who believed just the opposite. They were utterly repelled by my quest to marry a younger woman from the Philippines. There was just too much of a stigma attached to this. Too much of the "older-man-seeking-supple-flesh" thing. Also, there would be too much of a power differential in the relationship. I would have all the power in our relationship, and I would be the one in control. This is highly unfair and exploitive. I am a villain for wanting this 20-something woman from the Philippine provinces.

One of my friends showed me a 1996 article from *The New York Times*. It described men who seek younger foreign women through correspondence as "losers." Further, the women who get into such a relationship suffer an "inherent imbalance of power right from the start."

I hated how *The New York Times* exploited a convenient cultural stereotype and how this writer was somehow able to conclude that all men who use the post office and the Internet to find romance were all somehow "losers." That's why I had begun to despise journalism. Even a publication as prestigious as *The New York Times* was often guilty of crude reductionism, knee-jerk liberalism and intellectual laziness.

My response to all this was simple: I was the one who was oppressed here, not Liza. I was oppressed because I was a man with a dual ethnic/national identity that made me an outsider in both worlds. I had wasted too much of my adult life trying to be something I was not: a white American. And I had spent that entire adult life courting the grace of white American women, whose affection, I reckoned, would bring me the validity I so desperately craved.

Yes, I am courting a younger woman, and that's because I want to have children, the children I never had because I had become too self-obsessed in my pursuit of validity. Another thing: She also wants to have children, and she wants to have them with me. So what is wrong with this?

And yes, she is a woman from a fishing village in a poor country. So does this make me some kind of cruel exploiter because I am from the upper middle classes of the richest country in the world? Some of my friends said yes, and I should be ashamed of myself.

They do not consider that it is my home country that she's from. Does that matter? Could it be that I was seeking a re-connection with my home culture, a culture that had been lost through my years of American self-indulgence? Through my economic strength, I will be able to lift her to another level, one in which she doesn't have to worry about money, doesn't have to live in squalor, doesn't have to struggle to pay the rent and support her brothers, sisters, mother, cousins and anyone else who wants to come stay with her for a while. Since when does a partner's economic power not figure into the equation of a relationship?

And who was it that caused all this Philippine poverty in the first place? It wasn't me! Wasn't all this poverty and lack of opportunity caused by the imbalance of economic power that exists between the superpowers and the less powerful Third World? Oh, let's not go there! Let's just fixate on age differences. What incredible bullshit! Liberals are such toilet-heads sometimes, I reckoned, especially those of the aforementioned knee-jerk variety.

And so it all came down to this: Here I am, a middle-aged Filipino-American man living in America, somewhat successful, very educated, and very frustrated about the relationships I've had here in the U.S. I decided to find a Filipino woman to marry and have children with. I used the magic of the Internet to find a woman who suits me. She happens to be half my age. So what?

I am able to give this poor woman from the provinces a more comfortable life in America. In return, all I ask is that she love me and cherish me and give me children and be a good wife and mother and be with me for as long as we live. Is that such a bad thing?

Yes, my friends said. It is bad because you are 46 and she is 23. It is bad because you have money and she does not. It is bad because you are a powerful American and she is a helpless girl from the Philippines. You are exploiting her.

No, Liza's friends said. It is not bad at all. Age doesn't matter. Power differentials? What the hell is that? What matters is what's in your heart. You apparently love Liza and she tells us that she loves you. You will have a good marriage and a nice house and nice cars and you will have beautiful children. It is all fine. You are a good guy, George.

What to believe?

What to believe?

I didn't know. All I know is this: When I am with Liza, when I am looking into her dewy eyes, when she gently squeezes my hand, I am happy like I've not been happy in a long, long time. When I am with Liza, all the pain disappears, the pain of losing past loves, the pain of endless intellectual endeavor, the pain of losing my mother and father, the pain of never being able to attain full acceptance in America. With just a squeeze of the hand, with just one long, meaningful kiss, Liza takes away all of my pain. That's all I know.

Yes, mom and dad, I have found the Filipina girl of my dreams, of your dreams. I'm sorry that I didn't find her until after you both had left this Earth. I know that you wanted to have beautiful Philippine grandchildren, and you will have them now. See how beautiful and fine Liza is? So yes, of course, your grandchildren will be beautiful too.

This I promise you.

Liza and her friends finished off the crispy patas in due course. And after a round of dessert (mango ice cream), they all departed. Liza and I agreed to meet later in the evening, after she'd done her laundry.

I hung around the bar at Eddie's Hotel and chatted with one of the waiters. He had an important question he wanted to ask me: Where is Washington D.C. located?

"It's on the East Coast of the United States, a few hours south of New York by train. Why?"

"OK, excuse me," the waiter said. "Then where is Washington state?"

"The state of Washington? It's on the West Coast, near Canada, in the area known as the Pacific Northwest. Why?"

"OK, so Washington D.C. is not in Washington state?"

"Yes, that's right."

"That's what I was trying to tell my teacher, but she told me I was wrong."

"What? Your teacher told you Washington D.C. is in Washington State?"

"Yes, she's ignorant."

"She couldn't be an American. Your teacher, that is."

"No, she's not. She's Filipina."

"Oh well, maybe American geography is not her specialty," I smiled, trying not to inflame this guy's temper. "Just tell her that an American you met set you straight. Washington D.C. is not in Washington state. Got it?"

"Yes, thank you, sir. Thank you very much. I will tell her. Ignorant!"

I went back to sipping my San Miguel, but I noticed he kept on hovering around me, as if he had another question to ask. I wondered what other piece of geographical trivia he'd come up with next.

"Excuse me, sir," he finally blurted out. "I heard you tell the bartender yesterday that you are here to visit your girlfriend."

"Yes, that's correct."

"Is it a penpal?"

"Well, yes, I guess so. I met her through the Internet."

"Ah, I see. Yes, my sister also met an American through the Internet."

"Oh, and did things work out well?"

"No, she don't like him. He's too old."

"How old?"

"He's 60 already. Too old."

"Hmm, and let me guess…she's in her 20s."

"Yes, she running 21."

"Yes, most people would probably think he's too old for her," I said. "Some people think I'm too old for my girlfriend. I'm 46 and she's 23."

"Ohhh, you're 46? You look like 30s."

I was beginning to enjoy this conversation.

"So, you want to meet my sister? I'll call her and tell her to come here. You'll like her."

"What?? No, you don't have to, I mean, what, you want her to come here and meet me? Why?"

"Just for friends. You can tell her your story, and she can tell hers. Just for enjoy. It's OK, don't worry. She's a nice girl."

I hesitated, and before I could blurt out another comment, the waiter was on the phone dialing his sister. And so it was that 20 minutes later, a stunning young woman named Menchie, accompanied by her friend, Luz, came walking into the Beverly Room at Eddie's Hotel to meet with me.

After some greetings and small talk, they began peppering me with questions about the purpose of my visit to Cebu. When I told them I was there to see my fiancée to finish our visa paperwork, their eyes got real big and they became quite fascinated with my story. She seemed to hang on every word, as if it was some sort of lovely fairy tale. When I got to the end, where I proposed to Liza and she accepted, they clapped their hands and cheered.

"That is a very nice story," Menchie said. "I hope I can meet a nice guy, and it can happen to me some day."

"Me too," said Luz. "I want so much to live in America."

I asked Menchie about her America suitor. It turns out that she's had more than one—many more.

After her picture appeared in a Web site, Menchie received 31 letters. Most of the letters contained money. One man from New York sent $100 with his letter. In his letter he mentioned sex several times and also mentioned that he liked to wear women's clothes occasionally. He said he wanted to tickle her, and that frightened her. She didn't respond to him because he seemed *bastos*. She kept the money.

Another suitor, an Arab-American man from Cleveland, was also quite taken with Menchie. He sent her money, many photographs of himself and his parents, and offered to buy her an airplane ticket to come visit him in the U.S. She sent him one letter and stopped writing after that.

Another man claimed to be an NBA basketball player and offered to introduce her to Michael Jordan if she came to visit him in Chicago. He didn't offer to buy her an airplane ticket, though. And being no dummy, Menchie did an Internet search of the guy's name. There were no references at all to him, so he was clearly not a professional athlete.

Other letter-writers sent cash gifts, five dollars or ten dollars mostly, and she kept all of it. One man in his 60s kept sending her money even though she stated clearly in her one letter to him that she was not interested in a man that age. Nevertheless, he kept on sending desperate letters and enclosed small wads of American cash. She kept all the money he'd sent, which added up to more than $300. She rationalized that all the money she'd received from her various suitors was offered as a gift, and that it would be ungrateful not to accept. Sending it back would seem arrogant and would be hurtful to the suitors' feelings. Besides, the money might get "lost" in the Philippine mail.

Menchie, a wispy, long-haired college student, is from a poor family but has the perfect, glowing face of a model from the cover of *Seventeen* magazine. She grew up in a province in Mindanao (a southern island) and now lives in Cebu. When asked why she thought she was so attractive to American men, she laughed and said, "I don't know." She is depicted on her Web site wearing a short tight skirt and a form-fitting blue blouse bearing a "Guess?" logo.

"I learned that from my mama, how to dress. She had many admirers when she was young. When she was 16, she married a man who was 38. To me, age does not matter. What matters is that a man loves you and honors you and takes care of you. What good is it to have a man who looks like Tom Cruise, if he beats you? So looks don't matter; what matters is what's in the heart.

"I like the way American men look because they have light skin. The children of Filipino and American parents are very beautiful. But Filipino girls have to be careful when they meet American suitors. I heard that some American men are no good, that they beat their wives. I want to make sure I find a good man who will be a good husband and a good father and a good lifetime partner. I want a man who has a secure job and he's mature. One of my friends married an American, and she's not happy. She called me one day and she was crying. She said he always shouts at her and drinks and goes out with his friends, and he treats her like a maid. I don't want like that to happen to me.

"I had a boyfriend my age when I live in the province. He was young and very, very *guwapo*. And I was very much in love with him. But he married another girl there. Their parents forced them to do it. His parents wanted him to marry the girl. He wrote a letter to me and said he was sorry and that I was the one he really love, but what good is that? I was broken hearted and I didn't trust anybody any-more for about one year."

When Menchie finished, I shook my head and told her I sympathized with her. I said that she shouldn't give up because one day she'll find someone who's perfect for her. She just raised her eyebrows in that non-verbal Filipino way of agreeing with you. Then I turned to Luz and asked if she had a similar story. Indeed she did:

Luz worked in a restaurant in Cebu. She was a waitress, and foreign men always seemed to flirt with her. She had been experimenting with her hair color, and now it was reddish-brown with some blonde streaks. This gave her a very exotic look.

Taking a cue from Menchie, Luz also contacted an international matching service and put her photo on the Internet. She received several letters from men in Canada, Australia, England and the U.S.

Her one suitor from the U.S. was from Los Angeles, and he claimed to be a movie producer. Like Menchie, she is smart and techno-savvy, so she did an Internet search too and found that this man really was a movie producer, although she had never heard of any of the movies he'd made. He said he'd come to the Philippines and visit her, but has yet to do so. He said he's always busy with new projects, but will come soon. Luz is still waiting. He has sent her money, but only a little bit here and there, just to help her pay for return postage.

Luz did have one visitor, her admirer from England. His name was James and he said he was a stockbroker in the City of London.

"He came here last month, and he took me out. He was a nice guy, not so handsome, but nice. I liked him. He bought me some nice gifts. But then he asked me to come to his room and sleep with him. And when I said no, I can't, he was very mad. He said that he came all the way here from England, and he expected to have a special treatment. I told him, what do you think of me? And then he got mad again."

"We didn't see each other for two days and he didn't call, and then one day I went to his hotel room to just say hello and when I came to his door I could hear a lots of noises inside the room. He was with a girl. I could hear it. It was a prosty (prostitute). Then I heard another girl's voice. They were all laughing. He had two prosties in his room with him. That's what kind of guy he was.

"He called me the next day and I told him I did not want to talk to him any more. Then he insisted, and I told him that I will call the police if he doesn't leave me alone. Then he stopped calling."

Both Menchie and Luz told me stories about other men who'd sent them letters, and I reckoned that these women were very smart. Far from being the weak, helpless, prototype "mail-order brides" that the media love to portray, these women were opportunists, capitalists profiting off their good looks, and looking for a real ticket out in the meantime.

Does that make them bad? Does that make them good?

And how about Liza? Is she good or is she bad?

And how about me? Am I good or am I bad?

I didn't know, but I did know that I wasn't going to let *The New York Times* determine my virtue. Nor was I going to let my so-called "liberal" and "progressive" friends decide.

The time was quickly approaching for me to meet with Liza, so I finished my beer and I thanked the girls for sharing their stories with me. They thanked me too for spending time with them and telling them my story. I was surprised when Menchie drew herself up to me and hugged me tightly around the neck. Her hold on me lasted a bit longer than it should have, and she nuzzled my neck a little before she pulled away.

When she finally withdrew, she took a piece of paper out of her purse and wrote down her address and phone number.

"If you have a friend in America," she said, "tell him about me."

# 20

## *The Fixed Decision*

This was the end of my third—and I hoped final—visit to the Philippines. These trips had been joyful, but they were also very expensive. My credit-card balances were now bloated and my mind and body were weary from the trans-hemispheric travel. I wanted this to end. I wanted Liza to be with me in America.

I was confident that the visa paperwork had been executed correctly. We mailed her application, bio forms, sworn statements and photographs to the U.S. Embassy in Manila. We used LBC, a special courier service, because we did not trust the Philippine postal system. Letters routinely disappear in the mails here, especially letters that appear to contain something of worth. Thus, we paid the 150 pesos for next-day delivery service to Manila on LBC. Three bucks and change for guaranteed overnight delivery? No problem.

Liza thought it was outrageous that we had to spend so much just to mail an envelope full of forms, but I assured her it was worth the expense.

Now, as we rode in a taxi taking me to the Cebu-Mactan airport for my flights home, I watched the scenery roll past and thought about how much Cebu had meant to me. I also thought about how much this place meant to the history of the Philippines, as well as the history of European conquest of the new worlds.

As I pondered these things, I looked in the driver's rearview mirror, hoping to make eye contact with Liza, just like I had on that day in the taxi when we first started kissing. I was hoping to have another intimate eye-contact moment like that one to invigorate me during my long trip home.

But Liza didn't make eye contact with me. I don't know if she was purposely avoiding eye contact or just too deep in thought about something. Maybe she was just sad that I was leaving, and she didn't want to think about my being gone. All I could see were her thick lips, her high cheeks, her skin—the color of an exotic desert—and her dewy eyes looking to the side, focused somewhere, far, far away.

At the airport, she accompanied me to the international terminal and stayed with me until the checkpoint. We noticed there was a large statue of the Santo

Niño at the entrance, and Liza pulled me over to it. We stood before it, and Liza nodded to me and lowered her head. She was praying and she wanted me to pray with her, to pray for a safe journey, to pray for a happy future together.

After the prayer, we said our sad goodbyes. And as I walked past the security gate and looked over my shoulder, I saw my beloved, the lady of light, the girl of my dreams, the girl who I had been waiting for my entire life, smiling and waving at me through the glass windows separating us. And I waved back and blew her a kiss and decided not to make a big deal of this departure because we would be together soon. Real soon.

I remember something Jessica told me: that Liza cried and cried and cried when I left for home the two trips before. "Liza kept saying, 'George is such a nice guy. I love him so much,'" Jessica told me. It hurt me to think that Liza could be so sad. So it's best not to have a great big goodbye scene, I figured. Let's just pretend this is routine, just another departure, just a matter of course. After all, we'd be together soon, and it would be forever.

Liza's interview at the U.S. Embassy was set for March. She would be receiving her visa about two weeks later and then she could hop aboard a Philippine Airlines flight that would take her to Manila and then to San Francisco, where I would pick her up and drive her in my black Nissan pickup truck to her new home in Humboldt County, Northern California, USA, and there, in the land of fog and trees and mystery, all of her dreams—big and small—could come true.

So why make such a big deal out of goodbye? No need, I said, resisting the urge to look over my shoulder one more time. No need.

After another grueling trip home, I rested and then got on with the fall semester. The days and weeks started to seem indistinguishable from all the others. I needed Liza's light with me in gray Arcata. I got a glimpse of it in the form of a Valentine's card, which I found one day in my mailbox. It was dated Jan. 29, 1999.

---

*Darling:*

*Have a nice day! I think this is the happiest moment that comes into your life because it's your birthday and may you have more birthdays to come. I'm hoping for your success in the future and may all your dreams come true and please don't ever change the way you are. I'm wishing you all the luck and happiness always. Again, happy B-day to you, even this is late. God Bless you always. Take care. I love you.*

*Love, Liza.*

*PS: Happy Valentine's Day! It's nice to send this Valentine with lots of love. You know, I will always love you. I will spend the rest of my life to you, if you really love me too. Again, Happy Valentine's Day to you, sweetheart. Hope you enjoy this coming Valentine's Day! Love, Liza*

I hadn't been able to reach her on her cell phone for the last few days, so it was nice to get this card. These sweet words rang in my ears for the next few days, and my soul glowed from the promise of never-ending love.

It was a day just like any other in Humboldt County when everything changed.

It was drizzly, with big, black clouds in the sky warning of an imminent downpour. I wondered how Liza would cope with this weather, with 200 days per year of rain and gray skies. Then I remembered that it also rained a lot in the Philippines. Except there, it was hot. Hot before, during and after the rains. And there were hurricanes and floods too. So, in all, I reckoned she'd do all right here in wet and wild Humboldt County. The mention of an occasional earthquake terrified her, though, so I spared her the explanation that earthquake-prone Humboldt lies at the confluence of three major faults. Why get her riled up? She's got a lot of other things to think about, like visa interviews in Manila, crying mothers and stupid ex-boyfriends.

I taught a couple of classes, did some catch-up work in my office, answered some emails, drove home to my apartment up the hill from the university, and got the mail. There was a magazine, a couple of bills and another letter from the Philippines, from Liza.

Another one so soon? How delightful! I opened this new letter. What else does she want to tell me? That she will love me beyond forever? That our children will be beautiful and smart? That I am just impossible to resist?

---

*Feb. 20, 1999*
*Dear George,*

*Hello! How are you today? How's your Valentine's? I hope you enjoyed on that very special day. For me here, I'm happy w/my family and my friends.*

*You know George, I write to you because I want to give an apology from you. Last Feb. 13, 1999 my boyfriend came here together with his parents. And proposing marriage again. I was so shocked when they arrived here and his parents talk about it and it has been agreed. So, our wedding is already scheduled for this month.*

*Don't ever think that I was forced to agree about this matter. It is also my decision. You're right that I'm still young and anytime my decision will change. My decision to accept his proposal is fixed and final. Before we have this relationship, you know already that I have a boyfriend. Maybe we are not meant for each other. Let's forgive and forget the past. We will just accept the realities in life. God has a plan for each and everyone of us. I know that you can accept this because you already know about my situation. You're professional and it is not hard for you to find a new one.*

*This will be my last letter. Our relationship will ended this way. If you want, I am very much willing to return all the things you have given me or else I will sent it back to you. Thanks for your love, your care and your kindness. I hope you understand me. Thanks for everything and please give me peace of mind. God's love you.*

*In Christ,*

*Liza*

I was stunned.

I couldn't believe what I was reading. I stood there speechless, staring at the letter, alternately shouting in anger and whimpering like some wounded animal. I read it over and over, to make sure I'd read it correctly. I read it aloud again and again, more intensely with each reading, as if somehow the force of my will could make the terrible words morph into something different, that the force of my will could transform this letter into something loving, something caring, something Liza would've sent.

Not this! This was straight from hell!

Didn't she tell me she had dumped that loser once before? And when he came back whining, she told him again that it was over and that she was marrying me and coming to America. I remember her telling me that! She promised me it was me and only me in her life. Forever! And now this?

I looked at the handwriting closely and compared it to her other letters to see if it was hers, not her sister's or her mother's or some jokester's. Sadly, I could see it was hers. This was a letter from Liza. This was a letter from Liza telling me it was over. I'd been dumped. This was a letter from my dream girl telling me that the dream was over. This was a letter from the queen of my heart, telling me a divine wind from the Philippines had blown our love off its foundations and sent it swirling up, up, up into some dark unknown. This was a letter from the girl who was going to be the beginning of my new life, telling me that this was the end of everything, that everything was ending before it had even begun.

And all she could say was sorry and "thanks for everything," like I was some sort of common idiot, some cheap punk, who she could just dismiss with a flip of her hair and a beautiful smile and a frilly wave.

I didn't know what to do. I was devastated. All my hopes, all my dreams, all the missing things in my life that I thought I'd finally found—all were now lost again.

I collapsed in a heap and cried, and cried and cried like I hadn't cried in 5, 10, maybe 20 years.

The poor, little frail girl from the Philippines, the girl with the delicate smile and the shy manner, the girl who had caressed my hand outside the church with a touch that said, "You are mine, and I think that God sent you to me," the deeply religious girl who had pulled me to her side and asked me to stand with her before the statue of the Santo Niño and pray that our love would last forever, the girl with the name that sounded like a divine whisper, the girl whose family was so poor that she had to support them, had to share all her things with them, the girl who seemed so helpless, so much in need, so delicate, so beautiful—that girl had reduced the mighty, young Dr. George Estrada to a sobbing, pathetic heap.

Where was *The New York Times* now to tell me about power and powerlessness? Liza's mother and ex-boyfriend had seized the day, and I was wholly unable to stop them.

After a while, I don't know how long, I raised my head and confronted the truth. Liza was gone. The dream was over. I felt devastated and humiliated. How could I face all my friends and relatives with this news? I got up on my knees and prayed to God for guidance and strength. Outside, the rain fell in a constant, gentle drizzle. Every now and then the rain would get stronger, and I could hear the tap, tap, tapping of the water on the windows. It was raining in Humboldt County that evening. It always seems to rain in Humboldt County.

I felt sorry for myself, and sorry for the children Liza and I were never going to have. But even as I wept, I formulated a plan. I wasn't going to give up that easily. I was going to play hardball.

The next day at school, as I told my sorry tale to anyone who would listen, people offered different suggestions:

"Just go," said one of my journalism faculty colleagues. "Go to the Philippines and take care of business. Don't worry about your classes. I'll take them for you. You need to go get your woman."

"Just flick out your Visa card," said one of my students, an excitable guy with a shaved head. "Charge a plane ticket, just put it on your credit card and go. And bring a big knife with you to cut that boyfriend's throat."

This kind of advice I didn't need. I wasn't about to go committing murder, even though the thought did seem attractive momentarily. And ditching my classes for a week seemed irresponsible, despite my colleague's generous offer.

At home after classes, I kept calling Liza's cell phone number. She hadn't answered my calls for about 10 days, but I figured she would start soon. Suddenly, she picked up the phone.

"Liza, I got your letter. And so what's this all about? I thought you were coming to America to be with me. And I thought you had given up on that guy. You picked me, remember? That's what you told me. And I came to visit you three times, and we've done all this paperwork, and we've waited so long for this visa thing to happen, and we're so close now, so close. Your interview at the U.S. embassy is just two months away!"

"Yah, I know," was all she could say. I could hear noisy chattering in the background. It sounded like there were several people at her house. "But this is a fixed decision. We signed a marriage contract already."

"A marriage contract? For God's sake, marriage contracts aren't binding. They aren't legal. They fooled you into signing something, and now they're telling you that you can't back out of it."

"No, no, you don't understand. I'm getting married in two weeks."

"Liza, you can't do this. You promised yourself to me. I can't live without you. We worked so hard for this. We are just a couple of months away now. We are very, very close to achieving our goal. Don't follow what they're telling you. You're a grown woman. You can make your own choices."

She began to cry. "This is my choice. This is a fixed decision." Through her quiet sobbing, her words sounded rehearsed. "I'll send back all the money you gave me, and the engagement ring and the cell phone."

"I don't care about all that. I only care about you. You need to get away from those people. Run away from them. Stay in a hotel until I can come and get you."

"No, no, I can't do that."

The cell connection started breaking up. Her battery was running low.

"Liza, Liza...listen to me. Just get away from them. I'll send you some money so you can support yourself for a while. Then go to your appointment in Manila and after you get your visa, then you immediately come here."

Silence. More silence. The cell connection had been lost. About an hour and 100 redial attempts later, I got through again. Liza greeted me pleasantly, just like we were about to have a normal conversation. I stammered out something about loyalty and obligation and trust, but before I could finish, she interrupted me.

"George, I know this hurts you very much. But it's a fixed decision. Everything has been arranged." I could hear whispering in the background. Someone was talking in Liza's ear, coaching her on what to say. "There's nothing you can do about this now. It's a fixed decision."

"Liza, listen to me. I know what's going on. There are people there listening to what you're saying, right? They're telling you what to say."

Silence.

"Liza, I'm going to call you at Shoe Mart tomorrow. Be at the consignor's office at noon and then we can talk in private. You got it? Liza? Do you understand?"

"Yes."

"OK, I'll call you tomorrow at noon. And then we can talk. All right, hang in there, sweetheart. We'll make this right. Believe in me. Believe in us! You've got a great future here waiting for you. I want you to have it, and you will have it. We just have to figure out a plan. Understand?"

"Yes."

And then she hung up. What was she telling her relatives now? I'm sure they were all chattering very loudly and very quickly at her, as Filipinos tend to do when they get agitated, and trying to make her tell them what I'd said. What would she tell them? Would she tell them the truth? That George wanted to speak with her alone? That George wasn't about to give up so easily? That George was about to propose some sort of secret plan? Or would she play it cool and tell them that I had surrendered and said my final goodbye? How would she handle this? What would she say? It all came down to this now.

The next day, I called at noon, her time, at the Shoe Mart store consignor's office.

"Hello, Liza? Are you alone? Can you talk now?"

"Yes."

"So, like I told you, I can send you some money and you can get away from your family for awhile and then you can go to Manila and get your visa."

"No," she was firm. "I told you this is a fixed decision. This is my decision. No one forced me."

"Liza, I just can't believe that. It sounds like you memorized something to say, and you're not speaking to me from your heart. Is this what you feel in your heart? I thought you picked me over that guy. I thought you wanted me."

"Yes," she started crying again. "You already know what's in my heart. I already told you. I already told you. I don't have to repeat it."

"Then you still love me? Please tell me the truth, Liza. Do you still love me?"

"I told you many times what I feel about you," she was crying heavily now. "I want to thank you for all your kindness, for everything you gave to me. I'll send back all the money you gave me, and the ring and the cell phone."

"Liza!!! Listen to me. Don't marry that guy. He's a merchant marine, right? And he's away from home a lot. You'll be alone, and you'll be poor if you marry him."

"I know, I know that, but this is a fixed decision. We can't change this. There is a contract."

Liza cried for about 15 seconds and couldn't say anything else. Then she righted herself and spoke in the gentle, loving voice that I knew so well: "You know, George, I had a dream about you last night. You came to visit me one last time. Were you visiting me last night in my dream?" She started to laugh through her tears.

"See, you're still dreaming about me, Liza! How can you just end our relationship like this? You just can't do this, sweetheart. It isn't right. It isn't what you want. I know it! Just tell them that you changed your mind and that you're not going to get married. It's that simple. Just tell them. Tell them you're an adult and you can make up your own mind, and that you made a commitment to marry me and come to America. Just tell them, and walk away. It's that simple."

"Maybe in America," she said. "Maybe in America, it's that simple. But not in the Philippines."

Silence again. I didn't know what to say. I know that family is everything to the traditional, conservative Filipino. Disobey your mother and you disobey God. My mother had once told me that. Turn your back on your family and you have no family. You've lost everything. You are cursed forever.

"OK, OK, Liza. Let me think for a minute."

"George, you are a nice guy, you are a professional. You can get another girl. This is my fate. This is my life. Please, please give me peace."

"Liza…"

"I will send you back the money, the phone and the ring, OK? OK, thank you again for everything. Thank you for your kindness."

It was that damned rehearsed speech again. "Liza, please don't talk like that. This is insanity. Your parents can't tell you who to marry. They fooled you with that phony marriage contract. They can't force a grown woman to marry someone she doesn't want to marry."

"OK, bye."

"Liza, stop. Don't hang up."

She started crying again. "Please, George, give me peace. Give me peace."

More silence. I could hear excited chattering in the background. Liza was still on the phone.

"Liza, are people listening to you talking?"

"Yes."

Dammit, that's right. Some of her co-workers were friends with Liza's ex-boyfriend. She'd told me that once. Of course, they were there. Of course, they were listening in. This was an irresistible little drama. Better than a corny Tagalog soap opera. How could they not be insanely curious?

"Liza, do you have access to another cell phone? Do you know anyone who's got a cell phone? Can I call you on someone else's cell phone? I desperately need to talk to you and I know you want to talk with me."

Silence.

"Liza? Did you hear me? Do you understand me?"

"My cousin has."

"Your cousin? So, give me the number."

"Okay." She gave the phone number, and then she turned and said something to her friends in Cebuano—or was it Tagalog?—and I heard laughter in the background. I reckoned she was telling a cover story so they wouldn't suspect what was really up. I couldn't tell, though. I was the alien here.

"Liza, thank you. I'll call you, OK? I love you, baby. I will always love you. You are my girl forever. Don't forget that, OK?"

"OK."

A few hours later, I tried calling the number. No answer. I tried again. No answer again. And so it was for 20, 30, 40 more attempts. I started to suspect that I'd been had. I tried again, another 20, 30, 40 times. I was now sure I'd been had. This was a bogus phone number.

I called Liza's cell phone. A male voice answered. It was him, I could tell it was him. It was Wilson, Liza's ex-boyfriend and now husband-to-be, the man who had stolen her away from me; stolen her away from me with a trick so old and so clichéd that I couldn't see it coming. He had played the "family" card.

To me, this was despicable. He couldn't win the girl through the regular way, the manly way, so he went crying to his parents to help him. And so they did, by approaching Liza's mom with his marriage proposal, with the offer of a marriage contract and a good Catholic wedding right here in the Philippines. And why wouldn't mom prefer that Liza marry a man from the Philippines in the Philippines? This was a man from her home province of Daanbantayan, a man who could speak Cebuano, who knew all the traditions, who knew the deep culture, who knew how to act like a Filipino son-in-law, who knew all the right moves. This wasn't an Americano, an alien, this was a man of her own kind, knowable, predictable, all Cebuano all the time. It just made total sense to a mother desperate to keep her daughter close to home. This was the answer. Agree to this and she could keep Liza here for all time. Don't agree to this and Liza will be off to America, carried over the ocean by some divine wind, and perhaps lost to her clutches forever. The answer was so obvious; so clear, so blessed was this solution. God must have heard mom's prayers.

And so it was that Wilson's parents and Liza's mom had signed the contract. And so it was that they all got together and made a surprise visit to Liza's little boarding house on MJ Cuenco alley in Cebu City. And so it was that they showed her the contract and told her that she had no choice because this was "a fixed decision." And maybe she resisted, and maybe she didn't. But eventually she did give in and signed that damned, phony contract and now she believes she's obligated to marry this scam artist, this pathetic, little mama's boy who was now speaking to me on the cell phone that I had bought for Liza.

"Hello, is this Wilson?"

"Hello? *Kinsa mani?* (Who is this?)"

"Wilson, this is George, the guy you stole Liza from. Do you have any idea what you're doing to her? Do you realize what you've stolen from her? Do you think you can give her the same future I could give her here in America?"

"*Onsa?* (What?)"

I was getting pissed. This guy was pretending he didn't understand me. He was fucking with me. "Wilson, do you know what I'm going to do to you the next time I come to the Philippines?"

"*Onsa?* Hello? *Kinsa mani?*"

"I'm going to cut your fucking throat, you little prick. I'm going to KILL you, do you understand me? I'M GOING TO KILL YOU, YOU PATHETIC LITTLE SHIT, WILSON!!"

He clicked the phone off, disconnecting us. Wilson and his friends and Liza's family were now controlling all of Liza's lines of communication. I had no way of getting in touch with her now.

Over the next few days, I came up with many desperate plans. My agitated state of mind started to affect my work. I told some of my students and colleagues what I was going through. Most of them understood my dilemma and were very generous with their advice and words of comfort. At that point, it became clear that despite its rain and cold, Humboldt was a fine and warm place, with lots of tolerant and sensitive people. And I knew I had made the right decision to come to this obscure, little university tucked away in the Northern California redwoods.

As I walked through the campus on one misty afternoon, I looked around at all the big trees that throw their shadows on the people of Humboldt State University, and I looked at all the different people with their trust-fund dreadlocks and their Mary Poppins-chic attire and their day-glo hair and multiple piercings and I reckoned that no place is more interesting or eclectic than this. And I was happy as hell to be here, around such creative and supportive people. But I felt a surge of sadness when I realized that Liza would never see this beautiful little campus, never walk hand in hand with me through a grove of big trees, never watch me teaching a class.

I submerged myself in work, and after a few days I felt much better. But every now and then, I lay awake at night and thought of her. I imagined the soft slope of her cheeks, the fullness of her lips, the naughty curve of her eyebrows when she smiled, the warm, welcoming eyes. I remember how those eyes welcomed me into her life from the very start.

And I think of how everything changed in one moment. I imagine the scene; the crying, the shouting, people madly chattering in Tagalog or Cebuano or whatever. I imagine these same people surrounding her, forcing her to give in to their will, pleading with her, yelling at her. And I imagine Liza sitting in shock, helpless and vulnerable. I could hear her in my mind, softly weeping, sobbing, buried in grief and confusion, resigned to the inevitable. What was going through her head at that moment? Did she know this was coming? Did she have any advance warning of her fate? Did she imagine that she would never see me again? Did she imagine what she would tell me? Did she rehearse it? Did she imagine anything anymore? Did all of her dreams die that day? Did all of my dreams die, as well?

There were no answers to these questions now. I lay back down again and I thought more about her. And I thought of how she came into my life unexpectedly and restored my faith in everything again. And then I thought about how it was cruelly pulled it out from under me, like a discount carpet remnant.

A few days later, some money arrived from the Philippines by bank wire. It was from Liza. It was almost all the money I'd given her, minus about $200. There was a message accompanying the money, saying that she had spent the $200 contributing to a cousin's funeral. Sorry! She also said she'd be sending the ring and the phone soon. I sent a message back saying that she could keep the ring and the phone.

"George, you were a victim of deep culture," one of my colleagues from the University of Texas told me one evening over the phone. "Family is a big thing over there, you know that. You've got to do what your family wants. If you don't, it's a big deal. You will lose your family ties just like that."

That made me feel better, although that seemed somehow to be too tidy an explanation. There was more to it than that. There had to be. My instincts were burning with suspicion. A conversation I had with a cousin fanned the flames.

"You were tricked," she said. "Plain and simple. It's very obvious. This was all planned. She just wanted you for the money and the gifts—and she took you for a ride."

"No," I said. "That's not possible. You don't know Liza like I know her. The look in her eyes was genuine. The way she kissed me, the way she clung onto me in public, was genuine. The way she made me feel loved was impossible to fake."

My cousin laughed. "You don't know Filipinas. A lot of Filipinas are tricky. Filipinas do this all the time to lonely American men. They take their money and they leave them. You are just the latest victim."

I did not want to believe my cousin's harsh appraisal. Could it be that my lovely Liza, the creature of divine light, was nothing more than a cheap hustler? Could it be that she had played me for a fool? Could it be that I was that blinded by her light, that stupidly in love, that desperate for affection, that I was utterly and completely fooled?

I reckoned at that moment that anything was possible. I was also saddened by the probability that I'd never know the truth behind it all.

I did know one thing, though. I knew that I had tasted the sweet mangoes of Cebu, and found that they were the sweetest fruit of all. I had seen the country of my birth, the land of my ancestors. I came to reclaim the culture that I had rejected for the shiny New World, only to find that the home culture would reject the thing I had become.

I came here in search of self-revelation, only to discover that the only thing revealed would be the alien within me. I came here in search of love, but what I found was a lady made only of light, with thin substance that collapsed under the weight of family duty. I came here in search of answers, but was left with only riddles.

Full of Asian-looking people with Spanish names, full of Catholics who lust for bohemian pleasures, full of convenient cultural stereotypes that are shattered by the complexities of the Filipino soul, the Philippines will always be a riddle. Liza was just another one of these riddles.

The guidebooks to the Philippines I'd been using are useless, I decided. Filipinos are people, as complex and cynical and opportunistic as any American would be. Forget these old notions about Filipino women being traditional and conservative and loyal and loving and caring. Forget the stereotypes that would put all Filipinos into a convenient little box. Filipinos are complicated, individual, each with ideas and emotions that set them apart from one another.

Such is the greatness of the human experience. Such is the riddle of the Philippines. Such is the reality of America. I belong to both countries, and I belong to neither.

Somewhere out in the great beyond, it wasn't raining. And I imagined Liza was in that place, safe and warm, smiling at her mother, laughing and joking with her sister and brother, cooking rice and adobo and serving her family loyally, like a good daughter should, occasionally placing her hand on the shoulder of her husband, reassuring him that she is his and his alone. I loved Liza for being what she was. I envied and hated her husband and her mother for stealing her away from me.

And I imagined that deep inside, Liza was quietly crying, thinking about me, thinking about what her family had just taken from her, thinking about what we'd just lost. At the same time, though, she was totally content with being who she was and being where she was. Wild dreams are for other people, she might have been thinking. Not for me. I am meant to be here in my home country with my husband and my mother and my family. We are all happy here together. We may be poor, but we are happy. It is God's will.

My name is George and I am a Filipino-America. I am both American and Filipino—and I am neither. Maybe that too is God's will. This is my story.

# 21

## *A Shot in the Dark*

I was resigned to the situation, but something in me didn't want to surrender so easily. Maybe it was the American in me. Americans hate to lose. I tried calling Liza's cell phone many more times, to no avail. I also tried calling the SM consignor's office, where I'd been able to reach her before. No luck there either, but the girl who answered the phone tried very obviously to flirt with me, even so far as to ask for my home phone number so she could call me later. I wasn't interested.

I tried writing letters and sending emails to people who were willing to deliver them to Liza, but that didn't work either. I never got a response from her. In desperation and anger, I wrote a terse letter threatening to report her and her family to the immigration authorities for defrauding me out of money. She never responded to any of my love letters nor my hate letters. Why couldn't she at least send me a note telling me I was a despicable bastard and that she never wanted to hear from me ever again? That would have been better than getting nothing at all. Getting nothing was pure torture.

I gave up.

I went back to my life and my work. There were plenty of papers to grade and classes to teach, and each day became like the all the other days in rainy, cloudy Humboldt County.

Late in the spring semester I received some interesting news. The Society of Professional Journalists sent a letter informing me that *The Osprey,* my student magazine, had won first place in the six-state western region for Overall Excellence.

My passion for journalism and its highest ideals had been vindicated. I knew that all those things that keep journalism vibrant were not just a bunch of platitudes. Journalism, when done right, does have the power to shed light on dark corners, uplift the weak and give voice to the voiceless. When news of the award spread, my students started treating me like I was someone who knew what he was doing. That was the biggest honor they could've given me.

And it didn't stop there. In the next week or two, a flurry of additional awards came in. *The Osprey* took First Place for Best News Story and Best Human Interest Article in the California Intercollegiate Press Association's annual competition for student journalists. We also took several second-and third-place awards and honorable mentions in other categories.

This was unprecedented. Never had *Osprey* so dominated the state and regional competitions. We had scored a knockout punch. *The Osprey* was now a force in California student journalism—just like that! The RFK awards didn't come through, but it didn't matter. We were proud as hell of what we'd accomplished. We were a ragtag bunch of outlaw journalists working on a low budget up here in the redwood country, and we had beaten the tar out of the bigger, finer, big-city universities in the west.

We soaked in the glory of this moment for a couple of weeks, but when the end of the semester came, my mind started to turn to other thoughts. For some reason, I couldn't get Liza out of my mind. She was the glorious victory that had eluded me. I constantly thought of Liza, the mad heat of the Philippines and the sweetness of the mangoes I had tasted there.

I noticed at the local Safeway that they'd started carrying a new kind of mango—Mexican mangoes. They were smaller and they were yellow, with some black spots; not red, yellow and green like the mangoes I was used to seeing in the U.S. They looked and felt more like Philippine mangoes. Biting into one, I noticed that they more closely resembled Philippine mangoes too in flavor and texture than did the more common mangoes, the ones grown mainly in Florida.

I started buying these Mexican mangoes like they were going out of style. I ate mangoes throughout the spring semester, enjoying their succulence, milky texture and tangy backbite. They kept me company and slaked my thirst for the tropical lushness of the Philippines. They also reminded me of who I was and what I wasn't.

I forgot about the pain of loss by submerging myself in work. I worked on some academic papers for a coming conference. I shopped on the Internet and bought anything I could to fill the voids in my life. I worked on some magazine articles that I had put off for a while.

While doing research on the 'Net one afternoon, I found myself turning again to the *Filipino Dream Girls* Web site. Why, I don't know. Maybe out of boredom, maybe out of loneliness, maybe from the cynical thought that I'd find Liza's picture there again, trying to hustle another victim. Yes, I'd become bitter now, harboring hateful ideas about Liza, thinking maybe that breaking the hearts of lonely foreigners was something she did for sport and extra income. Maybe this Wilson character was her husband all along, and maybe she was playing me to get some nice gifts and a bit of cash.

My thoughts became hard and crass, like the thoughts I had when I was in grad school working on my dissertation, like the thoughts I had when I was a newspaper reporter—not at all like the rose-colored views of love and rainbows and beautiful light I'd had for the past 1 1/2 years while I was stupidly in love.

While clicking through the Web site, I found one slim, young girl, 23 years old, with silken black hair, white skin and a smile that was warm and welcoming. She was also wearing a very tight dress that ended well above her knees. What the hell! I got her address and I wrote her a letter.

About three weeks later, I received a letter from her, which included her cell phone number. I called that very day and we had a very nice conversation. She seemed like a modest girl, a bit shy and reserved, but also a little flirty. She said she'd love to meet me some day, and I said the same. She said she was particularly happy to know me because I am a Filipino-American, not a stranger. "You have a Filipino blood!" she said. I liked hearing that.

We had more letters and more conversations over the next few weeks, and before I knew it I was making plans to visit her in Manila in the summer. Because I am an idiot, I also made reservations for a side trip to Cebu, so that I could see Liza one more time.

My visit with Noreen in Manila went very well. She was a delightful girl, with a giddy laugh, a beautiful, slim body which she showcased underneath tight jeans and a shiny, black, form-fitting blouse. Despite the provocative clothing, she had a disarmingly shy way about her. She was fun to be with and she made me laugh a lot because she said silly things. I was immediately smitten. I was not in love and didn't want to be because I didn't want to go there again so soon after a major heartbreak, but I was definitely taken by her.

On our dates, we were always accompanied by a friend or two—the ubiquitous Filipino chaperone. And when I boldly asked her to spend the night with me one day, she politely declined, saying she needed to preserve her virginity for her husband-to-be, whoever that may end up being. That traditional Filipina conservatism again! Somehow, it made Noreen with the tight jeans even more mystifying.

Here she was, a girl dressing very sexily, like a coquettish American coed, but acting like a virgin. She was a riddle that needed to be solved. When I left Manila a few days later, I promised I'd stay in touch with her. I told Noreen about Liza and the breakup, but I didn't tell her I was going to Cebu to make one last, desperate attempt to win her back.

I flew to Cebu and decided to stay in a different hotel. I didn't want to face all those inquiries I'd surely get at Eddie's. I didn't want to go through the agony of explaining and re-explaining the situation to all the waiters and counter girls I'd come to know.

On the way to the Holiday Plaza Hotel, the young cab driver asked me where I was from and why I had come to Cebu. I told him that I was there to see my fiancée one last time, to see if I can persuade her to come back to me. I explained that Liza's mother had forced her to marry someone else, a boy from the province.

"Tsck," the cabbie said, making that Filipino clicking sound that indicated "what a shame." He added: "That kind of story, I think maybe I see that only in the movies, not in real life."

He seemed like a sympathetic type, so I asked him if he could do me a favor. He said sure, he'd be glad to. I fished one of my business cards out of my wallet.

"Go to the SM department store, and go to the barong section," I instructed him. "Ask for Liza and show her this card. Tell her I'm here now in Cebu and I want to see her. Tell her to call me at the Holiday Plaza. When you're done, call me at the hotel and tell me what she said. Got it?"

I gave the cabbie a $10 tip. "Yes, sir," he said enthusiastically.

When I checked in at the Holiday Plaza, it was uncannily like the Eddie's Hotel experience. The counter girls were all dressed alike in tacky business suits with big bowties. Some of them were tittering at my presidential surname, wondering if I was somehow related to Joseph Estrada. Some were smiling flirtatiously and eyeing me like I was a rock star. Across the street there were two nightclubs, and I noticed older men, guests of the hotel, walking across and entering the clubs.

My room was smallish, but comfortable. Of course, there was an air conditioner to keep me cool in the tropical heat. There was also a sign on a table offering a massage for a small fee. I could only imagine what else was available after the massage. I also noticed that my bed sheets weren't entirely stain-free. I wondered what sort of blood-borne pathogens might have been in those dried stains, but I was too tired to complain about it.

About an hour later, I got a call from the cabbie. He said he had seen Liza at SM and had given her my card. He also said that she seemed shocked to learn I was in town.

"Did you tell her I wanted her to call me at the hotel?"

"Yes," said the cabbie. "But she said she could not. She said she has a very jealous husband, so she cannot entertain you during your visit."

A very jealous husband. I'd be very jealous too. I thanked the cab driver and moped in my room for a while. I decided that I needed to just go to SM and see Liza in person. Maybe seeing me in the flesh would revive old memories, old passions. Maybe not. I just needed to see those dewy eyes again. I just needed to bask in her light one more time.

I caught a cab a few moments later. And so it was that I marched into the SM mall, felt its cool air conditioning kiss my sweaty brow again, and heard its joyful, happy music sweep away the pain of a hungry nation. I walked past swarms of teenagers gabbing on their cell phones. I marched past storefronts promising better lives through expensive sunglasses, Nike shoes and Hilfiger shirts. I walked past the Texas Chicken where Liza and I had many pleasant lunches and gazed into one another's eyes and dreamt about the future. I walked past the LBC office where we had sent off our final visa documents to the embassy in Manila. I walked past the jewelry counter where I had bought her engagement ring and then—there I was, smack in the middle of the barong section once again. I looked around for Liza, but she wasn't there. Two of her co-workers were, though, and they immediately noticed me.

"George!" one of them yelled out. "How are you? My goodness, what a surprise! When did you get into town? Liza is not here. She's at lunch."

I told them I'd be back in half an hour, and when I returned, there she was, looking as radiant as ever. When she saw me coming, she flashed that big, spectral smile, as if she were very happy to see me, as if she were still in love with me, as if nothing at all had changed.

"Hello, Liza," I said, walking up to her slowly.

"Hello," she said. "When did you get into town?"

"I just arrived. I wanted to see you one more time."

She looked away and started arranging shirts on a rack. "I'm married," she said, showing me her ring.

"Your husband is a very lucky man," I said, gallantly. "He better treat you well."

"He will. He's very nice."

I felt some tears coming and I turned my head away. I saw three of Liza's co-workers a few feet away from us, leaning on a glass counter with their arms around one another and watching us. Two of them were sniffling and wiping tears from their eyes. They were obviously very moved by this scene. This was way better than any Philippine soap opera, after all. I decided to keep this short, since I didn't want to start crying too.

"Thanks for sending me back the money," I told her. "It was the right thing to do."

"Sorry I couldn't send back all of it. My cousin…"

"Yeah, I know. I got your message."

After a few more trivial exchanges—why get heavy now?—I wished Liza good luck and offered her my hand. She reached for it and squeezed it gently, giving my finger an extra little squeeze.

I knew that squeeze. I felt it on the day Liza and I met in front of the basilica on my first trip to Cebu, the day I first told her I wanted to marry her. I remembered the precious little affections I felt in that squeeze a year and a half ago. I could feel her say, "I have found you, and you are mine," in that little squeeze from that happy moment. I will never forget the sight of her delicate gait, her long black hair, that warm smile of hers, shooting beams of eternity at me in the drizzle of the day.

In this goodbye squeeze, I felt something more. I felt her saying to me: "I love you with all my heart, but it wasn't meant to be. Please forgive me. You are a gentle soul who deserves more than this, and I will always treasure your love. Please, please forgive me."

I squeezed her hand in return, then turned my back and walked out of the Shoe Mart Department Store one last time. And so it was, with tears streaming down my face as I walked through the SM mall—past the Baskin-Robbins, past the McDonald's, past the Texas Chicken, past the Jollibee—that I finally forgave Liza.

And so it was that I finally figured out that this is where she was meant to be after all—working in a mega-mall, in a store that sold the unattainable American dream to poor Filipino folks. Such a girl was not meant to be living in the dream itself, because the real American dreamworld was harsh and rough, and this girl was kind and pure and innocent and totally devoted to her family. And she loved her mother so much that she gave up her dreams of a better life to stay here in the island forever, to serve her forever, and be her loving daughter forever.

I saw then and there what a beautiful person Liza truly was, and how selfish a person I was, and I continued to cry at the thought that she would not be a part of my life.

I returned to Humboldt County and did a lot of thinking. I stared out the window through the constant drizzle at the thicket of big trees in front of my apartment, and thought about her.

Could it be that she was totally sincere, honestly in love with me, and completely intending to fulfill her promise until Wilson and her mother came rushing in with their mad plan? Was she that foolish, that she would fall for a phony "marriage contract" argument, this bit about "everybody has signed it so you have to sign it too"? That was madness! What adult woman would believe that? Could it be that in the Philippines, all women are that vulnerable to manipulation? Could it be that Liza was that frail, that delicate, that weak, that she couldn't assert her own will?

I started feeling sorry for Filipina women, but also knew that many of them were not exactly helpless and weak. Many, in fact, were fully aware of this international mating game that has existed for a century or more between Americans and Filipinos, and many had become adept at using their attractiveness to hustle money and other commodities from their foolish lovers. I thought about Menchie and Luz, the two women who received money regularly in the mail from desperate American lonelyhearts. The power and the money was in THEIR hands. And they were not necessarily the helpless and desperate little urchins that the media and many people make them out to be. If they wanted to, they could be powerful players in this little game, just like any liberated American woman could be. And a man with a frail heart could be a victim in the hands of a canny, young manipulator—in the Philippines or in America.

Which was Liza?

And what was her mom?

Was her mom the kind that would be so selfish that she would violate her daughter's wishes and commit her to a marriage contract without her knowing? And why would she do this? Just to make sure that her favorite daughter would not ever leave her? To make sure that Liza would always be there to serve her, to give her money, to be her slave? How could that be love? Wasn't that just pure, raw selfishness? Wasn't that oppression? Or did mom know something that Liza didn't?

Did mom sense that this stranger from the West was just wearing a mask, just fooling her daughter with promises of riches and a better life? Who was this stranger who looks like one of us but who comes from Babylon bearing these decadent gifts? He speaks with a devil's tongue, brings trinkets to win your heart and offers parlor magic—a cellular phone!—to fog your mind.

Let us defeat him and send him away. Let this marriage contract with another man be a spear through his heart and a club to his head. Let him lie bleeding on the beach at Mactan and let him die. And let us send his Western ways back to hell where they came from. Filipinos for Filipinos, my daughter. Cebuanos for

Cebuanos. Stay here forever with me, with your family. Let this mad alliance with Western devils be done!

I had a revelation: Mom was Chief Lapu Lapu and I was Ferdinand Magellan. The Cebuanos had won again.

# Epilogue

Joseph Estrada, the actor-president, was removed from office in 2001 and jailed on charges of corruption. The man whose name made me something special in the Philippines during my trips there had fallen from grace.

But grace fell my way on Dec. 2, 2001, when my son, George Abelardo Quiros Estrada III, was born at St. Joseph Hospital in Eureka, California. He has the almond eyes, the flat nose and the light brown skin of a Filipino, which he is; but he has the stocky build and fiery temperament of an American, which he is. When he grows up, he'll discover that he is both and he is neither.

We named him George III, to honor my father and, of course, to honor me. We gave him the middle names Abelardo and Quiros to honor my wife's late father. Our nickname for him is "Popoy," which means little boy in a Philippine folk dialect. Somehow, we can't bring ourselves to call this little guy "George" to his face yet. That powerful name is for American presidents and Anglo-Saxon kings. We come from peasant stock. "Popoy" will do just fine for now. "George" will come later.

His mother is sleeping at this moment, tired from taking care of the little guy all day. Noreen is radiant, beautiful, devoted and loving and I am perhaps the luckiest man in the world to have found her. She gets a little perturbed when I talk about Liza because she thinks (incorrectly) that I am still obsessed with her. (By the way, Trujillo is not Liza's real last name. I changed it for this story to protect her privacy.)

Noreen and I bought a lovely house in Eureka, with three bedrooms, two baths, a family room and a big backyard—all spread out on about one-third of an acre. Last spring, I earned tenure at Humboldt State University. My wife watches baseball with me, and we dream of the day our son might become a left-handed pitcher for the Oakland A's. She's catching on to the American Dream very quickly. We are two immigrants riding the divine wind of a great dream, and we are very happy to be doing so.

I finally found the love I was searching for all my life, and I found her in the Philippines, the land of my ancestors, so the quest was fulfilled and the story has a nice ending.

The happy coincidence is that her family is from Cebu, where Liza and I had our day in the sun. The difference in our fates was that Noreen's mother fully approved of our relationship, and blessed our future with all her heart. Noreen came to America on a fiancée visa in November 2000 and we got married one month later at San Francisco City Hall, the same place where Marilyn Monroe and Joe DiMaggio had tied the knot many years before. If it was good enough for these American icons, it was good enough for this boy and girl from the Philippines, we figured.

Our son was born one year later. He has not tasted any mangoes, but as soon as he decides he wants some, we'll surely let him have his fill. Mangoes are the stuff of life, even here in rainy, gray Humboldt County.

Noreen spent most of her life in Davao City, a big city located on the southern coast of Mindanao. The favored fruit there is not mango, but durian, known for its spiky skin, pungent odor, mushy texture and complicated taste. Durian takes getting used to, but once you develop a taste for it, you're hooked. It's not simple and sweet and instantly likable like mango, but its complexity and addictive aroma bring you back for more. I have tasted the durians of Davao and found them to be complex, compelling and quite addictive.

You can't stereotype durian, much like you can't stereotype the Filipino people. They may have similar dreams, much like we in America all dream of happiness and riches. But each individual goes about achieving the dream in a different way. Anybody who tells you that all Filipinos are traditional and religious and loyal and smiling and this and that needs to stop reading *The New York Times* and start opening their minds. Reality is complex, and is meant for those who dare to challenge convention, those who are willing to take risks, those who dare to pursue their dreams even in the face of fierce opposition.

I dared to dream about finding love in my homeland, and I went there in search of it. I did find it, but I got a lot of discouragement, made some wrong turns and took a couple of bites out of some strange fruit before I finally reached my goal.

It's raining tonight here in Humboldt County. It always seems to rain in Humboldt County. Somewhere out in the great beyond, it isn't raining. And I imagine there are millions of young Filipina women out there in that place, safe and warm, smiling at their mothers, laughing and joking with their sisters and brothers, cooking rice and fish and serving their families loyally, like good daughters should. But in their minds they may be dreaming of another place, a land of plenty, a land of freedom and choice, a land that they could live in someday, a land in which their individuality and feminine power can come fully into bloom.

Or they may be perfectly happy with their roles in life: obedient daughter, loving wife, and great mother to the suffering masses.

Maybe Liza is one of the happy ones. Maybe she is not. Maybe she is both. Maybe she is neither.

Maybe she herself will never know the truth.

0-595-27955-4

CPSIA information can be obtained
at www.ICGtesting.com
Printed in the USA
FFOW04n1801030816
26493FF